PARENTING CHILDREN IN UNSTABLE TIMES

PARENTING CHILDREN IN UNSTABLE TIMES

Ruth P. Arent, M.A., M.S.W.

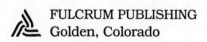
FULCRUM PUBLISHING
Golden, Colorado

*This book is written so that children may find love
and listen to love—wherever they may be.*

Library of Congress Cataloging-in-Publication Data

Arent, Ruth P.
    Parenting children in unstable times / Ruth P. Arent.
      p.   cm.
    Includes bibliographical references and index.
    ISBN 1-55591-132-3 (pbk.)
    1. Parenting. 2. Child rearing. 3. Parent and child. 4. Family.
I. Title.
HQ755.8.A72   1993
649' .1—dc20   93-23064
                                                         CIP

Cover design by Susan Orlie

Printed in the United States of America
0 9 8 7 6 5 4 3 2 1

Fulcrum Publishing
350 Indiana Street, Suite 350
Golden, Colorado 80401-5093

Contents

Preface

IT IS MY RESPONSIBILITY, as a professional in the world of children, to provide a useful guide for parents and other caretakers. In order to be effective, all strategies must be timely, optimistic, realistic, and usable. That's the mission of *Parenting Children in Unstable Times*—to present new material and update, expand, and enrich my previous book, *Stress and Your Child*. I encourage readers to appreciate their opportunities to help children proceed through complex, disturbing times with as much stability as possible.

Prologue

CELEBRATE THE INVULNERABLE CHILD! Take your hat off to the children who overcome instability, claw their way up the educational steps, hesitating occasionally when necessary, then perch on the top landing and go beyond. They are invulnerable—models of strength and wellness.

It isn't that these children don't have problems or difficulties to overcome. Somehow they have acquired the skills to get back on their feet. They survive and mature whether their parents help or hinder. They succeed "in spite of" or "because of" the instability they know—boy or girl, black or white, Hispanic, Oriental, or Native American—the kids you seldom notice. Too often adults are too busy observing and agonizing over the others—the ones who have faltered or crumbled.

Herald the invulnerable child as the hero or heroine who contradicts the assumption that parents are the cause of everything that happens to a child, from school failure to schizophrenia, and the assumption that certain traumatic happenings to children are *always* harmful. Both assumptions are wrong. We welcome that good news.

As you read disheartening reports and disturbing statistics, let this news encourage you to visualize invulnerable children.

More personally, help your children be as stable as possible, bearing in mind that all children have a reservoir of invulnerability and, in combination with the stability that *you* provide, your children can be happy and successful.

Introduction

As a PARENT you are the family manager. You make an endless number of decisions. Some the children will applaud, others will bring on protests—big and small, loud and soft. As manager, your influence is powerful, your caring essential, your rewards both questionable and great.

Parenting is not a popularity contest. There will be times when your children will be delighted to tell you that you make them mad or that they hate you. You will welcome the precious times when the message is, "I love you," whether scrawled on the back of a Valentine or whispered quietly as your child snuggles into a pillow when falling asleep.

In your efforts to raise stable children in unstable times, your role as family manager is pivotal. The many themes and strategies in this book are intended as practical support for you. A goal of stability, mutual respect, and healthy self-esteem for everyone is obtainable.

> *Stability encompasses mutual respect, which in turn evolves from the communication of persons with healthy self-esteem.*

Working definitions may be useful. **Stability** means that positive ties and predictable responses and behaviors will be forthcoming or maintained, even under difficult circumstances. **Predictability** means, to a child, "When this happens, I can expect mom to do this or dad to say that." This renders a sense of safety. It does not imply inflexibility. Throughout this book, specific factors influencing stability and instability are described and explained.

Mutual respect means a regard for another's needs, feelings, and, in the case of parents, authority. Self-respect is basic. Mutual respect empowers someone to withhold cruel, hurtful, abusive acts or words. Respect, from a child's point of view, also implies acquiescence, deferring to the mandates of the family manager. Respect implies that each person is important.

Mutual respect stems from your parenting style, your managerial skills, the decisions you make, and the plans you negotiate. Can respect be maintained when sad, disagreeable, or disruptive things occur? Most of the time. It fosters recovery and it benefits a positive parent-child relationship.

What about teenagers? Aren't all teenagers disrespectful? Isn't that part of growing up, of becoming independent? Pushing away from parental management, being rude or even defiant, should not be equated with disrespect. A smart remark, an insulting, critical remark may annoy you or make you mad, but the child's basic respect for you may still be intact. It's just that his or her behavior is abrasive, unkind, or selfish.

Mutual respect is the basic, underlying tie between parent and child. Sometimes it's taut, sometimes it's loose, but it is an artifact of the parent-child history—Big Person Taking Care of Little Person—and the power and trust this provides and implies.

> *The self-esteem of a child is nourished by parental respect, inspiring achievements—tiny or large—and rewarding relationships.*

Self-esteem allows a person to be unique. It means an appreciation of self that permits an individual to have personal likes, dislikes, differences, feelings, interests, ideals, *and* relationships. Looking to others for commendation and approval is not necessary. A person with healthy self-esteem realizes that no one is always loved by everyone nor will all actions and decisions be endorsed or applauded. Having healthy self-esteem encourages a person to express concern for others and gives a person the ability to handle disappointments or failures without a profound sense of defeat. As family manager, it is important to gauge how decisions you make and the subsequent consequences impact your child's self-esteem.

What are **unstable times**? Is it possible to manage a family today without some unpredictability and uncertainty? I don't think so.

Unstable times mean that there are too many choices, too many arguments, and too many possibilities that must be confronted before making decisions. In order to feel competent and experience repose, an individual must first sort out a single solution or course of action from a multiplicity of choices and then accept the consequences of the decision without self-recrimination and/or guilt. Furthermore, the person must be satisfied with, and even celebrate, a decision. Parents must be able to derive pleasure from their parenting decisions that result in evidence of stability in their children, and they must not overreact if the children are having some problems.

Coping in unstable times goes beyond a simplistic shift from "the way it was done in the olden days to how it is done now," because there is no one way "it is done now."

The familiar expression, "Happiness is an inside job," can be translated into, "Instability is both an inside and an outside job"—global, societal, familial, and personal circumstances contribute to unstable times. The 1990s abound in contradictions, confusions, and conditions that threaten family stability. *Parenting Children in Unstable Times* explores some of these circumstances. (Some are and some are not under parental control.) A parent, as manager, becomes the *interpreter*, helping children understand and cope as well as possible.

Parents may benefit from certain themes or basic threads that impact many situations. Briefly these include that in order to take care of others, you must take care of yourself; parental attitudes strongly influence the adjustment of the children—in stable times and in unstable times. Further, it is possible to be self-affirming even when things seem bleak, scary, or sad.

Other themes: Children are entitled to facts—they can cope with most anything if parents are honest with them, answer their questions, and give them the facts. Lies, half-truths, and omissions can be disastrous.

Parents must not pretend that they don't know what they know and see what they see. Parents must share themselves, be real, be human, be strong, and be vulnerable. Children model from their mothers and fathers. It is essential that parents don't hide behind facades, retreat under protective shells, or swim in nonstop denial if there are problems. Be proud of who you are. Let your children applaud. All families have ups and downs. Parenting is trial and error, generously mixed with experience, guided by some basic beliefs.

The plan of this book allows for an emphasis on child management, individual and family problems, societal problems, major sources of instability to overcome, and the downside of instability. As listed in the contents, there are seventy-two subsections ranging from how to bond to infants and toddlers to homeless families, TV violence, death, divorce, and therapy.

This is an upbeat book as reflected in the structure of each section: the status of the problem, the indicators of children's instability, procedures for parents, and reassurances. While few readers will read cover-to-cover, no matter which areas you select, you will find practical suggestions, support, and one repetitive goal—to encourage readers to search for the strengths and wellness of all people and apply procedures to fortify the self-esteem and well-being of each person.

It is my hope that you will enjoy your parenting as much as I enjoy mine. When, as adults, your children are respectful to you and friends among themselves, it is very rewarding. Tumultuous times of the past, times of blatant instability, provided my children with experiences that helped them to become successful adults.

PARENTING CHILDREN IN UNSTABLE TIMES

PART I

PARENTS CAN FOSTER STABILITY

1

What Parents Want for Their Children

"I WANT TO PROTECT MY KIDS from some of the horrible things I read about. It makes me sick when I think that Becky may see someone shot here at school or in a restaurant or even in a church. I'm old-fashioned. I want my daughter to be a happy, spirited little girl." Mrs. Clay was talking to the school counselor. Ten-year-old Becky was listening.

"But, mom," Becky interrupted. "I already know about bad things. I see them on TV and Debbie and I talk about them all the time."

"That makes me sad," the mother lamented. "Kids don't deserve to be upset and worried. That's not what I want for you."

Becky answered, "I'm not upset, mom. Come off it!"

"But it's not what I want for you," her mother said and shook her head. What do parents want for their children? In addition to a healthy sense of self-esteem and age-appropriate stability, the list includes:

• Trust
• Enthusiasm and joy about life—a ready smile, a sense of adventure
• A sense of balance, good decision making
• Relationships that are satisfactory, lots of friends

- An ability to accept and reaffirm strengths and wellness
- A healthy body, few fears and worries
- An excitement about learning—a positive attitude about school
- An appreciation of needs and feelings—their own and those of others
- Self-acceptance—a comfortable acceptance of limitations
- Pride as a member of the family
- Rewards that come from attaining goals—small, large, personal, societal
- A sense of comfort when alone
- No drug or alcohol dependency
- An openness to spirituality—an understanding of levels of awareness—the mind-body-spirit connectedness

This is a pie-in-the-sky list. Nevertheless, it provides a working agenda for parents. Procedures to help children attain these ideals are woven throughout this book. In the introduction, stability, healthy self-esteem, and mutual respect were highlighted. The issues of joy of life, trust, making good decisions, and balance are now explored.

JOY OF LIFE

The joy of life is something children learn from you. It is a spirit of adventure, a spontaneous outburst of happiness, and an appropriate reaching out to others: "Gee, you look nice today," or "I like the color of your hair," or "You were thoughtful to hold the door for that lady who was pushing a stroller." The joy of life includes a love of learning and excitement from many different experiences.

TRUST

Children learn to trust at home. Trust is built on secure bonds. Babies and little ones feel safe when they are totally dependent. Older children feel safe as they struggle to become independent because they trust that their parents will understand when they make mistakes or misbehave. Without trust, every experience creates anxiety and the child feels unbalanced. Trust requires that parents be discreet—that they do not tell the children's carefully shared secrets, or report details of the children's sayings or actions that might be embarrassing. The child trusts that his or her folks will be humane and respectful.

MAKE GOOD DECISIONS

Children can make good decisions if someone teaches them how. Parents, as managers, are teachers, and they can instruct a child how to decide what to do and what not to do so that the child feels good, under control, and pleased if a difficult situation does not get any worse. The fundamental approach is, "Bill can learn to stop, think, and choose!" He can stop before doing or saying something self-defeating or unkind, think of his options and choices, and choose the most sensible, useful response.

A SENSE OF BALANCE

Balance implies reason plus emotion—using common sense while handling your feelings. "I did what I had to do and I feel okay about it, even if I did feel scared or sad."

The child with balance learns how to react appropriately to different people and different demands. This understanding provides a sense of, "I can handle this." This can be expressed in many ways: "I know when to speak up and when to be quiet," or "I know I can disagree with Aunt Sarah and she won't get upset," or "When my mom expects me to be some kind of miracle worker, I tell her to cool it." The child's understanding and behavior add up to balance. Even when it is necessary to deal with others who may be out of control or irrational, the child can learn, "I can keep my head even though Jimmy is acting crazy." In more sophisticated terms, older children learn, "I can be rational in an irrational situation."

Balance and appropriateness go together. They reflect healthy self-esteem. But kids don't go around dissecting their behavior and parents accept that kids are impulsive. We can expect that school-aged children will learn to explain what they do while acknowledging that immaturity and spontaneity may prevail.

> *As a parent, you are a model for your child. Children learn by imitating. Take advantage of this and be the kind of person you want your child to be.*

A word of caution: What parents want for their children is a wish list. Your motto must be, "Work in Progress." Your relationship is lifelong and will endure times of harmony and disharmony. Your transition from manager to teacher, counselor, and friend takes years. The most important *procedure for parents* is to observe and praise, observe and praise, observe and praise, when good things happen to your good kids. This bundle of reassurances will sustain your positive attitude—the same one you want for your family.

2

What Parents Need to Do
Parenting Skills that Work

IT's NOT FAIR TO YOU to attempt the impossible. Family life today, with the complexities and conflicts of the nineties, means that decisions amount to tradeoffs. You can only do so much in one day; you can only be in one place at a time; you can only attend to one task at a time. That's how it is, and you, your spouse, and other family members need to be reminded of this frequently. Your relationships are important; the family is a top priority, but you must safeguard your well-being and that's why the Superparent concept must go. Everyone can understand and make the necessary adjustments.

1.
Take Care of Yourself

You must first take care of yourself. This requires that you:
- Don't even consider trying to be perfect—to be Supermom or Superdad
- Become self-aware
- Be assertive, self-protective
- Encourage yourself to grow
- Accept the rights and privileges of parents; welcome reassurances

> *Forget that the concept of Supermom and Superdad was ever introduced.*

BE SELF-AWARE

Parents today are frequently *spanked* in the press. We are sternly reminded that spouses and children suffer from neglect as we seek self-fulfillment or become absorbed in a search for the inner self. Likewise, self-help groups are now accused of diverting time and energy away from the family, most especially the children.

I maintain that self-awareness and appropriate assertiveness are essential to stability. Stability doesn't mean being strict or rigid or unwavering. Stability implies leveling off, keeping in balance. Stability further implies the ability to prioritize and manage. Therefore, if, for a time, your priority is digging into self-actualization, so be it. The family can adjust. Family stability is not threatened—rather, it may benefit from your pursuits.

Parents who care about themselves invariably manage to find time to care about others. Though you may shorten the time with the kids, you model the healthy self-esteem that you want them to emulate.

Self-awareness is a practical description, a sketch of you that describes your individuality. Self-awareness does not require Freudian analysis. It does not take years. It does require reflection and courageous answers to questions such as those suggested in the personal inventory below.

Your children take you as their models. They reflect your emotions. They learn to relate as you show them how to. That is why your self-awareness is so important. When you demonstrate that you like yourself, you show your children a model of healthy self-esteem.

SELF-AWARENESS INVENTORY

Which of these statements are true for you?
- I am open with my emotions. When I am happy, sad, worried, or frightened, I show it or talk about it.

- I explain to my family about when I like to be touched and when I don't like to be touched.
- I tend to be set in my ways, almost rigid. I criticize others when they don't agree with how I want things done.
- I am inconsistent and sometimes this upsets me.
- I frequently do not finish what I start.
- I enjoy life. I find that I smile and laugh—even giggle—a lot.
- I tend to feel critical of the children and need to be aware of how I express my disappointments.
- I enjoy loving people and hope that others see me as loving rather than cold and restricted.
- I am not a very patient person. I tend to have a short temper.
- When I take time to read a book, enjoy music, or watch a sunset, I feel rejuvenated.
- Assertiveness is not a problem for me. I used to let people walk all over me, but now I set limits. I need to remind myself—often—about boundaries and my right to be myself.
- I want to encourage my children to be creative. When I write a poem or do a sketch, I share this with them. I need to spend more time writing or designing clothes, two of my favorite things to do.

After taking this personal inventory, you may feel relaxed and satisfied that you measure up quite well to your ideal of a person who strives for full-time stability. The answers with which you do not feel comfortable may cause discomfort for your children as well. You may be criticizing yourself: "I should be more expressive," or "I guess I really expect too much from my two-year-old."

> *You are not obliged to share all your adult knowledge with children. Weigh what you say against your measure of their capacity to carry a burden successfully. This requires parents to be duly aware of the individual child and age-appropriate understanding.*

If you don't measure up to your ideal, here are some suggestions that you may find useful.

Take the first inventory statement: *I am open with my emotions.* You may respond, "I've got to work on that." You recognize that an essential part of helping children achieve stability is to urge them to express their emotions. Almost every family needs to work hard in this area.

Love	Bitterness	Concern
Jealousy	Fear	Uninvolvement
Forgiveness	Unhappiness	Depression
Frustration	Pleasure	Guilt
Loneliness	Anger	Relief
Impatience	Enthusiasm	Uneasiness
Happiness	Compassion	Joy
Worry	Disappointment	Restlessness
Excitement	Delight	Empathy

Consider this list of emotions or feelings, and picture yourself expressing any one of them. Watch yourself in the mirror. Listen to your voice on a tape. Notice how people react to what you say. Listen when your child says, "Mom, when you're worried, you don't talk to anybody. I don't know if you are mad at me or worried about something." Ask a friend to describe how you express your feelings. "Helen, I have never seen you show enthusiasm. You smile briefly when I give you good news. You smile briefly if the children bring home good grades. You never say, 'That's great,' or 'I'm proud of you.' I wish you could show excitement—give a big hug or use different words."

It takes practice to:

• Accept a description of yourself
• Read or ask for suggestions from someone close to you
• Figure out how to change
• Implement the change

Choose only one or two feelings to work on at a time. Take disappointment and pleasure, for example. You will begin to feel comfortable when you can express your true feelings in these areas. If you choose to concentrate on anger, describe the ways that you express it. Look at such habits as making belittling remarks or sarcastic comments, clamming up, slapping, scowling, hitting furniture, or walking away. When children perceive that you are angry, they want to know why, because your anger creates anxiety. If you do not answer their questions, they may unnecessarily blame themselves. Use terms the kids can under-stand when you explain an issue or a problem.

Feelings can be seen but not heard. Feelings can be heard but not seen. Your kids will sparkle when you sparkle. Practice talking about feelings with your children.

Consider a happy, positive example from your self-inven-tory, such as, "I enjoy life." What a nice way to describe yourself. Suppose your little girl spills flour all over the kitchen floor. You may want to bark at her, but instead you say, "Why, it looks like snow, and winter is my favorite season." You clean up the mess together. You are aware that the child feels guilty; she didn't spill the flour to make you mad. Are you aware that the impatient mom or dad might have spanked, yelled, or sent the child to bed?

What is a support system?
It's a system of trusted people who provide support when needed and congratulations when deserved; it's people you have fun with.

You may be struggling to find upbeat examples of your interactions with your children and become aware that you want many more. The difficulty may reflect that you could benefit from help with self-awareness or self-discovery. Don't hesitate to use the many self-help programs, books, groups, and services available. For example, programs for Adult Children of Alcoholics provide an understanding of how adults handle emotions and problems because of childhood-strained family relationships. This can serve as a base from which to gain self-awareness and may encourage changes that help to achieve stability.

Be Assertive

Assertive people exude confidence, make commitments that spur them on to action, manage to control unnecessary out-bursts, and use affirmations on a day in, day out basis. From your self-awareness inventory, perhaps you have been re-minded that assertiveness is a problem for you. Assertiveness is essential. Again, children will take you as their model.

Assertiveness requires that:

- You are your own best friend. You do what you want to do because you want to do it—as long as no one else will be hurt. You don't do what you do not want to do and you feel comfortable about this.
- You are a good communicator with family, friends, or strangers. You tell the truth, express feelings, and are a good listener. You give others the freedom to be themselves, and this lets you be yourself. Your communications denote love, caring, concern, and respect. You solve problems effectively without always giving in. Problem solving is a form of communication.
- You pursue what is important to you. You don't sit back and just hope that you will get a new job; you pursue it. You don't just hope that your new acquaintance will become a friend or lover; you take the initiative, extend a welcome to the relationship, and follow up on it. You take an active part in all relationships. With your children, you stay involved as a nonjudgmental friend, in combination with parental responsibilities, to provide information and guidance.
- You are able to consider the needs of others but do not let their needs run your life. You make your wishes known. You feel comfortable with the decisions and choices you make, and realize that you cannot always get what you want.
- You make certain that the consequences of inappropriate behavior are understood and carried out. This teaches the child to hold back before striking out or saying things that may require discipline. This pattern gives the child the message that certain behaviors are not acceptable to you and there is a price to pay. It puts the responsibility on the child. The parent, however, is the teacher—the one who establishes the consequences and carries them out. Certain consequences can be negotiated with older children ahead of time, but the parent must follow through, by cutting the allowance or making sure the child doesn't watch TV, for example.

A family cannot experience stability if parents do not take an in-charge position. By being in charge, you are taking care of you. Let's look at what happened last week at the Murphy residence. Susie took a small cup and threw it at her brother, Sam. Sam wasn't hurt, but he could have been. Susie has to learn that this kind of behavior has consequences—that mother won't ignore it. Susie is sent to her room. Mother's appropriate use of parental power benefits everyone in this situation. Mother does not make excuses for Susie. She doesn't say, "Susie is tired today," or "I'm sorry that she is jealous of her brother."

The in-charge position involves teaching the concept of *options* or *choices*. This is useful after age five. David, age ten, threw a snowball at Billy and hit him in the face. Mother carries out the consequences: David has to come in the house. She introduces options or choices.

"Why did you throw the snowball at Billy?" she asks.

"I hate him. He calls me names," David replies.

Mother says, "You had options or choices to make:
1. You could have come to me and told me that you hate Billy.
2. You could have thrown a snowball at the fence.
3. You could have gone off and played by yourself.
4. You could have come in the house to watch TV or read.
5. You could have called Billy a dirty name.
But throwing a snowball at him was not okay."

David may say, "I never thought of that. I was mad." Encouraging self-control is part of mother's job. The system of repeating the options or choices, many times and in many situations, can help David.

Eventually David will be able to tell his mom, "Guess what? Today when I got mad at Mary, I called her a dumbbell. I wanted to grab her ponytail, but I remembered about choosing." He will learn to choose a behavior—to use self-control.

Options and choices are important. When situations arise, a parent should provide *five* options for children under seven and *three* for younger kids. The children will accept the pattern of, "What five options can you think of, Sammy?" or "Tell me three other things you can do instead of hitting." During middle school years, when some friendships seem quite fragile, the use of options and choices can help foster stability.

Use Affirmations

Affirmations are positive statements about yourself that reinforce your appropriate assertiveness and well-being. Sample affirmations for you to consider are:

- I deserve to have privacy time.
- I am a good friend.
- I accept that I need help learning how to use a computer.
- I write well. I am happy that I am creative.
- I deserve to have my children be thoughtful.

Write down your affirmations in a diary or journal. As it grows, you will be pleased. Your demonstrations of assertiveness are reinforced when you keep track of successful conversations or encounters. Keeping a journal is a way to recall and evaluate, enjoy, and question things that you do and say. Some parents record only parent-child-family happenings in order to evaluate their style of parenting and other important concerns.

If you do not like to keep a journal, it is suggested that you record your affirmations on a tape recorder and review them frequently. You may be both surprised and delighted at your collection of good tidings.

Assertiveness is especially important for single mothers as a weapon to overcome common feelings of guilt and inadequacy. Nearly one family out of five is a single-parent family headed by a woman responsible not only for the care of the children but for part, if not all, of the family income. These are not women happily waving the banner of feminist liberation. In their role as mothers, they often fall right back to "old-fashioned" ideals. They are beset by feelings of guilt. They castigate themselves for every tiny problem or major crisis—a splinter in a finger to a child on drugs. They need constant encouragement to be assertive and to affirm their successes and strengths.

> *The definition of the stable family includes the parent as manager. This is assertiveness in action.*

Accept the Rights and Privileges of Parents

Parents are people too. You have rights and privileges. You are adults and do not have to justify or defend, to your children, your every action and decision. When parents are self-accepting, everyone benefits. You have the right:

- To be yourself, with your strengths and weaknesses
- To be spontaneous, to come out with unrehearsed remarks and suggestions
- To know where the kids are going, with whom they will be riding, and when they will be home
- To enjoy the children, baby the babies, and let kids be kids
- To set limits for the good of everyone
- To make decisions without the approval of others, as long as no one is being hurt
- To break promises when necessary
- To change your mind
- To be wrong
- To be taken care of at times
- To realize there are stages in which child-parent anger is to be expected
- To have privacy
- To ask for help, without being criticized, when you feel you need it
- To have fun with the kids
- To get involved in the schools that your children attend

When you maintain your rights, your children can and do learn respect. Respect is basic to stability, and even with ups and downs, you can feel confident that your family has strength and definition.

2.
Bond to the Children

Bonds are ties that denote safety. A bond conveys the message that someone cares and can be trusted to love you. Too many unhappy children today have been described as unattached, unbonded, throw-away youngsters. Bonding is taken for granted in a stable family. At the same time, it is a good idea to assess what's going on under *your* roof.

How to Bond to Infants and Toddlers

You can bond to infants by:
- Affectionate handling—stroking, massage.
- Expressions of delight—smiles, smiles, smiles.

- Introduction of limits balanced with freedom.
- Verbalizations such as, "I love you," or "You are so important to me."
- Listening to what children share.
- Observing and anticipating wants and needs so that the child can depend on you.

Parent-child bonds prepare children for intimacy and trust. The unbonded child suffers from minimal or damaged self-esteem. This child displays insecurity and a hunger for approval and closeness or much anger.

Suppose that you perceive your children feel distant from you. You may have heard one of them say, "I feel like a piece of furniture around here." You describe family relationships as unemotional. There are many ways to improve such a situation.

You can start to overcome detachment distance with affection. Affection builds bonds. Babies thrive on lots of holding and rocking. Young children may want to sit on your lap or cuddle as you read to them.

Not all parents enjoy holding their babies or cuddling. Perhaps touching is a problem for you. You may enjoy the children but remain emotionally aloof. Nevertheless, nonverbal messages communicated through touching must not be overlooked. For older children, you may want to explain why you are not an openly affectionate person and how you can be very loving without it. "I come from a no-touch family. I never saw my mother and father touch each other." Verbal communication in this situation is most important.

Reaffirm your feelings of love with words and availability. Be ready to go over homework problems, mend favorite jeans, prepare cookies for a birthday party, or fix up a doll for show and tell. Work on becoming demonstrative.

How to Bond to Older Children

- Be relentless about asking questions that denote love and concern. "How was school today?" "Did you have a good time at Freddie's?"
- Be willing to be unselfish, such as giving up a meeting to go to the child's conference or game.

- Tell the child repeatedly that he or she is very important to you.
- Display habits that support your commitment. You should be on time, go to school, move away from the TV, and answer the child's questions thoughtfully. Become a master listener.

Ties can be established and strengthened at any time. This can be difficult, but the rewards are meaningful. Children as old as fourteen can be placed in a new adoptive situation and significant, happy bonds can develop. The stronger the bonds, the greater the chance of achieving stability.

3

Parents as Caretakers
The Art of Child Management

MUTUAL RESPECT MEANS respect goes both ways. Young children who are self-focused need to be guided into mutual respect. Help them progress from the, "I respect you because you're big and powerful" stage of the preschool years to, "I get it. You and I don't agree, but you're okay mom, and I am too."

3.
Build Mutual Respect to Support Stability

Parent-child mutual respect stems from the bonding and connectedness of self-accepting individuals. The core of *mutual respect* is safeguarded by reasonable limits, discipline, negotiation, and open communication. All this takes time to develop.

Young children do not verbalize the word respect but experience the concept or feeling. Small children defer to big people. *Parent power provides a sense of safety and an undercoating of fear.* Children learn to appreciate that if they do not respect parental authority, they may be isolated or punished, spanked, or neglected. They know they had better listen and obey. They will learn the concept of *mutual* respect.

Teenagers may rebel against parental authority and still

respect their parents. They may question what their parents say and do and exclaim that they don't respect parental decisions: "That's nuts, Dad. *Why* did you buy *that* bike?" Nevertheless, deep-seated family ties remain in place in spite of such protests. They can thrive on *mutual* respect.

Mutual respect requires parents to respect children as well. Parents demonstrate respect when they acknowledge:

1. A child's need to be his or her own person
2. A child's right to opinions that differ from the parent's opinion
3. A child's right to relationships with other adults without feeling threatened
4. A child's right to live in a family where adults, as managers, display consistency and integrity

With parental respect, children learn self-respect. They sense that they are important and lovable. Displays of self-respect announce a growing appreciation of self, so basic to inner stability and to the development of moral values. Appropriate assertiveness and self-respect commingle.

Help Children Progress to Mutual Respect

Parents can help children progress to mutual respect. These steps may increase a child's respect for the parents.
- Help children understand the difference between respect and obedience. Define mutual respect so they will understand it.
- Teach the child to tolerate personality differences without feeling disrespectful. (If mom is too bossy, help the child learn to accept her as she is, even though she is hard to get along with or embarrasses him in front of his friends. If she is too passive, this too must be accepted.)
- Point out admirable qualities of each parent, such as honesty and cleanliness.
- Build respect in one specific area, if not in all areas—for example, in money management or integrity.
- Be optimistic. Learning to feel respectful may take a long time and may be difficult. If a child is critical, remind the child that parents can and do make mistakes and they do change.
- Help teenagers understand that they may learn to respect parents whom they have not respected before. They can let go

of the judgments they held against their parents. "I never really liked my dad when I was younger. He was drunk a lot, and I couldn't stand the way he yelled at everybody. Now I'm older and he has stopped drinking, controls his temper, and has a much better job. He is quite a guy; I respect him."

- Above all, set a good example. Show respect for yourself, your spouse, other adults, and children.
- Talk about family ties (bonding) and limits.

Mutual Respect Builds from Bonds

Parent-child attachment or connectedness is basic to mutual respect. It provides emotional links; some are strong, binding, and supportive, while others may be casual, fragmented, or unreliable. Most children crave affection. Parents who are not particularly affectionate or demonstrative can have strong bonds with children; however, the children may need verbal statements or reminders to be convinced. "I didn't get hugs and kisses from my parents, but I always felt close to them. I guess I'm the same way as a parent." Children may perceive inconsistent limits or discipline as a sign that their parents don't care. Again, your statements and explanations are important: "I'm not very consistent about how I scold you, Mary—but that's me. It has nothing to do with the fact that I love you very much."

Limits and Discipline Contribute to Mutual Respect

Limits enhance and stabilize relationships. Children feel a lack of respect when you set limits that are not adequately explained or which they consider unfair. In using limits to enhance mutual respect, consider your answers to these questions:

- Do your kids complain that you say "No" to an endless number of requests?
- Do you consider yourself a very strict parent?
- Do you take the time to explain your limits (except during a crisis)?
- Do your children have a chance to complain, protest, and ask for more consideration?
- Do your children push until you change your mind?
- Are you ever unfair?

- What kind of comments do you hear from the other kids, or their parents, about the limits that you set?
- Do you use words such as "appropriate," "mannerly," "polite," "mature," "immature," "considerate," "inconsiderate," and assume that these words make the limits acceptable to the kids? (These words are not likely to comfort the kids if they feel your lack of respect.)
- Are you reluctant to set different limits for each child, adjusted to age?
- Do you tend to be more lenient with one of the children?
- Do you and your spouse agree on limits?
- What happens if you don't agree?
- Do the children try to play one of you against the other?
- Do you frequently feel that you are at the end of your rope and (impulsively) impose a limit that you regret later on? What happens then?
- Are you comfortable with apologies?

Your answers to these questions set the stage for the changes necessary for building respect. An honest analysis of your answers can help you establish a sense of fairness and still support your *take-charge* style of management. Without fairness, mutual respect will not grow or survive. Fairness keeps relationships harmonious and enhances stability.

In conjunction with limits, parents are urged to be *comfortable as a disciplinarian.* Discipline conveys the message, "I mean what I say and I care." Without guidance, which encompasses discipline, a child has no one to respect and the possibility of mutual respect is lost. Furthermore, the child feels unloved.

In order to build mutual respect through discipline, a parent must consider that:

- The age, understanding, and personality of the child will determine what works and what does not work.
- Words—scolding—may be useful as discipline for one child and not useful for another. Some kids must experience other consequences such as removal from the room, loss of allowance, or reduced play or TV time. *Making the punishment fit the crime* is hard to accomplish in this day of many options. Let us suppose that Hank is watching TV and starts a fight with his brother. His mother tries to reason with him, tells him that

they should take turns choosing which channel to watch. Hank snaps, "Butt out, mom, it's none of your business." No kid should talk to his mother like that. What discipline would make sense in this situation? Hank is a big fourteen-year-old; his mother is not going to wash his mouth out with soap. She will probably choose to send him to his room.

- Consistency builds respect. If misbehavior warrants discipline one time, it warrants it again and again. When a child can predict the discipline, this provides security and respect and serves to inhibit forbidden behaviors.
- Name-calling is a common pitfall. Don't get mad and swear at the child or explode with, "You stupid, thoughtless, no-good kid." Such explosions can sting for a long time—sometimes for a lifetime. Sarcasm has the same effect. These reactions do not build respect.
- It's important not to embarrass your child in front of friends. I recall when I was a child and would invite my friends to stay overnight. I would be sent to my room because I had been sassy or annoying. I considered the punishment unfair. I learned not to invite anyone because I was not willing to take the chance of being humiliated. Humiliation does not enhance respect.

After an incident, provide a chance for the child to talk with you about whether he or she thought you were fair or unfair. Discipline must point the way to improvements. That is one of its most important benefits. If discipline prevents improvements, or if it creates resentment and fear, don't look for respect.

Corporal punishment can:
- *Cause physical harm*
- *Train children to use physical force rather than reason*
- *Interfere with learning (especially in the classroom)*
- *Increase aggressive behavior*
- *Teach children inappropriate ways to control others*

4.
Negotiations Build Mutual Respect

Some disciplinary patterns can be negotiated with your children. Together you can decide appropriate consequences for various misdeeds. It takes time to develop the art of negotiating with children. Negotiations are important not only because they can repair problems, but because they can also prevent them. Negotiation builds and maintains mutual respect. The message behind negotiation is: *You are important to me.* It is particularly important to try to anticipate what will need to be negotiated.

How to Negotiate with Your Children

1. Present the problem to be solved or the need for a plan. "We are arguing too much about feeding the dog. What do you think we can do about this?" or "I need to be away next weekend. I want to decide, with you, which sitter to hire or what arrangements would be best."

2. Allow the children to make suggestions. Listen with an open mind. Then share your thoughts or ideas.

3. Together, discuss the pros and cons and, together, decide what to do. If the plan is a rubber stamp of your ideas and excludes all the suggestions that the children made, be sure that you let them express their feelings. If you are only giving *lip service* to the children's input, they will sense that the negotiations are fraudulent. This undermines respect. Use negotiations only when you are open to ideas or suggestions that may not agree with yours. When children have input and then experience the plan or witness improvement in the problem, respect is enhanced and stress is prevented or reduced.

4. Specify the areas in which you are not willing to negotiate, such as disciplinary consequences for some misbehaviors.

Items to negotiate

Bedtimes	Smoking
TV	Allowances: amount and how spent
Household chores	Babysitting
Tidiness	Grades at school
Bathing	Boundaries in the neighborhood
Number of dates	

Remind the children that situations will come up for which no one is prepared, and this is part of living together. Children can be enormously forgiving and surprisingly flexible.

How well do you know your son or daughter?
1. Name your child's best friend.
2. What does your child like to do in his or her spare time?
3. Name one of your child's favorite music groups or recording artists.
4. What does your child like to do on Friday nights?
5. Name a famous person or television or movie star your child would love to meet.
6. Of which accomplishment is your child most proud?
7. Who is your child's least favorite teacher? What is his or her least favorite subject in school?
8. Name something you do that really upsets your child.
9. What would your child like to be when he or she grows up?
10. If you could buy your child the gift he or she wants most, what would it be?
11. Which household chore does your child dislike the most? Which one does he or she like?
12. Where would your child like to go for a vacation?
13. What has been your child's biggest disappointment this year?
14. What causes your child the most stress?
15. Name something your child really likes about you. What does he or she dislike most?
16. What would your child like to do more often with you?

How well do you know your mom or dad?
1. If your parent drinks coffee, what does he or she like in it?
2. If your parent is a football fan, name his or her favorite team.
3. Name two of his or her friends.
4. What was his or her favorite subject in high school?
5. What does he or she like to do to relax?
6. What causes him or her the most stress?
7. Name something you do that upsets him or her.
8. Did he or she smoke cigarettes as a teenager?
9. Name a food or drink he or she can't stand.
10. Name a famous person he or she would love to meet.
11. Did he or she have a nickname as a child? If so, what was it?

12. What was his or her most enjoyable extracurricular activity in school?
13. What is his or her favorite family occasion?
14. How old were your parents when they got married?
15. Name something he or she thinks is special about you.
16. What would he or she like to do more often with you?

4-H Youth Development and Family Living
Education Programs,
University of Wisconsin, 1987

Benefits of Negotiations

The main benefit of negotiation is that it provides a way for kids to ask for changes and for parents to ask for changes, too. As a parent, insist on your rights: the right to be arbitrary sometimes; the right to be human; the right to make mistakes; the right to be in charge.

———

In conclusion, mutual respect can only evolve if both parties feel good about themselves. The old expression, *you can't give what you don't got,* applies. If you are not self-accepting, your relationship with others cannot build from give and take.

If you feel uncomfortable about a lack of mutual respect with your children, try to assess, "Do I need to be more affectionate or responsive in order to enhance bonds?" or "Are my limits and discipline too severe or too lax?" or "Do I need to work on my self-confidence?" We all feel *shaky* once in a while. Tell the kids. They will understand. Kids are great. They want stability just like you do.

Parents!!
Stories about your childhood, your interests, talents, feelings, and dreams are important. Such self-disclosure builds mutual respect. Your children want to know you. Take time to answer their questions too. Share the treasures and mementos of your youth.

PART II

THE QUEST FOR STABILITY
INDIVIDUAL AND FAMILY PROBLEMS

Adaptations and Adjustments

The key to stability is adaptation. When disturbing or disruptive situations occur, the stable person takes on an attitude that helps to deal with the problem.

Some children are more adaptable than others. Some are more vulnerable and fragile. Others seem strong and flamboyant. Nevertheless, every child must cope with physical or emotional rough spots. That's part of growing up.

This part of the book is concerned with the rough spots that derive from individual and/or family problems. Some may be considered universal—generic to all children—such as those inherent in the stages of development. Others are due to unusual circumstances. There is a wide variety of problems and you will note that some are temporary while others are ongoing or chronic.

4

The Family Grows
Ages and Stages

5.
Fetal Health and the Newborn

Can you imagine making certain that you safeguard the well-being of your yet-to-be-conceived child? The lists are out and worthy of review for six months prior to trying to conceive: no smoking; men—drink in moderation; women—no drinking; avoid exposure to lead, noxious fumes, pesticides; women computer specialists—maintain a distance of three feet from your computer screen; avoid eating salmon, swordfish, tuna, shark, and lake whitefish, which may contain toxic levels of chemicals and mercury. Start your vitamin C supplements—they can prevent genetic damage in sperm and baby neurological and bone disorders. And without a doubt, every prospective mother must know if she is HIV positive. Babies born with AIDS or the AIDS virus need special care that must be planned in advance. Wow!

Fetal health is next in line—a major concern in medical circles and justifiably so. Both parents are reminded that their yet-to-be-born child is already participating in the family. In addition to nutritional and health matters, parents are reminded that the fetus enjoys music, becomes familiar with voices, reacts to parental stress, and much more.

Does this mean that your child may be stable or unstable or excitable or calm because of the prenatal environment? This has some influence, perhaps, but genetics and many other factors will be the important determinants.

Medical attention is an imperative during pregnancy. Premature babies who require crisis, life-sustaining care and remediation of related problems cost thousands and thousands of dollars per week. One insurance company reports that for every week an expectant mother is kept pregnant, the company saves as much as ten thousand dollars in health insurance costs.

In 1991 the March of Dimes Birth Defects Foundation published the following: Fetal surgery is a frightening thought and probably sounds impossible. But on June 15, 1989, it happened.

Beth Schultz was in her second trimester of pregnancy, when a routine ultrasound exam revealed her son's stomach, spleen, and intestines had passed through a hole in his abdomen and were damaging his lungs.

Corrective surgery after birth was considered, but there was fear the lungs would not develop enough for him to survive. If it weren't for years of research by a team of doctors at the University of California in San Francisco and funding from the March of Dimes, surgery before birth might not have been an option.

6.
Welcome the Newborn, Enjoy the Infants

Most babies do very well. Mother Nature does a first-class job. Indeed, the tree tends to grow straight. Can an infant seem "stable"? Some are more placid, sweet, and adjustable than others. My grandson, Tristan, at a year, is an easy-going, wide-eyed champion—he loves the world and is surrounded by love and it shows. It's his nature, we say thankfully. Unfortunately, some babies are irritable, hard to please, colicky, and seemingly create tensions that plague both the caretakers and the child alike.* The most devoted parents can run out of patience and resourcefulness, or feel tired and terribly frustrated. "I'd sell this kid for fifty cents," a distraught parent may declare at three o'clock in the morning. "I think I'll exchange this one for a new model."

Baby stability can be equated with growth, development of social skills, periods of self-entertainment (playing with cradle gyms, rattles, own hands, and so forth), and episodes of kicking and fussing.

From the newborn period to eighteen months, your child will cut teeth, handle spoons, strive for independence, become demanding, babble, learn words, and flourish as he or she becomes mobile. Remember that babies have individual personalities. Some may be more responsive than others. Don't put yourself down because the baby cries—babies cry for many reasons. Each forms attachments to loved objects—mother and/or father and/or caretaker. (See *Bond to the Children*, page 17.) Even the most stable babies have tempers; you want them to express themselves. It denotes wellness and budding self-esteem.

PROCEDURES FOR PARENTS

In order for you to safeguard your stability, given your new responsibilities, pressures, and adjustments, it is suggested that you:

- Accept that you cannot always be well organized when you have an infant. There is no way to predict when your baby will be awake and demanding or for how long. You may experiment with feeding schedules and feel frustrated when you discover that they work only when a baby is old enough for them to work.
- Take care of yourself. Let some tasks and chores go. It is okay

---

*Some babies have significant problems during the early months. I consider it unwise to relate this to instability. Many physical and neurological factors contribute to problems; in addition, nervous parents need *time* to practice and adjust to their new lifestyle.

for the dust to settle on the furniture. Dishes can wait for tomorrow morning. Frozen dinners can be delicious.

- Get as much help as you can from grandparents, paid helpers, friends, and neighbors. Let grandma rock the baby. Welcome those casseroles.
- Don't overlook your needs and the needs of your spouse. This can be a good time to enrich your marriage as you deal with frustrations, worries, and the joys of parenting. Sharing baby care is rewarding.
- Take time to fondle, rock, sing, and talk to the baby. Remember that infant care is a loving process, properly flavored with delicacies.
- Try to maintain your friendships, especially with other couples who were in a Lamaze class with you or who have young children. Your feelings of, "This is more than I can handle," will diminish when others are reassuring. Stable parents tend to have stable infants.

REASSURANCES

"Infants thrive in spite of us," my grandmother would remind me. Then she would laugh and say, "I'm anxious to see how the professional baby raiser raises her babies," and I would deftly change the subject. I have selected two important reassurances for this section; one deals with birth place and procedure and the other with child care.

First, place and type of delivery may have no effect on a child's personality. Whether you have a home delivery, nurse, midwife manager, traditional hospital with all the new equipment, or a cesarean section, your child can become a very happy, stable, little person. Place of birth may affect parental attitude with important physical, emotional, and economic considerations, but there is no one-to-one established formula that says, for example, that home-delivered babies do better than those born in a hospital. Each situation is unique. There is no need to fret because someone chooses different procedures from your own.

Second, child care arrangements affect parental stability. The child care dilemma may be difficult for the parents of young infants. In many instances it is necessary for both parents to return to work; nevertheless, it is a conflict. Mothers love to mother, especially nursing moms, and handing over a six-week-old little one for someone else to tend for eight or more hours a day can be painful. Reassure yourself that babies can benefit from a number of close relationships. (See *Working Parents: Multiple Caretakers Help Raise the Kids*, page 133.) In a family, the number-three child learns to love mom, dad, and two siblings—and that's a bunch. So too with other caretakers.

Your comfort with the provider is the number one consideration. The child will sense your comfort, and this will facilitate the smoothness of the daily transitions. To secure that comfort, take time to evaluate the person who will help nurture and care for your infant. Periodic evaluations and observations make sense. Stop in at odd times. Compare your impressions with those of your spouse and other parents. Be businesslike. You are paying for quality care. You and your children deserve the best.

One important advantage of daycare is routine. Most caretakers with a number of infants to care for establish patterns that benefit everyone.

7.
Parenting the Toddler to Five Years of Age

Each child displays his or her own personality right from the start. Each is describable: "Joanie is a bubbler, Helen is the quiet one. Jim's sense of humor is delightful. Bill takes life seriously, and Mack is off-the-wall." Preschool children will handle some situations more readily than others; yet, on some occasions, they may fall apart.

INDICATORS OF GOOD PROGRESS:
THE PRECURSORS TO STABILITY

Eating: The child eats most foods, tries to be tidy, has likes and dislikes.

Naps and bedtimes: The child seldom protests, has only occasional nightmares, is comfortable with favorite toys or blankets, and after infancy usually sleeps through the night.

Toilet and bath: There are no problems here, no fears or resistance. Occasional bedwetting may still occur.

Nervous habits: While the child may suck his or her thumb or chew nails or fingers when upset, there are no ticks, cringing, or soiling.

Social behaviors: Your boy or girl has worked through stages of clinging, is independent, curious, friendly, somewhat affectionate. He or she understands about taking turns, sharing, being friendly. The child accepts changes easily and enjoys grandparents, teachers, other people and places. The child may be selective about playmates.

Intellectual development: He or she registers excitement in new things, explores, questions, remembers well, understands about feelings and that people are sometimes happy and sometimes sad, sometimes afraid and sometimes angry.

Self-control: There are few, if any, temper outbursts. The child accepts limits or recovers rapidly from protests. The child uses words rather than hands or fists to express anger.

Emotional: All children display fears. Understand that fears are a natural part of the world of the preschool child. We hear about their imaginary monsters—terrors under the bed, the Wicked Witch, and other creatures. These are honest fears. They serve a useful purpose as they help children to distinguish between reality and fantasy. An imaginary bear may haunt the bedroom although no other fears are displayed. What should the parent do? Trust that the make-believe character will eventually fade away. In order to help, leave a light on, or rearrange the furniture, or allow the child to sleep in a different room for a while. If sleeping patterns are seriously disturbed, you may want to look for other stressors and consult the pediatrician or family doctor. There will seldom be a need for this.

REASSURANCES

These reassurances build from similar considerations regarding infants. For parents of toddlers and prekindergarten children, be assured:

• *Daycare is not a form of parental deprivation that is detrimental to a child.* This is a conclusion of the National Research Council (1992). Careful placement, supported by parent-child ties, is essential.

- Children at daycare do not seem to be at higher risk for physical or sexual abuse, and they don't differ significantly from home-reared children when it comes to disease and illnesses they experience.
- In a daycare setting, children learn values, taking turns, people are different, and social diversity—plus they have the traditional benefits of preschool experiences. Have fun. (Read *All I Ever Needed to Know, I Learned in Kindergarten* by Robert Fulghum.)
- Children in daycare settings become accustomed to adult authority and limits and rules. This can be especially meaningful to a child who is overindulged at home, perhaps as parental compensation for guilt because of daycare placement. Some situations offer prekindergarten "academics" that prepare children for reading, listening, participation, numbers, and so forth.
- Remember that children are resilient. They can also be forgiving. Affection from you, lots of it, can rescue a difficult situation, especially if there has been a shortage of attention because of your personal turmoil.
- Ask yourself if you take the time to keep your child informed of your plans. If you move too rapidly from one obligation to another or bounce into a spontaneous social engagement without taking time to brief your child, the youngster may feel discarded and unimportant. Even little ones must have careful preparation and honesty.
- When you echo the phrases, "You are important to me. I love you," you foster stability. Even though you have become a bit dictatorial, exhausted from improving and hanging on to a myriad of rules, your kids will benefit. Spoiled brats without limits are frightened and feel very unstable. Be proud of the love and the limits you provide.
- Remember that most young children do not experience tumult. They are always learning ways to express themselves and fend for themselves. One strength builds on another.
- These early ages and stages may be called the Era of Experimentation. You are experimenting to develop a workable formula for parenting and the children are experimenting with life.

> *Children with other children—these can be the happiest moments of the day, free of family stress, surrounded by age-appropriate toys and equipment, and adapted into a routine. Kids can make great friendships and have a wonderful time.*
>
> *Become an Activist*
> *Most child care providers earn minimum wage. Even zookeepers make more money. Take time to raise awareness. Child care givers need respect, plus rewarding compensation.*

8.
Parenting the School-Aged Child:
Five to Twelve Years of Age

As your children zoom into the school-aged years, there will be times when you will be thrilled to see how stable and sensible they seem, while at other times, you may ask, "What did I ever do to deserve this?" This may mean the kids are fighting, messy, forgetful, or even cruel.

School-aged kids are faced with three major jobs: (1) to make and keep friends, (2) to learn at school, and (3) to develop self-confidence and self-discipline. Preschool guys and dolls live a more free-floating lifestyle, and parents make many of their decisions. The school-aged child becomes his or her own decision-maker in new arenas. *Parents can help. Parents must help.*

SOME SOURCES OF INSTABILITY

- The influence of older kids is imposed on young ones. The fifth-grade girl insists on high heels, makeup, and values such as *being thin* and *being cool*. Little girls are not mature enough to cope with sexual come-ons that could result from provocative makeup and clothing. Parents are caught in a bind. If you say no, there may be clashes at home. If you say yes, you may give your blessing to a situation that may foster problems at school or on the street.

- The influence of affluence: Children of wealthy parents become confused about what is important and what is not important. Some have never had to take responsibility for anything; some have learned to care more about things than people. Some may try to buy friendships and experience immeasurable anxiety and uncertainty in their relationships. (See *Affluent Families,* page 196.)
- Girls mature at an earlier age. Puberty starts earlier, accompanied by preadolescent emotional swings. Some girls begin menstruation at nine years of age. They may be self-conscious because they have larger breasts than the other girls in the class. Many girls in the fifth grade might be labeled "adolescents" because of their physical development, yet they are treated like little fifth-grade kids by teachers and older children. This is confusing. Their self-images may become uncertain; they may become depressed and defensive. They want to go unnoticed; they may hate to be different, but their bodies and emotions are more mature. They exhibit the instability of the teen years. Parents must take time to visit school and observe the other kids in order to give support at home.
- The child begins to use logic; parental magic diminishes. The child under seven, even when testy or rebellious, has an underlying confidence that parents are right. This faith in parents is essential to family stability. At the same time, the child may believe that a family tragedy happened because he or she had been naughty or done something he or she was not supposed to do. Around age twelve, the child may be expected to question parental magic. Without realizing it, the child begins to question the faith in parents that has been so important. He or she begins to use logic. It is as if, in the developmental process itself, a bit of the secure foundation has been chipped away. It amounts to an invisible erosion of stability, an artifact of a stage of growth.
- Television creates turmoil. Children may easily become addicted to TV, and parents struggle to control how much TV the children watch and the shows that they select. Children need help to understand that commercials intend to sell and do not necessarily present facts with any objectivity. Kids want the merchandise—a lot of it. They can't have it all, and this causes misunderstandings between children and their parents. When

the children emulate weird decisions that heroes or heroines make, there is relatively little a parent can do. This may result in crude gestures, words, and behaviors. TV can corrode stability. (See Chapter 12, *Social Issues that Affect Stability*, page 198.)

- Children become more perceptive, more inquisitive, and more aware of family and social problems. They begin to experience anxiety from uncertainties that they were never mature enough to understand before. They confront issues about job changes, separation, divorce, death, violence, and illness. They watch the news and hear about race riots, the problems of the Native Americans, rapes, murders, and kidnappings, and they want reassurance. Children become fearful. In helping your child manage the anxieties that stem from family or social issues, make certain that you do not make guarantees that you cannot back up. Provide very specific cautions, limits, and guidelines to establish as safe a lifestyle as possible—which streets to go on, when to be home, not to talk to strangers. Social and family problems can be confronted with honesty and definitiveness accompanied by love and affection. It is best to be explicit as you take time to answer the children's many questions and encourage them to express their fears.

Help Children Handle Friendships

When kids have friends, they are happy. When they are not happy, the world is coming to an end. To a child it is a mini-tragedy when he or she is not invited to a birthday party or when no one will sit next to him or her on the school bus.

Parents Can Teach Their Kids How to Get and Keep Friends

Even first graders can understand some of the concepts. Older youngsters have no difficulty at all.

Ask your children: Can you keep a secret? Encourage your child to respect a friend's plea to, "Please don't tell anybody." Too many times, spreading stories or telling secrets leads to a fight and the end of a friendship. Trust is a word a youngster can learn.

Ask your children: Do you share your feelings as well as your toys? Do your children and their friends tell each other when something makes them happy, sad, disappointed, or angry? Remind them that everyone has good days and bad days, in and out of school. Understanding that, they will try not to let someone else's bad day cause them to have a bad day too. Help them find ways to be loving and understanding with their friends. Teach them to express their thanks when their friends are generous or thoughtful.

Ask your children: Must everybody like you? Help them understand that they don't have to like everybody and everybody doesn't have to like them. People are different; some will enjoy each other and some won't. It's best to avoid people you dislike. There is no need to be nasty.

Ask your children: Do you try to be just like your friend? You may notice that Sarah and Sue, daily, wear the same color sweaters and identical socks. This may remind you of when you did the same thing. Dressing alike is a badge of friendship, but you may want to say something about being an individual.

Ask your children: Do you worry that your best friend won't be your best friend anymore? Why? Because he walked off the playground with somebody else? Help your children learn to share their friends. No one owns anybody else, and most kids have lots of friends.

Ask your children: Are there times when you are jealous of your friends? Discuss jealousy because it can needlessly undermine friendships. "Bill gets to play soccer and I don't." Be frank. Explain that you can't afford the uniforms or provide transportation. Be sensitive—and humorous—all kids don't have to have personal computers or televisions. Material things are not what caring and loyalty is all about.

Ask your children: Does being popular mean giving in to peer pressure? Explain that even though someone may try to talk you into doing something you don't want to do, you don't have to do it. Everybody wants to be popular, but that doesn't require you to give up your opinions or to act like all the others. It may be hard not to go along with what kids tell you to do. Your best friends will understand. If your child is very popular, others may expect or ask too much. It can feel scary to have so much power over other kids. Help your child to use power responsibly to keep relationships harmonious and communications open.

Ask your children: What do you do when you get into a fight with your friends? Be prepared for an assortment of answers. Remind them that relationships have their ups and downs. Most friendships, even in elementary school, can withstand fights. Young children generally recover from an episode more rapidly than their parents do. It depends on the personality of the child; a few bear grudges for a long time. Suppose Dudley and John had a fight. John called Dudley a punk and said he was stupid and a rotten friend. Dudley's feelings were hurt for days. If he habitually complains about the treatment he gets from others, he is playing the role of victim. Is this important to him? Is being alone and angry what he really enjoys? Is this his way of getting special attention from you? These may be indicators of instability. Dudley may not be self-accepting; he retreats from any name-calling, disharmony, or rejection. Dudley may need special encouragement, even help, if he bears a grudge for weeks. Fights between friends are part of growing up.

Ask your children: Are there gangs in your school? Are you a member of a gang? During elementary school years, many children are introduced to cliques and even gangs. When they are part of a gang, they feel protected and secure. Still, gangs create anxiety. Gang membership changes because children are fickle. A kid pushed out may feel destroyed. Outsiders find it hard to handle rejection. Louie may announce, "I wouldn't hang around with those kids for anything," and Laurie may say, "They're snobs," but each feels unwanted.

Finally, when possible, encourage your children to befriend your friends' children. Keep them abreast of your contacts with your friends—phone calls, lunch dates, or evening social life. Show them cards you receive and display pictures of friends who are special to you.

A friend is one who knows you as you are, understands where you have been, accepts who you've become, and still invites you to grow.

SIGNS OF STABILITY

This checklist can help reassure you that your child has

progressed well through normal developmental stages (five to twelve years old).*

Routines

Eating: Appetite varies, sometimes disinterested in food, not obsessed with weight or size, mostly enjoys eating.

Bedtime: No significant problems, no more bedwetting accidents, may still want favorite toys or blankets, occasionally wants to be in bed with parents or siblings. May depend on music, radio, or TV to help go to sleep.

Toilet and bath: No problems, wants to be very independent, modesty begins.

Nervous habits: Has learned to handle worries by asking questions, attention span has lengthened, seems more patient and composed. Parents should look for nail biting, tics, or squinting as clues of anxiety and ask child-appropriate questions. Questions may have to be repeated. The child may be reluctant to admit, "I'm scared of ____," or "I hate my nose."

Social behaviors: Friends have become very important, some teachers also important. Less demanding at home, willing to share with siblings more readily, strong sense of fairness and unfairness.

Intellectual development: Many special interests. Uses explanations and reasoning to avoid or recover from some emotional scenes, such as, "I couldn't help it," or "At least I didn't get mad," as examples. Wants to know a lot about his or her parents when they went to school, reads a lot, watches a lot of TV, likes school.

Self-control: Very individual profile; some children passive, others very explosive. Most require very little discipline—want to be liked by parents, teachers, coaches, and peers.

Emotional: There is an all-pervasive attitude of, "I'm proud of my family." The children have learned to accept their family lifestyle and its various rules and regulations. At our house we had a trampoline with strict rules for its use. Children in this age range seldom questioned the rules.

---

*You are encouraged to refer to Gesell and Ilg, *The Child from Five to Ten*.

REASSURANCES

As you read the list of signs of stability, you will be able to pinpoint the wellness and strengths of your children. What great reassurance this is for you!

9.
Parenting the Adolescent

Adolescence is a time of predictable instability. Parenting the adolescent can be a test of your nerves, your stamina, and your sense of humor. Teenagers are the great experimenters of the world, and they don't even appreciate that. They are flexible and opinionated, lonely and peer oriented, critical and on the precipice of new adventure. There is no systematic, one-step-at-a-time way to become grown up or independent. We all have leftovers from our teen years—some we revere; some we want to forget. No one is one hundred percent mature or stable. With happiness and secure relationships as goals, combined with economic security and a confident sense of self-esteem, parents can help teens move toward stability. The mission: Help each person be the best that he or she can be.

When Barry is rude to his mother, she snaps back, "Control yourself, young man. Show some respect." It may be a losing cause. Barry continues to mutter dirty words declaring he's been cursed with the world's worst parents, and he'll never treat his kids the way he's been treated.

"Control yourself" is a phrase children hear from toddler days forward. The adolescent endures the same dictate. It applies to every facet of life—behave in school, be cautious about drinking, hold back your sexuality or practice safe sex (remember these are the days of AIDS), don't abuse your car, and so forth. "Control yourself" is translated into the message, "grow up."

Adolescents are still children. They do learn to control themselves and they do grow up, but to do so with an increasing sense of stability, they must have parental management and guidance. In other words, they must have parental control and that's where conflicts fester. *You can have struggles and stability at the same time.* It's a matter of balance and demonstrations of mutual respect.

Statistics remind us of the magnitude of teenage problems

today—that some adolescents were not able to control themselves due to many circumstances, lost faith in the future and acted out adolescent impulsivity, curiosity, and vulnerability. They were not bad kids. Many just never had a chance. These kids didn't have you to provide guidance and stability.

SOME SAD STATISTICS

School dropouts: One million students drop out of school each year. One American student drops out of school every eight seconds. More than seven hundred thousand of the kids who graduate from high school cannot read their own diplomas.

Teen pregnancies: In 1991 five out of every twenty births was to an unmarried mother. Every sixty-one seconds, a baby is born to a teen mother.

Teen suicides: (U.S. Centers for Disease Control) Federal Survey, 1991: twenty-seven percent thought seriously about killing themselves; one in twelve attempted suicide, of which two percent required medical attention afterwards. Annual rate of actual suicides: eleven per one hundred thousand. Actual attempts are significantly more likely for girls than boys, in contrast to adults where there is a four-to-one ratio, male to female.

Teen violence: In 1991 national totals compiled by the FBI showed a 92.6 percent increase in arrests of juveniles for murder in the past four years. One out of every nine deaths of young boys is by gunfire.

Teen mental/emotional distress: Twelve percent of 63 million children (or a total of more than 7.5 million children) have a diagnosable mental disorder.

Teenage alcoholics: There are more than five hundred thousand teenage alcoholics. There are 125,000 elementary-school-aged kids who get drunk at least once a week.

Explanations of statistics extend beyond the individual to the circumstances in which teenagers are trapped. Perhaps four major conditions have etched the downside of stability: the breakdown of the family, a myriad of problems at school, availability of drugs and alcohol, and a depressing, oppressive economy. It is unreasonable to assume that all inexperienced youth can weather such conditions successfully. Thankfully many do.

The purpose of *Parenting Children in Unstable Times* is to promote stability—not to dwell on the past or permit pessimism to infect your parenting. In addition to the following procedures for parents, see other specific suggestions included in indicators of instability, page 47.

PROCEDURES FOR PARENTS

- Express yourself. Declare your values. Let your children know where you stand. They may rebel, but knowing your position substantiates stability though the kids may not accept, agree with, or respect what you say.
- Respect privacy. Encourage open discussions. Trust is the ultimate teen-parent connection. *Teen secrets must be safe with you.*
- Continue as family manager. Don't abdicate your position of authority just because your youngsters may get angry. Your skillful handling of unfair accusations and a myriad of threats is evidence or your stability. You have the right to impose curfews, take away the car keys, turn off the TV, and be informed of your child's whereabouts and progress at school.
- Be a sincere, generous praiser. Teens can be inordinately hard on themselves. They may also scoff at your compliments or belittle their achievements. Parents must continue to nourish a child's self-esteem even though your child expresses no appreciation at this time. Praise is a worthy task; appreciation may be long delayed.
- Get involved at school. Get to know the teachers, counselors, coaches, and others. Be your child's advocate, keeping in mind that some teachers or grading practices are unfair, and some decisions disrespectful of the kids. Recommend schedule changes, classes, and extracurricular activities. If you're not your child's advocate, who will be?
- Take time to examine some of your behaviors that may be setting a poor example. Are you a procrastinator? Is there a chance you are drinking too much, are a couch potato, or are unwilling to negotiate with the kids? Look for changes you need to make. Your teenager may point out that you need to be more flexible or consistent. Maybe you need to consider a more generous allowance or liberal use of the car.
- Be forgiving when necessary and humble when appropriate.

- Be available. Come home for dinner. Turn off the TV and listen to the kids, read over assignments, and ask about their friends.
- Use your sense of humor.

These statements provide the foundation for promoting stability.
1. I love you.
2. I realize that sometimes you are stressed out. I am not going to pretend that I didn't notice. I have great faith in your ability to cope.
3. I'm here to help in any way I can.

Three statements to avoid:
1. You'll get over it.
2. When I was your age, I ... .
3. It's not as bad as you think it is.

One further suggestion: Develop the habit of a scheduled time to talk to your kids. Consider an interview style conversation without lots of advice or judgmental remarks. Such a plan is described in *Take Time to Talk** and has been widely acclaimed.

INDICATORS OF INSTABILITY AND ADDITIONAL PROCEDURES FOR PARENTS

In spite of your efforts, your teenagers may display a number of indicators that they are unhappy or insecure. Some teenagers are more vulnerable to problem situations than others. When indicators begin to show up, they are apt to be dramatic and persistent. Often, they are the culmination of years of indiscernible stress.

Eating
Indicators: Overeats, starves self, vomits compulsively.
Parent procedure: Parental lectures usually do not help. Many teenagers with weight problems are willing to counsel with a doctor. At the same time, many with anorexia or bulimia are secretive. Tell the child that you know what is going on. Offer to

---

*Ruth P. Arent, *Take Time to Talk, A Plan for Parent-Teen Communication.* Arent & Associates, P.O. Box 2501, Littleton, CO 80161.

get help. Although teenagers resent monitoring, assume an in-charge attitude when necessary. You may have to take your uncooperative teenager to the doctor against his or her will. Keep in mind that weight problems can denote depression.

Sleep
Indicators: Sleeps too much (missing school, escaping social life); screams; has nightmares; refuses to sleep except in short naps or under duress; needs sedatives, pills, or alcohol to relax; afraid of quiet—insists on TV, radio, or stereo.

Parent procedure: Spend time with your son or daughter before bedtime and talk over problems, gossip, make plans, help with school work. This closeness can build stability which may prevent sleep problems. Often, anxiety about sexuality disturbs sleep. Open discussions about sex may reduce anxiety.

Toilet or Bath/Shower
Indicators: Is compulsively clean or dirty, is severely consti-pated or has problem diarrhea.

Parent procedure: Most teenagers are very private about these matters. Girls may be particularly reluctant to discuss personal hygiene. If the teenage girl is tense at night, suggest that a bubble bath may be a great place to read or study.

Nervous Habits
Indicators: Has tics, pulls hair, bites nails, handles part of the body compulsively, cries very, very easily.

Parent procedure: Unless severe, ignore them.

Social Behaviors
Indicators: Is extremely withdrawn or extremely aggressive, out of control, talks about hating people, wants to be violent, defiant to the point of breaking the law, steals, destroys property, runs away (or threatens to), feels unwanted, can't be alone, feels extreme self-pity or suspiciousness, hyperactive, overreacts to everything.

Parent procedure: These are the most vivid indicators of instability with the exception of self-destructive behaviors. They may be the most difficult for a parent to handle. If discipline is indicated, remember that it must be programmed to the indi-vidual. Grounding may be to little avail. Taking away allowances usually doesn't help—friends help out and some adolescents may steal. For the middle-school-aged child (under fourteen), sometimes moving to a new school is a worthwhile change. Moodiness is normal. Unusual mood swings may denote disguised feelings, as a child appears hyper, then depressed. Counseling may be necessary.

Intellectual

Indicators: Quits school, turns off to learning or is obsessed with academic success, refuses to read, watches TV indiscriminately.
Parent procedure: The unhappy teenager may want to quit school. Talking will not turn this around; he or she has heard your ideas many times before. Parents should insist that the student go to school. At the same time, ask why your child is disinterested in learning. Is this being confused with not wanting to go to school because that child wants to escape from social contacts? If so, that is the issue with which to deal. Is there a problem with a member of the faculty? Most teenagers want to learn, even though some work hard to hide it. Be open to a temporary reprieve or leave of absence while maintaining specific academic goals. (See *Schools and Schooling*, page 167.)

Self-Control

Indicators: Is *unusually* controlled or uncontrolled; demonstrates exaggerated or sporadic behavior, perhaps drug or alcohol induced; has temper tantrums; is cruel and tactless; self-destructive behaviors—cuts, pills, unusual accidents, abuses health.
Parent procedure: It is impossible to regulate someone else's behavior no matter how much you care. Whether prone to temper tantrums, drinking, swearing, or arrogance, self-control is the key. *Be sure that your child understands the consequences. Be assertive in talking about problems. Your behavior and consistency may help the high school student manage his or her behavior.* Teenagers in junior high may be more reasonable and more respectful of parental wishes and authority. Set a good example. Keep your temper under control. When your child keeps his or her cool and doesn't blow up, acknowledge and commend repeatedly.

Regarding self-destructive behavior: *Take charge.* You must be involved, not a bystander waiting to see what will happen next or if this particular episode is just some silly performance. Explore what precipitated the act. Perhaps it was fury over an unfair grade or impending parental separation. Whatever it was, it was important to your child. Do not embarrass, do not belittle. Plan the next steps together—talking to a teacher, taking more time to explore feelings about home problems or lack of friends. If necessary, seek help—the healthy way to confront painful, complicated situations. (See *Suicide: The Choice with No Return*, page 300.)

Activities

Indicators: Is totally disinterested or totally absorbed.

Parent procedure: Younger teenagers sometimes just want time out from piano lessons or soccer. Find out if this is the case with your child. Often they threaten to quit an activity as a way of checking out how interested *you* are in what they are doing. Sometimes it is for financial considerations that they have never mentioned to you. They always have a reason, even to the point of saying, "Well, Lisa doesn't have to take ballet anymore, so I decided to quit too." Try to insist that children stay with the activity, especially music lessons, because they may be most grateful as adults. It may mean some quarrels, but it reflects your mature judgment. How many of your adult friends have said, "I wish my folks had made me stay with the piano?"

Loneliness and depression are two of the most worrisome problems that teenagers share. To combat feelings of isolation and sadness, kids defer to peer pressure and conformity. Conformity may require them to give up their own values and healthy sense of individual identity. They may sacrifice strong parental messages that have been potent.

Peer pressure offers synthetic self-esteem and, as a member of a group, a welcome sense of instant popularity.

Parents, be on the lookout for signs of loneliness and depression. Your awareness, plus the actions you take, may keep your adolescent from making decisions that cater to a compulsive need to do as others do. Your stability, encouragement, and availability can act as a deterrent to peer pressure.

Other indicators: Makes self-derogatory remarks such as, "I'm ugly," or "My nose is too big," or "I hate red hair." Has a persistent "I can't do it" attitude, and a need to blame others for all problems.

In Summary

As a parent, you may observe indicators of instability and pass them off as transitory teenage problems. Be conservative. Discuss your observations with your child and propose changes or improvements.

If societal issues, such as loss of a job or money, are the major problems, be honest, not unrealistically encouraging. Point out the child's strengths and help picture how to benefit from them.

REASSURANCES TO FOSTER A STABLE PARENT-TEEN RELATIONSHIP AND COMMUNICATION

Most adolescents tell the truth. Just give them a chance to ask and answer questions and express their feelings. They will tell you about the things they like and the things they hate. They have great wisdom and sensitivity. They may be impulsive and dramatic. They want to be happy. They want relationships that count. They want to feel free to make their own mistakes and want to know that you are behind them, no matter what.

Most adolescents search for self-awareness twenty-four hours a day. They want to face their own problems. They want help only when they ask for it.

Adolescents are still kids, though commonly cheated of childhood. They are bombarded by confused values and the raw material of relationships and human weaknesses that were not splattered in front of teenagers twenty or twenty-five years ago. They are not protected from painful situations and issues that were sanctified and kept away from kids. They act out in order to discover who they are and what works and doesn't work in society. *They do not act out to hurt you.*

Adolescence as a developmental stage is unstable. Stress is a way of life for most parents and teenage kids; no one is at fault. These are times of ambivalence in the parent-child relationship. The parent must be the family stabilizer, the steady fulcrum that keeps the seesaw of ambivalence from falling over.

For some teenagers, these are also the happiest years of their lives. They love school, friends, babysitting, their new clothes, and the family lifestyle. They have a sense of self that smoothes out the rough times.

10.
Parenting Teen Parents

It is appropriate to include mention of teen parents in a section devoted to adolescents. About 500,000 children are born to teenage mothers each year—340,000 of them to white girls. Many of these girls were raised in fatherless homes, had no or limited sex education, and are ill-prepared for maternal responsibilities. Many unwittingly or unknowingly infect their babies with alcohol, crack, nicotine, or a positive HIV blood problem. This profile may describe your daughter or her best friend. You may be in contact with a teen parent through work that you do or in a volunteer role that you fill. Some teenage parents are stable and loving. Others are unstable, needy, and stressed-out, and have great difficulty bonding to a child.

Certain procedures and reassurances may be helpful when you are involved with these moms.

- Avoid preaching or profound, stern lectures on morals, self-control, growing up, or responsibility. What these kids need is encouragement—*practical mothering suggestions*—time off, and, frequently, money (or an opportunity to earn).
- Offer to baby-sit if you can manage. Immature adolescent mothers benefit from time with their friends, sports, and entertainment (movies, concerts, etc.). Time with peers is important. Support from friends is immeasurable—basic to an accepting, positive self-image. "The kids really like me even if I have a baby." And a good self-image promotes maturity and stability.
- Little girls performing big-girl tasks need as much encouragement as you can offer. Commend the girl generously for well-managed baby care, homemaking, personal grooming, and responsible money management. Too often adults overlook the fact that accomplishments need reinforcement. Smile and remark when the baby is clean, the toddler is happy, or when you note a myriad of signs that the infant/child is well taken care of.

- Don't take over for the girl-mother and absolve her of her responsibilities. This may extenuate or exacerbate dependence. When she had a baby, she plunged into independence, whether she wanted it or not. Promote independence, supported by your concern. If teen mother and child are living with you, be certain you insist that you are not a substitute mother. The girl herself must plan, make appointments, and care for the baby as much as possible. Having a baby is not a free ticket to dump on the grandparents.* The girl may have been naive, but facts are facts and she's got an important job to do; it has already begun.
- Be cautious about your involvement in the teen mother-father relationship. Some teen fathers are devoted, concerned, and involved. Recognize, however, that the mother-father relationship may never evolve into a lasting, mature marriage.

REASSURANCES

You undoubtedly have mixed feelings about the fact that your teenager plunged into parenthood. You undoubtedly are aware of the pitfalls commonly associated with the ongoing problems and challenges the teenager faces.

You are urged to discover and focus on the happy, bright side of the situation. Be certain that you stipulate and repeat positive reassurances—in three divisions—for the baby, the mother, and yourself.

- *The infant:* Her smile is lovely, her weight gain is excellent, he's walking early, listen to all the words she says.
- *The mother:* Your report card is excellent, you're managing so well. I'm proud of you. I could never have handled things as competently as you do.
- *For yourself:* I deserve every delightful greeting I get from this baby. I am able to stand back and let my daughter (or son, son-in-law, or daughter-in-law) handle things without interfering or passing judgment. Encourage the parent to write personal affirmations and you do the same.

---

*See *Grandparents as Parents*, page 142. Note that drug-infected teenage mothers are more prone to abandon infants than any other group. They pursue drugs, not mothering.

5

The Individual in the Family Setting
Possible Explanations for Instability

T. BERRY BRAZELTON, M.D., is one of the most respected heroes of parenting. His television series, lectures, and books encourage millions of parents as they struggle through parenting. He reminds us that healthy, strong families handle necessary adjustments, large and small, by following a pattern of turmoil, regression, reorganization, and growth. The highs of parenting grow from conquering the low points, and the process of trial and error lends itself to family strength.

The development of interactions and a coping style defines each family as a unique unit and typifies each unique member therein. At times the interactions are upbeat and successful. At other times the family may be infected with hostility, mistrust, and unsettling threats that add up to instability. The old adage, *a chain is only as strong as its weakest link,* describes a family. When one person is unhappy or in trouble, this threatens the stability of the entire unit. This chapter covers the causes of such unhappiness and trouble, indicators of instability, procedures for parents, and reassurances intended to establish or reestablish the well-being of the individual and the group. This information may help parents as they experience the trials and errors of parenting.

There is no perfect family. Children feel family pride, however, even in homes that others might criticize as being dysfunctional. Families may experience times of excellent parent-child relationships—times when the parent-child relationships feel comfortable and safe. All families experience some turmoil, times when members would be glad to tell you they are happier with their friends, classmates, or other relatives than they are with the people at home. Perhaps it is the intimacy or overexposure that creates tensions and misunderstandings. As we have seen, communication and mutual respect can do wonders to alleviate problems and foster reorganization and growth.

11.
The First Child and Possibly the Only Child

In the military, it is understood that certain officers have "rank and privilege." In the family, the number-one child is often awarded the same favors. Male or female, the baby receives a lot of attention, fanfare, acclaim, and power. He or she doesn't have to share parental love and devotion. He or she feels very important. Everyone wants Jimmy or Janie to be happy, to not cry, to explore, and to be free to make all kinds of discoveries. The child develops an abundance of attention-getting mannerisms and tricks. The parents frequently act like a fan club, and the child thrives on the applause and feels secure. Many parents smiled when they read that an expensive government research project established that there are no negative effects of being an only child. They would have been happy to tell you that they knew it all the time.

> *Single-child families are rapidly becoming acceptable, if not the norm. The only child relates easily in the adult world. The old cliché, "The only are lonely," may be true. The child may not have round-the-clock companionship, but may appreciate and enjoy privacy and time alone.*

Two problems arise that may foster instability: First, when children are permitted to act like "spoiled brats"; and second, when the children feel smothered or overprotected and are corrected or commended for everything they say or do. They resent these intrusions and believe they can never measure up to parental expectation.

The child who becomes a master at controlling the household may act like a "spoiled brat." The adults may choose not to set limits or are too lax about teaching manners or social skills. Jimmy or Janie may be allowed to interrupt adults, be a picky, fussy eater, and dominate the play when children come to visit.

"Spoiled brats" may become anxious children. As little guys, they cannot visualize limits and, therefore, feel unprotected. Having too much power can be scary. In a sense, they are robbed of their childhood.

The Preschool-Aged "Only Child" Displays Instability

- Disturbed sleep pattern denoting anxiety.
- Extensive temper tantrums to get what he or she wants.
- Nonstop demands for attention.
- Inability to be distracted.
- A self-defeating willfulness that causes a lot of child-parent battles.
- Inability or unwillingness to amuse himself or herself.
- Destructiveness.
- Selfishness with toys.
- Appearance of self-consciousness and lack of spontaneity as if preparing for a presentation: "Look, my tooth's loose!" or "See the picture I made."

When the parents of an only child ask me for advice, I frequently suggest, "Pretend you have five kids and then figure out how much of a fuss you would be making about this incident." If one kid had the flu, one was in a school play, one had football practice, and another had to go to a piano lesson, you might say to Jerry, "I don't have time to help you pick up your blocks right now. I'm sure you can do it by yourself." This pattern of *adding four kids* is surprisingly helpful. In effect, it redistributes your energies, money, and time, and gives you a chance to back off from some of the intricacies in the life of your child. You let the child have more freedom and you permit yourself to ease up from stress.

The School-Aged "Only Child" Displays Instability

- Extreme secrecy.
- Rudeness and disrespect: "Stay out of my life!"
- Efforts to belittle and criticize the parents.
- Indications the child is embarrassed to have his or her parents around in front of friends, teachers, and classmates.
- Nonstop demands for material things or service.
- Bids for attention on his or her terms; a tendency to interrupt and to challenge adult authority.
- Very dependent, seeking help or advice when perfectly capable of doing the task independently.
- Unusually inept in relating to other kids. May want the limelight, insist on being the boss, be intolerant of other kids' weaknesses or demands, teases others ruthlessly.
- Unusually passive with other children as if grateful for the company.
- Evidence of many psychosomatic problems that come from parental overanxiety. Parents may have the attitude, "He's our *only* one. We have to take special care of him." Reactions may include asthma attacks, hives, or allergies, for instance.
- Very choosy and fussy about what he or she will eat or wear.
- May be angry at parents because he or she is an only child and feels deprived. An only child tends to romanticize about the happiness and fun that siblings have. It may be difficult to picture that jealousy, fights, hostility, rivalry, and competition are also parts of sibling relationships, and that there are times when such children may hurt a lot.
- May be intensely involved with an imaginary brother or sister. This is predictable up to four or five years of age.
- May be stormy and stubborn about being forced to play with others, share toys, take turns, etc. May appear disinterested or turned off by babies. May show that they really do not like other kids.

PROCEDURES FOR PARENTS

Your most formidable tasks are to assume and maintain an authoritative role, provide boundaries, and dwell on mutual respect. To carry these out:

- Repeatedly establish your rights and privileges so that the child accepts who is "boss." This important lesson will help considerably when the child goes to school and must defer to a teacher and other authority persons.
- Set limits on what you buy or provide. Parents may feel defensive, "But he's our only child and this can make up for the fun he would have if he had a brother or a sister." That is a nonproductive position.
- Don't look to the child to fill your needs if your marriage becomes rocky at times or if you are a single parent. Don't burden the child with your dependency needs. Don't get "too close"; this is an invasion of an appropriate parent-child relationship and may result in the child becoming overanxious.
- Provide as many social situations as possible—play with cousins, friends, neighbors, and daycare or school companions. Children are naturally gregarious.
- Don't push. Keep your expectations realistic and express any disappointments in a supportive way. "Only children" can become too anxious to please and overly dependent on your approval.

REASSURANCES

There are benefits of being an only child, synonymous with the characteristics of a first child. Such children:
- Are highly motivated toward a goal
- Are intellectually curious
- Set high standards for themselves
- Tend to mature earlier; may be very verbal
- Enjoy the philosophical position that their parents are aware of world problems and the overpopulation crisis and are abiding by the controls that are essential
- Usually feel very much wanted and appreciated

"Only children" are very likely to do better in math, English, abstract reasoning, reading comprehension, and even IQ tests. They may tend to be less sociable and more prone to spend time in intellectually artistic or solitary activities than children with siblings. They are not very often conceited or lonely.

The only child is usually encouraged by the parents to show

interest in both male and female activities. The mother is happy to see sensitivity and female characteristics in her only child. At the same time, the father welcomes male qualities such as dexterity and orderliness. The androgynous attitudes seem to provide a special degree of comfort to both parents and prevent, for example, a single boy from being forced into all-boy activities that he may not like.

Although the single child may miss out on the normal give and take of a sibling relationship, he or she thrives on having the single-minded love, warmth, care, and attention of both parents. Often, "only children" will announce, gladly, that they do not want a brother or sister.

12.
The Only Child Isn't an Only Child Anymore: The Second Child Arrives

"I've got a new sister so now there are two of us. But I'm still bigger and older," little Roger announced. Roger, as the number-one child, appears to love the baby. Other young "first children" display ambivalence. They are not hesitant to ask you to take the baby back or give it to a neighbor. It's hard to learn to share mom and dad. The adjustment varies with age, preparation, self-assurance, and the relationship with the parents, as well as the time he or she is involved with the baby's care and the quality of time alone with the parents. Older first children may appear more sophisticated, even ultramature, and maternal or paternal.

School-aged children may not show any jealousy until the new sibling is mobile or starts to talk. When the brother or sister gets into the older child's toys, knocks down his blocks, turns off the TV that "number one" is watching, you may expect outbursts and normal displays of disgust and anger.

Five-year-old Sarah loves her Barbie doll. She carefully lays out her clothes as she prepares to take her to a dance and then to a beach party. Toddler sister, Molly, picks up one of the dresses, clutches it, and waddles out of the room. Sarah can't stand it and says, "Get that kid out of here. I hate her!" Don't overreact. Distract Molly; Sarah will recover.

Siblings Without Rivalry by Adele Faber and Elaine Mazlish has become a classic. The book emphasizes avoiding comparisons, being aware of favoritism, building the self-esteem of all kids, allowing expression of bad feelings, and creating ways to let go of anger and jealousy. Faber and Mazlish remind us that parents can help the child know he or she can be civil, kind, and assertive. How to handle fighting is artfully explained.

The adjustment to a new baby may be genuinely exciting and smooth. If, however, you notice any of the following behaviors, the first child may be upset.

INDICATORS OF INSTABILITY

The child may:
- Resort to baby behaviors, regress, wet pants, talk baby talk
- Be very passive, act depressed
- Overplay the role of mother's helper
- Exaggerate displays of talents such as playing the piano or reading out loud
- Act out anger against parents; hit, spit, be defiant, call names
- Become excessively demanding and unreasonable
- Act aggressively toward the baby

PROCEDURES FOR PARENTS

The best strategy to follow is to make certain that the first child has certain privileges. He or she can:
- Stay up later
- Have time alone with you
- Not be exploited to help take care of the little one
- Have an opportunity to express jealousy and love
- Have privacy; the child may be permitted to not share some things

Children Don't Need to be Treated Equally.
They Need to be Treated Uniquely.

Instead of giving equal amounts
"Here, now you have just as many grapes as your sister."

Give according to individual need
"Do you want a few grapes, or a big bunch?"

—

Instead of showing equal love
"I love you the same as your sister."

Show the child he or she is loved uniquely
"You are the only 'you' in the whole wide world. No one could ever take your place."

—

Instead of giving equal time
"After I've spent ten minutes with your sister, I'll spend ten minutes with you."

Give time according to need
"I know I'm spending a lot of time going over your sister's composition. It's important to her. As soon as I'm finished, I want to hear what's important to you."

—Adele Faber and Elaine Mazlish*

REASSURANCES

The siblings may or may not become close. If they don't mesh, it is not your fault. Different personalities can clash. But they do live in your home, and they must learn to tolerate each other, to share, and to use self-control. Tolerance and sharing are essential ingredients in all relationships.

---

*Adele Faber and Elaine Mazlish, *Siblings Without Rivalry*, New York: Avon Books, 1987, page 99.

Most siblings become great friends. As a toddler, the little one may adore the older one and emulate his or her every step and gesture. It is great fun to watch. Older siblings may confide in each other, be strong allies, and give each other a rough time.

Caution: Many health experts are becoming increasingly concerned about the negative effects of ongoing sibling teasing, belittling, and tormenting. You are urged to pay attention to any systematic, unkind habits your children develop and take active steps to stop them. Sibling abuse can be very destructive and lead to serious self-esteem problems with lasting scars. Therapy may be useful.

13.
The Baby of the Family

Recently, at a wedding reception, I watched an elderly couple greet a lovely girl, "Oh, you're Lisa, *the baby!*" Lisa protested, "I'm not a baby. I am a twenty-year-old woman."

Lisa used to enjoy her position in the family. She could turn on her little-girl charm and her parents would give her almost anything she wanted. They would explain, "But she's so little and she's our last." At other times she bore the brunt of parents' annoyance. Her older brother and sister would set her up to do something forbidden, and when she got caught, they were nowhere to be found. Lisa's protests were to no avail. "It'll have to be a lesson, Lisa, on when to say no." Nevertheless, being the baby was fun. Besides, there was nothing she could do about it.

If the youngest is pushed to grow up in a hurry, there may be many problems. The child gets the feeling that he or she is a burden and that the parents are tired of dealing with little people. They appear to want an instant grownup. The boy or girl facing unrealistic expectations from the parents imposes unrealistic expectations on himself or herself. This creates stress.

On the other hand, some discover that their efforts to grow up and be more independent are thwarted and discouraged. The message from the folks is, "We love having a baby in the house and can't bear to face the day you leave." This makes some children very angry, while others enjoy such acclaim. A lot depends on the number of children in the family and the friendship patterns that have developed.

INDICATORS OF INSTABILITY

The youngest child may display:

- Babyish mannerisms, whining, tattletale games, and manipulative, coquettish behavior.
- An attitude of helplessness.
- Unexplained outbursts of anger denoting insecurity or reaction to too-high expectations.
- Possible resentments expressed to older siblings because of their detachment from parents. In effect, the baby feels as if he or she has been left holding the bag.
- Unsatiated need to get older siblings in trouble.
- Pouty, passive behaviors as a bid for attention.
- Incredible need to be on stage—the main attraction.
- Compulsive need to live up to brothers and sisters.

PROCEDURES FOR PARENTS

- Sit down and discuss the child's feelings about being the baby of the family—what feels great and what may be a problem.
- Intervene if older children persist in teasing and taking unfair advantage of the littlest one. Children understand about fairness.
- Make sure your leniency and permissiveness with the baby doesn't arouse jealousy in the other children.
- Set limits if the baby persists in tattling, bothering the others, interfering with their toys, messing up their rooms, and demanding to be noticed all the time.
- As the baby matures, let go of the word "baby." "Our youngest" is more respectful.
- Be tactful. Even though you really may be thrilled to have this "last child," make certain that your enthusiasm does not leave the other children feeling unimportant.

The older brothers and sisters of the baby constitute a built-in support squad, and they are important teachers in almost every way imaginable. Even though youngest children may feel overwhelmed, the benefits of being part of a group are numerous.

REASSURANCES

Circumstances may benefit the youngest child. Sometimes the family is considerably more stable than when the older children were born, or it may become more stable by the time the "baby" is a teenager. For the affluent, a gift of a car or stereo or college tuition may be possible for this child while the older kids had to work for theirs. Parents don't need to be defensive and neither does the youngest child.

14.
The Mature Youngest Child

As the youngest child matures, it is not unusual for him or her to feel a special sense of responsibility toward the parents. He or she has lived in the home more recently and so is more aware of the problems and pressures that the parents face. It is natural to want to reach out to them, and depending on the age of the parents, the youngest child may offer to stay in the home to help. If one of the parents is deceased, the youngest child may feel very strongly that it is his or her place to take care of the surviving parent. The resulting conflict between being independent and being a caretaker may be difficult. The child may decide to follow the independent lifestyle of the older siblings and then feel so guilty at abandoning the parents that he or she decides to return to the home. The youngest may be the one to negotiate with siblings about joint responsibility for the parents.

15.
The Middle Child

Child development experts give the middle child a lot of press. There are numerous articles in the women's magazines about how to make certain the middle child has a proper and special place in the family. Who is the middle child, and does he or she have distinguishing characteristics? In the family of three, the one born in the middle may be the second girl, but the third child is a boy. Is this little girl a middle child? The girl may prefer to see herself as the little sister to one sibling but as a big sister to her brother and may not feel as if she has been squeezed in between.

Being the middle child is more attitude than placement.

INDICATORS OF INSTABILITY

Those who perceive themselves as the center of a cookie may have difficulties acquiring stability. Look for:
- An exaggerated sense of insecurity, or shyness, or a tendency to be a tattletale in order to get the others in trouble.
- An unwillingness to express an opinion, as if what he or she has to say, "isn't important anyway."
- A tendency to find excuses to be away from the family.
- An all-pervasive anger, perhaps masqueraded behind ill-nesses such as asthma, allergies, skin problems, or eating disorders.
- Many signs of jealousy. Belittling remarks, such as, "How come she gets to do that and I don't?" or "It seems as if you have to be a baby in this house for someone to come and kiss you goodnight."
- Efforts to be controlling—sometimes openly, sometimes covertly.

Each of these behaviors should be seen as a plea for love. This child needs to feel appreciated for special talents and for his or her uniqueness.

PROCEDURES FOR PARENTS

- Avoid making comparisons. "At your age, Janie was helping with the dishes, and Julie is still too young."
- Structure schedules so that you have time alone with each child. The little one can go to bed a half hour early. The older child can go to his or her room to read or listen to music. Now you can spend undivided time with the middle child. This may not be possible every day, but consider once or twice a week as minimal.
- Ask yourself how well you know your middle child. Describe him or her as best you can. *Then fill in the blanks.* What does

the child like or dislike about school? Who are his or her friends? What badges is he or she working for in scouts or Camp Fire Girls? Will he or she make the soccer team? How well does your spouse know this child? Does he or she happen to be a favorite of either of you? Do you note symptoms of stress and rationalize that this is just a phase that the older one went through too? (See Chapter 4, *The Family Grows: Ages and Stages*, page 31.)

- Compare the amount of attention you bestowed on your first child at this age, and ask yourself if the middle child is receiving a fair share. If not, begin today.
- Have you left a lot of the caretaking to the other child, who in turn may be impatient, angry, or disdainful? If so, start a plan that will change this situation.
- Make certain that the preferences and opinions of a soft-spoken middle child are not overlooked.
- Program the middle child into activities different from the others.
- Make the same effort to get to the middle child's piano recitals or ball games as you did for the first child.
- Take time to talk to the middle child about feelings. A middle child may ally himself or herself with the youngest for protection from the first child and receive, as a bonus, a more generous amount of the loving than the youngest one gets.

The personality descriptions of first children emphasize their aggressiveness and need for power and approval. The descriptions of the other kids are less definitive. But all children in the family need approval and have the right to take turns being bossy. Middle children are frequently described as easy-going, less intense, sweeter, and more considerate. These complimentary adjectives may describe your child. *Don't let the nice description deter you from observing whether the middle child is unhappy.*

Reassure the child that you do not have a favorite child in spite of such accusations. Molly's mother blithely says, "My favorite is the one I am with at the moment. When we are all together, I don't have a favorite." Middle children need to hear this a lot.

16.
The Wrong-Sex Kid:
"But I Was Supposed to Be a Boy"

I was an unwanted child—a mistake. It was not unusual for me to be told, "I never wanted any more children and certainly not a girl!" I picked up the message that girls are like leftovers, sometimes useful, seldom outstanding, and with limited potential. A sad lament such as this is disturbing. It never loses its sting.

I have heard little ones ask, "Then why didn't you give me back and get a new one?" Parents are quick to respond that they would never do that, but the child's underlying fear of being unwanted remains. Older kids may just joke about it, even though their stability may be affected by the unresolved hurt.

INDICATORS OF INSTABILITY

If the "wrong-sex" kid is a girl:
- She may act like a boy—demand trucks, cars, guns, or male-type clothes to try to make up to the parents for what she visualizes they are missing. She may act out her feelings of being unwelcome and unwanted by belligerence, defiance, or pre-delinquent behaviors such as lying and stealing.
- She may overplay her femininity to win her parents over. She may acquire seductive mannerisms as early as two or two and a half years old. She may strive to be like mother—a good cook and dressmaker, for instance. She may become very competitive with her mother for the father's attention. She may display an exaggeration of sex stereotyping or a total rejection of your reassurances that she is loved and appreciated. As a young adolescent, she may become sexually promiscuous.

If he is a boy:
- He may exaggerate his masculine interests in order to impress his mother and father that he is acceptable because he is Superboy. He may show off—do risky things such as climb dangerously high in a tree. He may become self-conscious about everything; he may make weird faces and seem strained

and tense all the time. As an adolescent, he may take to drugs to ease the pressures resulting from the self-consciousness and feelings of rejection.

- He may become overly ambitious to prove that he is a worthy member of the family. He may put himself under too much pressure to succeed at school or in athletics or may become emotionally disturbed. He may avoid peer friendships.
- He may just give up and become very passive, convinced that he is in a no-win situation. Consider Martin, now ten years old. While his parents haven't mentioned their disappointment in several years, he thinks about it every day. His passivity comes across as depression, low self-esteem, and lack of ambition. At this point, he needs professional help.

Other family dynamics can add to the stress these "wrong-sex" children feel:
- The maturity and adjustment of the mother and father.
- A possible division. Mother wanted a girl; father had to have a boy. This polarity itself may indicate problems in the home.
- The child was to replace a child who died.
- The family name was to be carried on by a boy in spite of today's changing patterns in passing on names.
- The parents had, themselves, been "wrong-sex" babies and unwittingly set up the same stress for their own children.
- There was a real desire for a mix and match family. There were already two boys, and they wanted a girl.
- An older child or children had ordered a brother or a sister. Such a fantasy may harm the sibling relationship for years to come.
- In some religious groups, such as Orthodox Jews, there are special services and celebrations to herald the arrival of a male. A young girl may feel she has let her family down by being a girl, depriving them of the tradition so important to the heritage. In the ongoing family lifestyle, the role of girls is difficult, although the family lifestyle is predictable and the relationships stable.

PROCEDURES FOR PARENTS

What can a parent do now? What do children need?
- If planning a pregnancy, consider amniocentesis (a procedure not without risks) so that you may know the sex of your child

before the birth. Work through any disappointments ahead of time with someone you trust, such as a doctor or minister, in order to let go of any attitudes that might permanently damage your child's self-esteem.

- If you were a "wrong-sex" child, let go of this emotional baggage. Reaffirm for yourself that everyone disappoints his or her parents on some level, at some time. Everyone has both feminine and masculine qualities and can achieve a well-balanced personality.

- Stop verbalizing your disappointment if your child is an infant or toddler. Babies cannot comprehend, and toddlers are in love with life and can withstand your remarks. Give children nonsexist toys, such as blocks, and both-sex toys, such as dolls and trucks.

- School-aged children need repeated reassurance that they are loved as a person, not as a male or female. If the wrong-sex concept is deeply implanted, it is difficult to erase the damage. *If you still harbor disappointment, get help for yourself;* examine your own hang-ups about being masculine or feminine.

- Try to avoid gender-specific expressions: "Well, that's not bad for a girl!" or "Boys are supposed to be able to fix their own bikes." The wrong-sex child will overreact. Be aware of his or her sensitivity, whether it is verbalized or not.

- Consider the name of your child and whether a nickname would be a good idea. Did you want a boy whom you planned to name George and have a girl with the substitute name, Georgia? Perhaps, if the child is young enough, it is time to try a nickname like "Gigi." Nicknames can offer a reprieve.

- Talk to your teenager and explain the history of your attitude. This may alleviate misunderstandings and guilt. Teenagers need reassurances with repeated expressions of love and welcome. If your child asks, "How come you're talking about this now?" explain that you are aware of the problems you have created and that you want to straighten things out. Furthermore, it may help prevent their imposing a "wrong-sex" burden on their own children.

REASSURANCES

If your child is already aware that you were disappointed because of his or her sex, it is time to confront this disturbing information. If you have never discussed it before, make light of it now. Explain to the child that most men want sons and most women want daughters. "We wanted a male to carry on the family name," or "We had three boys and hoped to have a girl this time, but you were loved from the moment I held you in my arms." The child, regardless of age, must hear that the momentary disappointment was only momentary.

17.
The "Late-in-Life" Child

The child whose parents are in their forties when he or she is born faces some interesting situations that may affect family stability. The deferred child is becoming increasingly common as couples marry later, remarriages occur in the forties, and some career-minded women prefer to wait until they have achieved certain goals before having children. It can be a matter of choice or a matter of chance.

"Was I a mistake?" If there are older children, with perhaps a gap of eight to twelve years, the child will, at some time, ponder about being an unwanted child. Parents usually draw the picture with such comments as, "You were a happy surprise!" or "We thought we were through with diapers, babysitters, and the PTA—and then you came along!" These intended-to-be-humorous remarks need to be backed up with a lot of reassurances and sincere indications that the couple is, indeed, delighted to have this child. I have heard couples say, "We worked hard raising the first three kids; this is the one to enjoy!"

If an only child, high expectations may abound and the child may be overstimulated, overprotected, and overworshipped. The affluent Yuppie family may overindulge their child in concert with expensive, trendy clothes, nurseries, and so forth.

PRESSURE ON THE CHILD: INDICATORS OF INSTABILITY

- Does the child seem to be forcing himself or herself to be independent in order to avoid being a burden on the parents?
- Does the child seem to avoid the parents in an effort to stay out of the way?

- Has the child developed habits of apologizing for all kinds of things that do not warrant apologies? This can be interpreted as a basic apology for interfering with their plans and mature lifestyle.
- Is the child reluctant to bring home friends for fear of messing up the house or bothering his or her older mom and dad?
- Does the child take advantage of his or her special position by being obnoxious, attention-seeking, and demanding?
- Does the child appear embarrassed when his or her parents attend a school function or scout meeting? How does he react when one of his classmates says, "I thought they were your grandparents"?
- Does the child seem passive with his or her parents? Does he or she take the position that the parents are unduly set in their ways and there's nothing he or she can do to change this?
- Does the child seem obsessed with his or her parents' age and worry about them becoming infirm or dying?

PROCEDURES FOR PARENTS

- Settle the issue once and for all. Make it clear that the child is a welcome member of the family who enriches the lives of all of them.
- Avoid the expression, "You keep me young."
- Don't push yourself to get involved in activities that you do not enjoy just for the sake of the child. Suppose that you are in your sixties and your child is in junior high school; you are extremely busy with your work and activities, and the child pushes you to become a skier, a jogger, a weaver, or whatever. Your other interests, other children, and commitments determine how many new pursuits you can undertake.
- Don't overplay all of the child's accomplishments to your friends. Many of them are into a grandparent role and may be burned out on the doings of eighth-grade kids.
- If you are a grandparent, it is important to show as much enthusiasm for your child's school, friends, and interests as you show for your grandchildren's activities. Your child may feel displaced by or jealous of his or her nieces and nephews.

REASSURANCES

Look at all the advantages the "late-in-your-life" child may have:

- The stability and maturity of the parents may mean considerably less friction about such issues as clothes, which were troublesome when raising the siblings.
- The family may be more secure financially. Older brothers and sisters are out of the nest, so there is more time and money for the new child.
- An add-on kid is sometimes overindulged by all the family. Relationships with nieces and nephews can be very loving and close and provide the companionship that may not be possible with older siblings and older parents.
- The child may have a setup similar to that of an only child and love every minute of it. (See *The First Child and Possibly the Only Child*, page 55.)
- The parents may feel rejuvenated and excited about being a part of younger parent groups. The attitudes of younger parents, as well as those of their own older children, may make parenting this child easy, delightful, and fulfilling.
- Current issues that face the child of today are brought home for your consideration. The child may challenge you about environmental issues, overpopulation, endangered species, and world health, including AIDS. You may have to confront prejudices or old attitudes you have had and be motivated to change them.

18.
Twins and Other Multiple Births

The days have passed when parents heralded a set of twins with the announcement, "We were totally surprised." Almost all parents-in-waiting have weeks, or perhaps months, to prepare for a multiple birth. This planning time provides an opportunity to think about possible problems and complications that twins, triplets, or quadruplets may bring. This includes costs, how much help will be needed, and what provisions will be necessary. How to meet the emotional needs of the babies is another important matter. The parents will have to visualize how to give equal attention to each child, how to try to keep comparisons down to a minimum, and how to find time to enjoy each baby.

There is a multiple-birth boom. Women who delay childbearing until their mid-thirties are considerably more likely to have twins because their reproductive systems start to drop two eggs instead of one. Women taking fertility drugs are having far more multiple births than anticipated. Inasmuch as a relatively high percentage of multiple-birth babies are low-weight preemies requiring extensive, expensive medical support, there is some concern about the dosage of fertility drugs with recommendations to lower the dosage to prevent multiple births. A quad birth may require as many as twenty to twenty-five persons to help with the delivery, crisis resuscitation, and intensive care. A hospital bill for triplets may be as high as $159,000 for a one-month stay.

In 1989 there were ninety thousand sets of twins in a new baby population of 4 million. In 1988 there were eighty-five thousand.

Triplets are on the increase as well: 2,385 in 1988 and 2,798 in 1989. Twins occur in one of every forty-five births, triplets once in sixteen hundred births.

Research about twins has fascinated social scientists, among others, for years. The believe-it-or-not similarities or unexplained simultaneous acts or decisions present a compelling statement that genetics plays a huge role in behavior. Stories abound—one twin was in school at 10 A.M. when pain struck her right knee; the pain lasted forty-five minutes. She later found out her twin sister had surgery on her right knee starting at 10 A.M. that morning, lasting forty-five minutes.

A Focus on Twins

Twins are fascinating and fun to watch. Family and friends may ask, "Is one brighter than the other?" "Do they want to be dressed alike?" "Which one is dominant?" "Do they mind being separated?" "Have they developed their own language?" "Do you have a favorite?" The most commonly asked question is, "How did you survive when they were babies when you had so much work to do?" Thoughtful parents reflect their philosophy of raising twins with the statement, "I want each child to have individuality and not feel that he or she only counts when *one of a pair*." Through normal give and take, each personality will become distinguishable. One twin is friendly and one twin is shy. Mary is self-confident, Marty is not.

As infants, some twins are easy to manage and some more demanding. A lot depends on size and physical well-being. Within three or four months, they learn to watch each other and react to each other, which can provide short periods of quiet time and rest for the adults. Days may seem much less frantic.

It may be difficult to maintain stability or a sense of control when the babies are small if:
• Fatigue prevents parents from cuddling and handling their twins.
• The small size of the babies creates unusual worry and concern to the point that parents may become overprotective.*
• The personalities of the babies (or just one of them) is demanding and difficult.
• Mother's recovery is very slow and this causes problems.
• Parents are not able to get extra help, even from the neighbors, older children, grandparents, or paid help.
• Expenses are overwhelming.
• Either child is ill or exhibits developmental problems.

There are three different kinds of twins—identical, fraternal same sex, and fraternal opposite sex—with similar and different problems. Identical twins can be confusing to all caretakers. The switches and tricks that the kids may play, as they grow up, are fun to hear about, but they can also be a puzzle to parents, teachers, neighbors, or friends. Competition may play a big role with some fraternal, as well as identical twins. Others may accept the dominant/passive positions and not be noticeably competitive. Boy-girl twins seem to demonstrate the more traditional sibling rivalry.

---

*Many twins are very small at birth, some due to preterm delivery. Although there are studies about problems relating to preterm deliveries and mother-child bonding, they are not included in this book.

In general, there are many advantages to being a twin.
- Companionship, fun, and their own games and jokes
- Loyalty, concern for each other, protectiveness
- Independence from parents
- Sharing
- Cooperation
- Understanding of differences

INDICATORS OF INSTABILITY

These disadvantages may result in immaturity or delayed evidence of stability or well-being:
- Physical problems associated with small size or prematurity
- Too much competition
- Lack of individuality
- Feelings of being a burden
- Favoritism
- Too much dependency on each other
- Feelings of being forced to do what the other wants to do
- Resentment from other brothers and sisters

Parents must observe and study the personality of each twin. Tommy, a withdrawn child, has adapted to Tim, who is overbearing and very outgoing. He does not struggle to be in the limelight, and, though he may feel jealous, he seems at ease with his position in the family. As a preschooler, Tommy's passivity becomes a problem in a hurtful or unsatisfactory way as he has difficulty making friends or feels unwanted and unimportant. Tim lets him be a tag-along. Other kids may not play with him. As he gets older, he may learn to select friends of his own.

Parents are urged to be on the lookout for these other problems:
- Unrelenting need for attention and approval—may stem from one twin getting more or neither twin getting enough attention because of parents' personalities, fatigue, or schedule.
- Combativeness—social situations become competitive, out of proportion; one twin must be the first served at the table, sit next to a visiting grandparent, and argue and quarrel to prove he or she is always right.
- Exaggerated dependency—child refuses to make a decision on his or her own; consistently defers to the opinion, leadership

or preferences of others; appears to react with hero worship toward the sibling.

- Too independent—child refuses to be associated with twin—won't dress alike, play same sports, read same books, eat same foods, etc. May denote unrelenting jealousy.
- Exaggerated overprotectiveness of twin—child feels the need to be the twin's protector at all times. This may interfere with how they relate to other children.

PROCEDURES FOR PARENTS

Questions you need to answer:
- Does one twin appear insecure as a person, not sure who he or she is?
- Does one twin act as if alienated from you?
- Does one twin complain that the other one is a burden?
- Does one twin cling to you as if fearful of the other?

If your answers cause concern, talk to each child, and make certain each feels respected. Make certain that your interactions with each child are unique. For example, one of your twins may court closeness while the other is uncomfortable when you ask personal questions. If one is struggling for identity, you may have to insist they enter different activities or be placed in different classes. Teenage twins may be adamant about separate activities and friends.

In general, twins enjoy each other. They benefit from their relationship. They may proclaim that they feel sorry for kids who have to go it alone.

There are more than 2 million pairs of twins in the United States. And twins tend to beget twins. A woman who is herself a fraternal twin has one chance in fifty-eight of bearing twins. A number of persons alive today who have lost a twin brother or sister at birth or in infancy are described as obsessed with being a twin and unknowingly suffer from unresolved grief. Nancy Segal, a twins researcher, says that they experience survivor's guilt. If this should be your situation, take time to find help for yourself. The unresolved problem may affect how you parent your twins, and you are entitled to clarity and happiness.

Parents need all the support they can get—especially the advice and encouragement that comes from participating in parents' groups. You may want to inquire about *Twins* magazine and its hotline (1-800-821-5533). Above all, in spite of the work load, enjoy the twins, the triplets, or the quads. Their antics can provide nonstop entertainment.

19.
The Replacement Child

The child born following the death of a sibling is in a unique situation. Many things will influence the life of this new child— the deceased's sex, age, personality, and the cause of death. Will the parents try to mold the new baby after the dead child or expect and accept differences? Chances are there may be few problems, but some uneasiness is predictable. However, most parents are happy to have the new baby; they do not become overprotective or unrealistic in their expectations. If problems begin to arise, consider these suggestions:

- While you are pregnant or the infant is still very young, talk to someone you know about your feelings. If, for example, the deceased child was a victim of sudden infant death syndrome (SIDS), it is advisable to seek out the support of members of the SIDS organization. This may require attendance at meetings and/or counseling. There is no time line for recovery.
- Try to stop all comparisons.
- Keep sentimental memorabilia to a minimum.
- Help all extended family members to accept the new baby as a very welcome addition to the family. Discourage a recital of memories and grief.
- Discipline yourself to avoid comments such as, "She is sweet, but little Mary was sweet too," or "She is a darling baby— almost two now, but Mary would have been six and just starting first grade." Such remarks keep the new child under intermittent stress that can damage self-esteem.
- Express depression away from the child. Young children have great difficulty understanding depression. They may even emulate depressive behaviors and not be aware of it at all.
- Enjoy the baby!

The stability of the family is influenced by the fact that the replacement child lives in the shadow of a dead sibling, causing parents to be unusually fearful. At the same time, the new child becomes *precious*—a perception that reveals parental awareness that one doesn't take for granted the health and survival of a child.

Reassure yourself that you are fine, a stable person maintaining stability for all as best you can, even though there will always be a sense of loss. In reality, one child cannot replace another—only be a new personality to add joy to the family.

20.
Adopted Children

Is keeping secrets from children a form of child abuse? Perhaps. Yet, unwittingly, for years adopted children were not told about their birth parents or roots. The intention was to protect children from the *then* unacceptable label "illegitimate." However, the secrecy resulted in great difficulties for many, including low self-esteem, ongoing fear of rejection, and problems with bonding and trust.

The scene is changing. While not always totally successful, *open adoption* is recognized as a healthy, honest process that benefits the child, the birth parents, and the adoptive parents. Open adoption includes the birth parents and adoptive parents meeting one another, sharing full identifying information, and having access to ongoing contact over the years. (All three components must occur to fit this definition.) The birth family is considered extended family like other relatives within the adoptive family.

> *The most important discovery about open adoption is that the adopted child is much happier and emotionally more stable knowing that his birth parents had indeed loved him very much (and still love him).**

---

*Kathleen Silber and Phylis Speedlin, *Dear Birthmother*, San Antonio: Corona Publishing Co., 1989.

Both birth parents are free to relate to their child without threatening the child's relationship with his or her adoptive parents. In order to achieve this, birth parents need counseling by trained persons in conjunction with guidebooks. Adoptive parents applaud the normalized adoption process and feel in control of the adoption procedures. Reportedly they do not live in fear that the birth parent may have a change of heart and come and reclaim the relinquished child. One adoptive mother said she never felt threatened by her child's birth mother because, "We can never have too many people love us, and our children are lucky that so many people love them."

A second reason the adoption scene is changing reflects the broad-minded thinking after World War II with the upsurge of multiracial adoptions. Children of diversified ethnic backgrounds are welcomed into adoptive homes that are open to sharing as many facts about birth parents and cultural backgrounds as possible. This precludes secrecy.

PROCEDURES FOR PARENTS

Problems regarding interfamily adoptions, surrogate mothers, and long-sought reunions are publicized and occasionally glamorized by the media. The issues are complex—both emotionally and legally.

Many adoptive parents want their adopted children to know more about their biological roots and welcome and expedite ways to enrich the lives of the children.

If you are "traditional" adoptive parents and you and your child are considering a relationship with the birth parent(s), keep in mind:

- The child's needs must come first. You, the adult, must consider what the impact of change or reunion may be on the child's stability, sense of security, and on the beliefs and adjustments this child has had over the years.
- Your relationship with the child should have top consideration. The new knowledge and perhaps the new acquaintanceship with a birth parent may or may not be fruitful, but regardless of the outcome, it must be orchestrated so that you, the adoptive parents, do not feel threatened.
- The purpose of reunions is complex: curiosity, amends for

previous "rejections," explanations, and for some, to open up a source of love. In addition, it serves to free up some children to love and appreciate their adoptive parents in new ways.

- Not all reunions or revelations are successful in spite of good intentions. Be prepared that your agenda may not mesh with the child's.

An agenda for all adoptive parents would require that you bear in mind that the traditional phrases like, "You are special" and "You were chosen" are very important and need to be expressed. Also, be prepared to handle common questions young children may ask, such as, "Why did my parents give me up?" "Will *you* give me up too?" "Am I lovable?" They seek reassurances. Children who have lived in a series of foster homes prior to the adoptive placement are particularly insecure.

If you are a "single-by-choice" parent or a partner in a homosexual household, help your adopted children deal with these aspects of your life. Your children will learn to appreciate the meaning of freedom of choice. Some children may experience stress due to outside judgments or pressures.

REASSURANCES

Your history with your adopted child is unique, and whether or not you endorse or reject the "new philosophies" is not important. If your adopted child should want to explore their biological background and if, for any reason, this disturbs you, take time to talk to an adoption counselor who can help explore your feelings. If a child wants to seek information, rest assured it is not a rejection of you. It does not have to undermine the stability of your family.

———

Some facts about the adoptive process. If you adopt a hard-to-place child, you may be eligible for financial subsidy. Other adoption fees may escalate beyond ten thousand dollars. If you are a working parent, inquire as to whether your company will help cover some of the costs. Recently, IBM, Proctor and Gamble, and others have begun to assist.

Although the baby shortage in the United States continues (about ninety-five thousand babies are placed each year), the recent trend of adopting foreign children continues. There are approximately fifteen hundred adoption agencies in the United States, and private arrangements through doctors, lawyers, friends, and family can be made.

There are more than one hundred thousand American children now in foster care awaiting adoption. Such children are considered *hard to place* for one of the following reasons: they are too old (about forty percent are eleven or older); they belong to a racial or ethnic minority; they have some physical, emotional, or intellectual problem. Although parenting a disabled child may be a very difficult task, bear in mind that most children *do* respond to loving, stable parenting and that children as old as seventeen can bond successfully. Seek as much information as you can about the child, knowing the depth of the challenge.

The rewards are immeasurable when you see love and peace in the eyes of your adopted sons and daughters.

21.
The Child of Teenage Parents

When teenage parents are happily married and have a growing, sincere relationship, the arrival of a baby may, indeed, be a celebration. When an unmarried, teenage mother, with or without the support of a devoted partner, has a baby, she may feel confused, ambivalent, and guardedly excited. How differently their stories may read! My basic concern is how to help teen parents provide the stability and parenting that their babies need. Many "babies raising babies" are doing a great job. Others are too immature, too needy, and too overwhelmed to meet the needs of infants or toddlers or school-aged boys and girls. This may forebode neglect and abuse.

Regardless of the circumstances, teen parents need support and guidance. They need someone to insist that they finish their education, and to help them prepare and practice parenting skills. You may want to recommend marriage counseling for some.

Consider your relationship with the father carefully. A viable relationship with the baby's father—perhaps even his extended family—adds to stability. The more stable the parent, the better the situation for the baby.

In the "happy" situations, teen parents have fun with their kids and don't seem to worry as much as older parents do. Fresh from school and homework, they find it easy and natural to ask for help or advice. They appear to be adultlike and display a stability uncharacteristic of many adolescents. On the other hand, in difficult situations, teen mothers have problems bonding to their babies. They regard their babies as a burden and make impulsive decisions that make matters worse. They may be neglectful, disinterested, and occasionally abusive. When grandparents take charge of the infants, there may be misunderstandings that can escalate to hostility and alienation. So much depends on the maturity of everyone involved—and their abilities to conceive what stability is all about and how to achieve it.

Grandparents as Caretakers

In the case where a grandparent, usually a grandmother, takes care of the child, there are important guidelines to consider.

- The grandparents should maintain a parenting role with the teen parent—setting limits, demanding respect, encouraging good school performance, and so forth.
- The grandparents should consider their own needs when arranging a schedule. Older persons can get very tired caring for infants and young children.
- The teen parent should find ways to compensate the grandparents. If money is impossible, then the teen can take on such responsibilities as house painting, lawn care, or car maintenance.
- The teen parent should frequently express appreciation and not take grandparent care for granted. If the teen fails to show appreciation, tensions may build, which can affect the child. Children are perceptive of tension, even if too young to verbalize. They may have disturbed sleep or uncharacteristic crying.
- The grandparents have the right to express an opinion about the teen mother's lifestyle, decisions, self-defeating habits, if any, and money management. Together they may need to

discuss self-awareness, social skills (manners, deportment, dress, job skills, need for friends, and so forth).

- The grandparents may encourage the teen mother to become informed about birth control, conception, and sex.
- The grandparents should applaud the many good decisions the teen parent makes. Parenting is a tough job, no matter how old you are. (See also *Grandparents as Parents*, page 142.)

Right now 150 teens are giving birth to their third child. There are over 1 million teen pregnancies a year; one-half result in live births. Many of the babies are undernourished, drug infected, and unwanted, and may become victims of a mother's desperation and loss of control.

The importance of teen fathers must not be overlooked. The benefits of two-parent love are commonly acknowledged. Successful two-parent parenting provides the stable base from which the child learns to trust and learns self-worth.

Do Not Accept These Myths About Teen Fathers

- The Super Stud myth: This teen father knows more about sex than most teenage boys.
- The Don Juan myth: He sexually exploits unsuspecting and helpless adolescent females.
- The Macho myth: He feels psychologically inadequate and has a psychological need to prove his masculinity.
- The Mr. Cool myth: He has a casual relationship with the mother and has few emotions about the pregnancy.
- The Phantom Father myth: He is absent and rarely involved in the support and rearing of his children.

Facts About Teen Fathers

- Some do not abandon their partners; they stay involved and have intimate feelings toward mother and baby and want to participate in the childbirth and child raising. Some want contact with the child without any responsibilities.
- They are no more educated about sex, sexuality, pregnancy, or contraception than nonfathers.

- Teen fathers are no different psychologically from adolescent males or adult men who father babies by adolescent females in regard to:

  Intellectual functioning   Interpersonal trust
  Personality adjustment   Self-image
  Coping style   Social support
  Anxiety

- The more support the teen father receives, the more he can provide support for the mother and baby.

> *Become involved ... make certain that schools where you live provide classes for teen parents and daycare for the kids.*

22.
The Child Born to a Single-by-Choice Parent

This youngster has a special role to fill; a woman elects to be a mother in spite of the possibility of censure from family and friends. The woman has a real need and commitment to motherhood. However, the child's burden to meet her needs goes far beyond a physical presence. These may result in unrealistic expectations with components such as the companionship a spouse might otherwise provide.

Single-by-choice mothers make important decisions that usually reflect stability and maturity—so vital to the child's well-being. One may foresee they will offer many compensations to these fatherless kids.

Like adopted children, each knows, "I was wanted," and this can launch a stable parent-child relationship from the onset. Honesty is the key. Appropriate revelations, without unnecessary, intricate explanations, will be important in order for school-aged children to understand where their family fits. Teenagers may ask piercing questions such as, "Am I from artificial insemination or not?" or "Who is my dad?" A stable communication and sturdy relationship of the mother and child will not be in jeopardy when children seek such information.

If the mother is a lesbian, there is no evidence that these

children are any more likely to become homosexuals than children raised in a heterosexual family. Rather, they express appreciation for love received from the woman or women who enjoy an ongoing, stable relationship—who model unselfishness and fidelity. A baby brought into a lesbian family may be expected to fill the maternal needs of both women. Although the recipient of a double supply of love and attention, there may be considerable pressure to understand and satisfy two moms. There may be times when teenagers are uncomfortable or embarrassed when discussing their situation at home.

REASSURANCES

A single-by-choice mom usually has a clearly defined sense of self before she has a baby so that she understands that for her, single means "go it alone." Basically, she may be free of entanglements, dependency problems, and parenting conflicts with a spouse. She is proud of her decision; today being a single parent is no longer taboo. Many older women, the biological clock-watchers, are open and willing to make arrangements for the children to have productive, if not close, relationships with men. They may arrange for a child to have male teachers, scout leaders, male leaders of youth groups at church, or Big Brothers. Male members of her family—her father, brothers, or male cousins—often bond to the child in a most satisfactory fashion.

Reassurances are important. Every single-by-choice reader is urged to read and reread this list:

- You are an independent person.
- You have made an important decision and can continue to make fine decisions on behalf of your child and your parent-child relationship.
- You will be faced with having to plan new ways of using your time and energy to realize your goals.
- You will be able to change your lifestyle to promote the most efficient, satisfactory methods of child raising. Take inventory of all the potential options in child rearing. You can select those that meet your goals and are worthy of your investment of time.
- With your new baby, you can tidy up and reorganize your life and welcome the rewards of the love of an adoring daughter or son.

You may foresee that in the seventeen or eighteen years ahead you will face issues about your career, your social life, and parenting. *Career* considerations stem from your role as sole provider for yourself and your child. Consider whether you will need more schooling. Would a transfer be advantageous? What new skills do you need? List your options and estimate, as best you can, the money you will need, skills you possess, and time you can afford.

A social life is important. You are entitled to your friends and all the joys and benefits that friendships offer. New kinds of recreational social opportunities are available for single moms and their children. Don't play the martyr—have fun and appreciate your need for companionship.

You are free to parent in your own style and are mature enough to accept that some folks will applaud what you do and others may be critical. Too often family members will unduly scrutinize the parenting of a single-by-choice mother more readily than they would a traditional family headed by your brothers or sisters. You may have to tell them you welcome their interest and love but are not asking for supervision.

Single-by-choice is a courageous decision with innumerable rewards.

23.
Favoritism Affects Stability

Favoritism may erupt at any time. Sometimes it is only a matter of the children's ages and how "cute they are." Sometimes it is a matter of different personalities and how they interact. One child is bossy, one is complacent, one is habitually ill-tempered, and another has a cheerful, happy disposition. You may be quick to note, "Susie is just like my sister, and we never got along," or "John is the spittin' image of my dad's brother and he was everybody's favorite." Such statements have an immeasurable impact on a child. In effect, they are labels that reflect attitudes and determine expectations.

Children learn to believe that mom prefers one type of kid over another. The same for dad. "He's dad's pet because he gets good grades and dad's a brain," can be an accurate picture. Mom has made it clear that Gayle's whining drives her up the wall.

"She's a whiner and I can't stand it," mom frequently exclaims. Gayle can't let go of the label, even though the whining is a symptom that she needs more attention.

Children label themselves, and many times they reinforce the idea that, "John is her favorite. I'm the troublemaker," or "I'm the helper." Such descriptions expose family patterns. Labels can be delightful or disastrous. Whether self-imposed or picked up from others, they influence relationships and the stress level of the family system. A child who gives himself a negative label, such as, "I'm sloppy," or "I'm dumb," has a built-in excuse for being the unfavorite kid. This hurts. It prompts anger, jealousy, fighting, and other behaviors that denote low self-esteem. When children accuse you of playing favorites, hear the accusation as an indicator of unhappiness, which undermines stability.

PROCEDURES FOR PARENTS

Parents are urged to:
- Confront labels. If they describe a problem accurately, work for a solution. "I'm sloppy" may mean Chris needs more shelves in his room, fewer toys to straighten up, or your attention when getting dressed.
- Establish complimentary labels for each child. "You are so thoughtful and dependable."
- Help children get rid of labels that no longer apply. "You used to be silly, but you're not anymore."
- Extinguish competition wherever possible so that no one feels inferior or unwanted. "Let's take turns on the trampoline and not go with a system where you have to do two flips before you can get on."
- Give the child who sees himself or herself at the bottom of the pile some special attention. This may relate to birth order. Youngest children may need frequent reassurance that they are important too—especially if the older child is an outstanding person.
- Note how symptoms of stress at home may disturb relationships outside the family. Work with your child to overcome bad habits that may stem from labels. "You seem to like being sloppy. Even your friend complains that you won't help clean up when you play at his house." "You seem to be proud that

you are the most sarcastic member of the family. We are learning to ignore you, but you hurt people's feelings. Your friends won't go for that."

- Listen to the defeatist labels the little ones may express. For example, "I'll never be as good as Patty. She is so pretty and smart, and I'm little and not smart." This may reflect that the first child has been dominating and demeaning. You have to address this issue. Act promptly to safeguard the self-esteem of all the children.
- Little kids usually admire big sister and big brother, yet they are jealous of their power in the family. Big sisters and brothers may echo similar complaints. You have not failed as a parent when kids protest, "But you always let Jennie have the front seat," or "You always help her and you never help me." These protests are warnings for you to heed. Are labels or favoritism contaminating your family?

Stress in the family is to be expected. Even animals adjust to a pecking order. Happily, as human beings, we can rearrange relationships so that *no chick feels unwelcome in the barnyard.* Children want to feel that they are all loved for their unique qualities. Even favorites can hate being favorites because they realize a sibling's feelings are being hurt. They want to be free of the problem, to see you as fair and appreciative of everyone.

6

Personal Problems that Affect Stability

THE PREVIOUS SECTION FOCUSED on a child in relation to the family constellation. This section shifts the emphasis to personal problems a child may have and how this affects stability.

24.
The Ill Child:
Living with a Chronic Illness or Disability

It is asking a lot of an ill or disabled child to display stability when forced to face complex, difficult situations twenty-four hours a day. Chronically ill children, such as youngsters with cerebral palsy, epilepsy, childhood diabetes, or cystic fibrosis, are helped to understand their limitations and the nature of their disease. Children with impairments, losses, or malfunctions may consider themselves disabled or handicapped. As best they can, they learn to adjust and master the demands of being self-sufficient, productive, and socially competent. Thanks to many new devices, machines, training programs, and therapies, the lives of disabled persons may closely parallel those of the nondisabled. When living or working with disabled persons, bear in mind that their world is both deprived and rewarding, threatening and satisfying, painful and comfortable, frustrating and gratifying. Be certain you don't attach the label "disabled" to someone whose behavior, attitudes, and achievements denote that he or she doesn't relate to the label at all.

Unfortunately, parental tensions and conflicts that preclude stability often result from the stress of dealing with a chronically ill or disabled child. The rate of separation and divorce is estimated to be as high as fifty-eight percent for parents of children suffering from conditions such as cystic fibrosis or chronic problems following a traumatic accident. Every parent is urged to seek support from other parents or groups. It is very important. *In order to take care of others, you must take care of yourself.* The stability of the family contributes immeasurably to the well-being of the chronically ill or disabled child. It is one thing that they can depend on.

It is important to remember that:

- The child with a disability is more like than unlike nondisabled or ill persons. The child has the universal needs to feel acceptance, competence, and love. With the exception of extreme retardation, the child with a disability may function normally in many areas and may have outstanding talents. These children are usually highly motivated to be independent and to find ways to be creative and productive.
- The adjustment of the child will be very much influenced by age, mental and emotional development, ability to conceptualize, and the nature of the illness. The time of onset is extremely important. Has the child had years of normal development, or has he or she been ill since birth? Is the problem the result of a recent accident or trauma?
- Problems a family faces, such as poverty, lack of medical or therapeutic support, or troubled relationships may affect the child's attitude and adjustment. The child knows medicines and doctors are expensive and feels guilt and shame.
- Disabled kids love to teach someone else what they have learned. This builds self-confidence.
- It is possible to integrate disabled children into many arenas such as schools, athletics, music, arts, drama, and so forth. Qualifications for placement in a regular classroom are tied to limitations resulting from the disabling conditions. Some

> *The granddaughter of a friend of mine was born with multiple abnormalities due to the mother's use of Bendectin. The child, bright, articulate, and enchanting, had numerous surgeries before she was three. Her abbreviated arm with pedestal fingers was not repaired. The child was unaware that it was a problem until several doctors asked her many, many questions. At that point, she became self-conscious and later told her mother, "I never realized anything was the matter until they told me so." She had adjusted and was a secure person. Others imposed their ideas of "handicapped" into her thinking.*
>
> *If a teenager has a leg amputated because of cancer, his or her attitude may be as poised as little Allison's, or the teenager may become demanding, difficult, and even withdrawn for some time. Depression and anxiety are natural reactions to such trauma, and will vary according to age and the child's personality. The stability of all family members is at risk during the traumatic times and the demanding adjustment period that follows.*

excellent TV programs promote such integration along with federal legislation. The success of the placement of your child will depend on the preparation and attitude of everyone concerned.

PREDICTABLE INDICATORS OF INSTABILITY

The child may be a very happy, well-adjusted person or unhappy, volatile, and difficult to manage. This is, in part, determined by the condition itself. The characteristic way a child copes may be predictable and seem stable. Nevertheless, all children experience frustration and stress. Occasional symptoms will show up. For example, the child with limited ability to speak has to act out by crying, being extremely obstinate, hiding, hitting, running away, or clinging. The youngster who is immobile may occasionally scream, be unusually irritable, throw things, or regress in other ways.

As a parent, you may hear yourself saying, "Oh! That's just Susie," and lose sight of Susie's frustrations. Be aware of changes that denote problems.

- Does your child seem unusually agitated?
- Is your child exhibiting more babyish, less mature behavior than usual?
- Is your child doing something unusual, such as bedwetting or thumbsucking?
- Are there unusual pleas for attention—holding, comforting, closeness?
- Is your child unusually anxious to talk to you, to tell of fears, bad dreams, or new frustrations?
- Does your child appear unusually listless, defeated, or unhappy?
- Has your child stopped trying to be independent? Does your child refuse to try to overcome some problem on which he or she has been working?
- Does your child cry or daydream excessively?
- Does your child talk about death or express a wish to die, or express nonstop self-pity or guilt at being a burden to the family?
- Is your child exhibiting self-destructive behaviors?

Some of these problems may be age-related, such as the wheelchair-bound girl who fears how she will manage menstrual needs or the paralyzed boy who wants to shave himself.

The Child Goes to School

A child may seem stable at home and exhibit problems at school. School adjustment reflects the child's personality, past experiences, and the way parents and teachers handle the situation. At school look for:

- Indications of being overwhelmed
- Fatigue
- Insecurity, crying
- Signs of jealousy or misunderstanding of classmates
- Show-off antics—aggression or marked passivity
- Exaggerated displays of disabling condition
- Vivid denial of weaknesses; bravado or unrealistic stories about achievements

Parents and teachers need to be encouraging and patient. Although most kids readily accept disabled peers without ongoing notice, *teasing* may be a problem that adults must intermittently discuss with everyone involved. New teachers, new classmates, the challenge of new activities, and the feeling of being one of the group can help the youngster let go of self-consciousness and problem behaviors. While your child may be one of seven million "exceptional" youngsters who need public concern, this child prospers from *your* special understanding.

The School-Aged Child with a Disabling Condition

School-aged children harbor a need for closeness to adults and attract it with their enthusiasm and sparkle. They may freely seek counsel, comfort, and advice. These patterns may be exaggerated by the disabled child. Above all, children want friends and acceptance at home, in the neighborhood, and at school. Some may continue to behave in babyish ways, and their more sophisticated peers may be scornful. Help them understand that all kids of this age are trying hard to grow up, and that is why peers may be intolerant of their babyish behaviors.

If a disabled or ill child has always been carefully protected, he or she may overreact to the characteristic thoughtlessness of peers. A disabled or ill child may perceive the tentative quality of peer interactions as callous, uncaring, or hostile. They may perceive that kids are staring at them or mimicking them when that is not so. Adults should interpret these misconceptions.

Many middle-school-aged children appear to emulate their older brothers and sisters in almost everything they do. This results in uncertainty and confusion. In effect, they are catapulted from childhood to adolescence with too little time to try out their own ways of doing things. The disabled child faces an even more complicated task when surrounded by peers who have interests and activities from which they are excluded. This creates feelings of alienation. The child may become more self-conscious, self-critical, and depressed. Help the child learn that everyone matures at his or her own pace.

The Adolescent with a Potential Disabling Condition

No date on the calendar is marked, "Adolescence starts today." The onset of puberty, the need to be with a gang or a clique, and the struggle to become independent and to set career goals and develop a sense of self-mastery are part of the adolescent realm. This may not describe the progress of the adolescent with a disability or illness, who at times appears *too young to be so old* and in other situations, *too old to be so young*. The disabled teenager may have great wisdom and a philosophy of life from which parents, friends, and siblings derive much strength and courage. In other respects (again, depending on the nature of the disability), the judgment and demands that the teenager displays indicate that he or she is still immature.

The years of preparation for adulthood have been full of adversity. The teenager has learned to cope. One sees compensatory behaviors, acceptance of limitations, courage, a spiritual acceptance of an illness or handicap, development of talents, parental support, and important bonds with friends, family, and professional helpers. One may also note low self-esteem, loneliness, repeated expressions of inadequacy and failure, anger over being a burden or worry to parents, discouragement, and confusion. At the same time, this teenager may have a great sense of humor, school spirit that won't quit, and enthusiasm for new activities, such as learning to play the guitar, that are an inspiration to everyone around. Some teenagers give the impression that they are out to conquer the world—and they do.

Others become increasingly depressed. As they begin to look ahead, they are angry about or they fear their dependency. Money matters can become very important. Resentment about their condition or illness builds up to larger-than-ever proportions. Questions about dating, sex, and marriage come up to cause heightened feelings of being cheated, inadequacy, and bitterness.

As the parent of a disabled teen, try to distinguish between the normal ups and downs of teenagers and any special attitudes or problems of your youngster. Your child needs to know there are times when all kids feel this way. Be certain that your child has a chance to talk with other teenagers. While this may sometimes be difficult to arrange, it is very important. Kids may benefit more from talking to others with similar problems than they do from therapy program activities or their parents!

In the case of the chronically ill teenager who must be hospitalized periodically, it is comforting to see the camaraderie that the kids build in the ward. As much as possible, they tease, scold, laugh, and joke with the staff. They show great sensitivity for those who are suffering and display an admirable bravery themselves. Visitors may show more depression than the kids. Nurses and attendants often complain good-naturedly that they get tired just trying to keep up with the high spirits of the kids. They also report that kids today get hooked on TV serials—an interest that sometimes interferes with the characteristic group quality of the wards in the past.

No ill or disabled person, teenager or not, can be expected to act like well people all of the time. However, be aware that this may reflect age and not how their health problems are handled.

REASSURANCES

Disabled or chronically ill children need:
- As much certainty as possible; uncertainty undermines stability. Many illnesses or conditions are difficult to diagnose; wrong diagnoses may have been made. Multiple surgeries may have had to be endured. The ever-present uncertainty of the progress of an illness or disability causes anxiety for the entire family. *The children need explanations they can understand.*
- To be surrounded by people with a positive attitude. Loss of hope is the worst disability of all. Most children remain very optimistic if those around them have the same attitude. If they feel very discouraged, accept their feelings and assess the situation. Depressions can deter some recovery. A depressed person is entitled to medication and counseling.
- Help and support to face changes. A child's hopes, dreams, outlook, and goals will vary with remissions, and new therapies, braces, or machines.
- Lessons on how to handle stress. Learning to give up something you love to do, like skiing, and substituting swimming in a warm pool may be very tough. Help the child feel enthusiastic about the new people they meet at the pool or in a yoga group

or in the physical therapy room at the hospital. Just staying active keeps the stress level down. Coping by retreating to a TV set may be necessary for some but may be overrelied upon by too many others.

- Experience in coming to terms with visible evidence of disability, such as hearing aids, crutches, a walker, or wheelchair. Most children adjust very well. They need to be surrounded by accepting family and classmates or to have a buddy or two nearby. Often the initial fear of isolation or of being conspicuous is a more difficult adjustment than becoming dependent on the equipment itself.

- Help in coping with an invisible disease, such as childhood diabetes, early-stage multiple sclerosis, or controlled epilepsy. These children are privately ill. With parents they are urged to be open and direct. No one at school has to know that they have a chronic illness unless they tell or have some kind of episode or breakdown at school. There may be days when they are not energetic. They may be pleasant one day and surprisingly short-tempered the next. They need a sense of emotional well-being that will permit them to talk about the disease without embarrassment. Acceptance is the key. Self-esteem leads to acceptance and an attitude that promotes friendships. In the world of children, friends come first.

- A chance to help others become comfortable with their disabilities or illnesses. Teachers, friends, parents of friends, teammates, or neighbors may be very uncomfortable, not knowing how to help or even to talk to an ill child about it. The child gains much by talking about real feelings, especially anger and fear. These experiences help the child make the point that, while a disability or illness may be a real nuisance, it can be put on the back burner of the mind. Little Kathie has childhood diabetes. As a fifth grader, she could remember times when she was dizzy, sweaty, couldn't sleep, and had to be rushed to the hospital. She says she's glad they found out what was the matter. Now her parents aren't so mad at her for being cross. She says she would rather have a shot every day than wonder what was the matter. She smiles when she says, "You know, I only think about it in the morning, and when I can't eat candy, and when I have to go to the doctor. I wish my mom and dad wouldn't talk about it so much."

- Freedom to ask for rest periods or to be given shorter assignments or to change deadlines. After a day at school or a therapy session at the hospital, the child may rebel against having to do the dishes or feed the dog because he or she is too tired.
- Encouragement, encouragement, encouragement—the kids need as much as they can get. Help each child discover strengths and talents that they never dreamed they possess.

The child whose illness causes a loss of control suffers an added source of stress. The youngster who experiences breathing difficulties or seizures, the child who stumbles or drops things, and the blind child who may fall against a misplaced chair need to know that even the nondisabled have clumsy moments and drop things or bump into things. Remind the child that all people goof now and then.

Children who must take medicine at school usually do not attract any attention at all. Some schools require the child to go to the nurse's office for their pills. It becomes routine. The child will smile or greet the secretary in the office on the way to the nurse's room without any unnecessary fanfare. The child needs to be aware when medication is changed so that he or she will not be frightened if there are any side effects. Parents would be wise to notify the teacher and school nurse of such a possibility.

PROCEDURES FOR PARENTS

As you read about the needs of disabled children, I am sure you are saying to yourself, "I could help her do that," or "I could talk to him about that," and you probably have in mind at least three or four things that you want to try right away. Or perhaps you are pleased and satisfied that your child's needs are all being met. Great! I invite you to read over this list of strategies—one of them might be a good addition to your present repertoire.

- Remember that the disabled or ill child is learning a different lifestyle from those who do not have such problems. This requires you to be tolerant of expressions of sadness and fear that you never imagined your child would have. *Be open and let the child express any feelings to you.*
- Prepare yourself to support the child in whatever school setting he or she fits into. Think through all the benefits of

mainstreaming, of special classes, and training programs. Mainstreaming can be a most successful school arrangement. Your positive attitude is essential.

- Keep in mind the importance of friends. Promote ways to keep the youngster in a social setting.
- Try to capitalize on strengths at all times.
- Listen to what the child wants to learn or to improve upon. Would mastering a word processor or computer games be helpful?
- Help your child set realistic goals in many areas—home chores, schoolwork, and outside interests.
- Encourage independent decision making whenever feasible.
- Make frequent efforts to help the child develop new interests and creativity. Provide toys, supplies, and books.
- Handle the subject of sex, grooming, and relationships with the frankness appropriate to the child's understanding. If your teenager has had a limited background in social situations, an understanding of relationships may be missing or misconstrued. Take time to read books together, rent videos, watch TV, and talk about the relationships that you observe.
- If your child shows a special talent (for example, a blind student who plays the piano, or a deaf person who composes) make certain he or she is planning to use the talent for monetary *and* emotional gain.
- Don't overreact to outbursts. Teenagers may be acting out for the first time. The ill or disabled adolescent may be reacting to years of forced overdependency, overprotection, and frustration.
- Keep in mind the wider scope of interests and job opportunities that are developing. This means new methods of evaluating work and forecasting for the future. Be open-minded about noncompetitive school placements, homeschooling, or training situations and living facilities that promote independence.

The teenager with a potential handicapping condition is confronted with the normal crises of adolescence. Combined with the ongoing difficulties of the past, these may upset some of the established ways he or she has learned to cope. This may be very upsetting to the child and the parents. Remain optimistic even though you know there will be regressions, demands, and problems ahead.

My grandson, Phillip, age five, cautiously watched as two caring adults placed a spina bifida victim on the playground grass. The little girl, about eight years old, managed to weave her fingers through the blades of grass and pushed several tiny pebbles back and forth.

The adults moved her several times. Phillip wandered over to them and asked, "Will she be okay?" hoping to hear that she would soon be walking. He quoted their brief answer to me, "She's handicapped and she was born that way."

I explained about spina bifida using my fingers to illustrate how the spinal cord was incomplete.

Phillip went on, "Gram, will she ever get married?"

I answered gently, "I'm afraid it would be difficult for someone to relate to her in a close way."

His immediate response was, "Well, maybe some other handicapped person will learn to love her and they could be happy."

REASSURANCES

Every adult in the life of a child is a teacher. Teaching involves the effects of our behavior on the feelings and learning of others. This requires insight into self. Once we understand ourselves, we can begin to understand others. *Understanding the needs of your ill or disabled child must take priority over understanding the disability itself.*

Welcome the reminder that our concern is for the integrity of the whole person, for his or her finiteness as a human being, and the comforts that can be established and maintained in the complex world of human relationships.

> *Let me win, but if I cannot win, let me be brave in the attempt.*
>
> —motto of the Special Olympics

25.
Living with a Life-Threatening Illness

The daughter of a friend of mine died as a teenager. She had nephrosis, and she had been hospitalized frequently. She couldn't stand straight and used to call herself, "the crooked one." Before she died, she wanted time with her sister who lived far away. She died at her sister's. The mother let the sister select a burial site. It was underneath a crooked tree.

Vivid, poignant stories of children with AIDS are becoming more frequent. The media invades the privacy of some AIDS victims and their families, which may add to their anguish and instability. On the other hand, the TV presentation of the life of Ryan White did wonders to help others understand the struggles of an afflicted little boy. His courage and honesty was straightforward. The entire nation mourned his death.

Children with a fatal illness may acquire an amazing sense of equanimity and an inner stability in spite of their condition. They know that they do not feel well—that something is very wrong. They rebel against being different from well people—family, friends, and kids on TV. Depending on age and development, first they want answers that are hopeful; later they want the truth about their future and about death. In many ways, answers provide them with a way of life, with a format for dealing with profound anxiety. Each child develops a way to cope whether it involves sharing feelings and fears or maintaining a kind of quiet privacy. Children adjust to their own emotional swings at separation from family and friends when they have to spend time in the hospital. They often become intuitive, philosophical, and spiritual.

The initial impact of the diagnosis of the disease will create more anguish for the parents than for the ill child. In some cases, it may be months, perhaps years, before the child is told the truth. The child must be given sufficient information to ensure cooperation with medical treatment and to respect his or her emotional well-being. You, in the meantime, must answer the questions of relatives and other children without alarming the child who is ill. The teenager, in contrast to a five-year-old, may demand immediate, honest answers about the nature of the illness and the prognosis. All ill children need much support, regardless of age.

> *Children can learn to cope with almost anything if you tell them the truth.*

INDICATORS OF INSTABILITY

During the months or years of an illness, there will be tests. The stability of the family will help each person even though it goes without saying that the tests threaten the stability itself. Again, the age and the personality of the ill child will be pivotal to his or her coping style, and outside support should be provided for the entire family.

Descriptions of children with a fatal illness may include such words as pensive, angry, searching, realistic, hostile, passive, intuitive, and unresponsive. When such children feel well, they are frequently described as conscientious, eager, delightful, reserved, anxious to please, and friendly. At certain times in the illness, their emotions range from deep depression to temper tantrums and refusal to talk. Realistically, all of those behaviors are manifestations of the child's awareness that they are ill, that they are different, that they may die. Their priorities may shift rapidly. For a while, a child may be intent on spending a great deal of time with parents, siblings, and friends. Within a short time, he or she may want to spend hours watching TV or reading, learning about aviation, or studying trees, or history. Young children may want someone close by with few demands for a response or cooperation.

In early stages of the disease:		
For the Child	**For the Parents**	**For Siblings**
Wants to feel better	Medical decisions	How to deal with
Wants parents,	Feelings	fear, anger,
doctors to make	How to approach	curiosity
him well	others	How to know when to
Fears treatments,	Spouse agreements	ask for something
separations,	or disagreements	for themselves
missing school,	Financial matters	How to deal with
and losing friends	Hospital stays, visits	jealousy for attention
	Concern for others	ill sibling receives

After remissions or in late stages of the disease:		
For the Child	**For the Parents**	**For Siblings**
Wants to be certain	How to communicate	How to give support
parent is near	with the sick child:	to ill sibling, parents
Wants doctor near	what to/not to tell	Questions about their
Wants help to talk	How to program a child	own well-being
about illness, death	during remissions or	How to satisfy the
Wants time, a chance	when "feeling better"	curiosity of well-
to say good-bye	How to balance expect-	meaning friends,
Wants to decide how	ations: normal child	classmates,
things will be	versus ill child	teachers,
distributed	Discipline, excuses,	and relatives
Wants to be reas-	sympathy as problems	
sured that death	Making plans for funeral,	
doesn't hurt	burial of the child—	
	anticipating life without	
	the child	
	Seeking answers, cures,	
	spiritual guidance	

PROCEDURES FOR PARENTS

How can parents help to alleviate such stress? If you are a parent with an ill child, I am certain that you give immeasurable support to your youngster. So that others may benefit from the lessons that you and other parents have taught us, this summary is presented.

- Remain at the hospital with the infant, toddler, or preschool-aged child. The child is apt to be more devastated by the separation and fear of abandonment than by the illness.
- Be prepared for angry outbursts and don't overreact. The child may scream, "I hate you!" because he or she feels that, somehow, you have let this happen.
- Express understanding, realistic reassurances, and some of your feelings. Downplay despair. Share about sadness and worry. Express yourself so that your child doesn't feel guilty: "If I weren't sick, then mom wouldn't be sad."
- Be certain not to make promises that you won't be able to keep. For example, safeguard against a promise that the child will never have to go to the hospital again or through painful tests and procedures. No one can be certain what lies ahead.
- At home, keep the family as near normal as possible. Continue holiday celebrations, routines, events for the siblings, and traditions. This helps the ill child feel less guilty about interfering with family life and supports stability.
- If the child is going to school, urge the child to be honest with teachers and friends. This prevents misunderstandings when the child gets crabby, can't keep up, or complains of not feeling well. If the child is embarrassed about handling this, offer to go to school with him or her and handle the problem together. Some young children may discuss heart disease, liver problems, cancer, or other diseases with peers in a matter-of-fact way. Others are reluctant to do so. The child may feel betrayed if you tell anything without his or her knowledge or permission.
- Older students will accept hospitalization more readily when you make arrangements with teachers for lessons and tests. There is no way to predict the outcome of a disease for a patient—for your child. Some teenagers with Hodgkin's disease or leukemia may become young adults—into their twenties—and will make every effort to be independent and self-sufficient. They are, therefore, entitled to the same skills, training, learning, and career counseling as others.
- Listen to the child's protests if he or she feels that you are being overprotective. Back off or explain your decisions. There will be

times when you can make decisions together about bedtimes, exercise programs, clinic schedules, or responsibilities at home. When not feeling well, most children accept dependency without too much of a struggle. They welcome freedom and responsibility when they feel better.

- If the child is being teased by peers, such as being called "hairless" because of a side effect of chemotherapy, be assertive. Parents' and teachers' assertiveness must be focused on being fair, kind, and empathetic.

- Reflect on your spiritual or religious beliefs regarding life and death. Share these with your child. Seek help for yourself from any sources that you respect. This support gives you more energy to cope with the many pressures that you face. It goes without saying that your ill child will benefit from your attitude and strength. (Parents sometimes report that one of the most difficult adjustments to be made after the death of a child, is where to direct and how to use their ready reserve of energy.)

- When you become aware that death is imminent, your presence is the greatest reassurance and comfort the child can have. Dying at home allows the child to be in a place he or she has loved, surrounded by people, especially parents, whom he or she loves. This is not always possible or wise. In the hospital, the dying child, though very weak, perhaps semiconscious, needs to know that you are there. If possible, having his or her much-trusted doctor there also eases the way. Be assertive and ask your doctor to stay nearby if at all possible.

Pressure on the child with a life-threatening illness cannot be compared with any other stress. We all want to know what we can do. Underneath, we all feel so helpless. Children may show us the way to compassion and humility. For this, we are grateful.

REASSURANCES AND THE POSITIVE SIDE OF THE SITUATION

- Reassure the child that you care—that others care, that the doctors and nurses will do the best they can do, and that they care too.

- Emotional ties for all members of the family may be strengthened. The appropriate and sensitive expression of feelings is a pattern that helps through the days and months of distress and as preparation for all relationships.

- Be supportive, express love, and be helpful.
- Introduce the realities of death and dying, even though this is sad and difficult. Discuss the concepts that Kubler-Ross describes and participate as the patient goes through the stages. This encompasses an understanding of the emotions a dying person may express—anger, denial, depression, and resignation. (See Appendix B.)
- Each person can work to clarify what counts most in his or her life. It reaffirms the importance of compassion, unselfishness, sensitivity, and nonmaterialistic goals.
- Other family members must adjust to a shift whereby the needs of the dying child may preempt others—at least for a period of time. Make certain you tell the others they are not being rejected if you can't attend a soccer game or piano recital or plan a family vacation.

In your interactions with a dying child, listen to his or her agenda. Let the child ask about the flowers in the garden or the puppy. You are there to comfort—not to ask questions that may require strength to answer. Show your love—touch and smile.

26.
Adjustments After a Traumatic Accident

The stability of a family may be dramatically threatened or strengthened as the result of a traumatic accident. Some members of the family may fall apart; others may display predictable or new strengths and caring. Everyone is afraid, and fear can elicit fury, tears, denial, and panic, as well as stalwart control and the appearance of coldness or detachment. Young children observe how their parents react and may imitate them.

Emergency procedures must preempt psychological or emotional considerations, even when the patient is a child. Doctors and nurses, aides, technicians, and law enforcement persons are trained to save lives first, although they try to minimize trauma, if possible. A parent may be permitted to ride in the ambulance with a child or be close to the child in the emergency room. Some hospitals provide as much attention, normalcy, and tenderness toward children as possible, given that medical procedures are top priority.

In most hospitals, parents are permitted to stay with children twenty-four hours a day to feed them, read to them, and so forth. This is in contrast to the old-fashioned dictates of limited visitation. When rooming-in for newborns became an accepted practice, hospital personnel became less resistant to having parents in patients' rooms. Nevertheless, hospitalization frightens children and the trend remains to move toward discharge as rapidly as possible.

Accidents Requiring Hospitalization

Kenny, age five, was in a car wreck in which his mother was killed. He suffered two fractured legs and a broken pelvis. They were en route to visit grandparents almost eight hundred miles from home. Kenny's father was in the service in Germany. It was almost twenty-four hours before the grandparents could get to the hospital. Doctors kept Kenny sedated, but by the time the grandparents arrived, he was alert and in a state of panic. In time, Kenny recovered and adjusted to the loss of his mom. His body healed, but he is not the carefree boy of preaccident days. Except for his underlying sadness, no other important symptoms persisted.

Common Responses to Hospitalization

At the time of a traumatic accident, a child may be heavily sedated. Depending on the level of sedation, some of the following behaviors may be seen.
- Evidence of panic, overwhelming fear
- Mutism
- Uncontrolled crying, screaming—especially at night
- Refusal to eat
- Almost total withdrawal from caretakers
- Physical symptoms of shock, such as blood pressure changes
- Extreme passivity, unresponsiveness

As the child improves, other symptoms may show up:
- Fears about being alone without someone nearby to help if needed

- Anxiety about disfiguration, handicaps
- Belated grief when appropriate
- "Hospitalitis"—child becomes cranky, hostile, restless, or very critical depending on length of stay
- Seeks guarantees that he or she will be welcome at home
- Anxiety about peer rejection, losing ground at school, poor grades, or having to repeat
- Exaggerated self-involvement
- Nightmares, disturbed sleep patterns, especially as sedatives or pain shots are reduced or discontinued
- Guilt over attention taken away from the siblings at home

Children have a remarkable capacity to bounce back. They want to make new friends among the hospital personnel and other patients. As they improve, they may strain to show each new accomplishment and how they have learned to compensate for a cast or immobility. This is wonderful to watch.

PARENT PROCEDURES AS PREPARATION FOR RECOVERY AND STABILITY

Strategies for support have to be modified for each patient, but some can be grouped together.

Physical needs, medical matters

During the critical days, be there, be comforting, and don't press for responses, smiles, or laughter. After the critical days:
- Be prepared for the child to be demanding, have a short attention span, and to cry easily.
- Share the facts in a supportive way. There is no use in making predictions that may not come true, but you can express hope, for example, that nerves in the arm will be restored. Talk about pain. There may be pain for a long time.
- Discuss with the physician and the child what signs of improvement to look for and a possible timetable. Even young, school-aged children can understand accurate reports and prognoses.
- With older kids, discuss their responsibility to stay with a medication program without constant nagging.
- Make it clear that there will be appointments that will interfere with school activities and outside interests. Talk about home

routines and plans, taking into account that the child may get unusually tired.

- If further surgery is necessary, prepare the child far enough in advance so that all questions can be answered but not so far in advance as to cause prolonged worry and stress. In some instances, let the child choose the date—for example, spring vacation for plastic surgery or skin grafts.

Nonmedical matters

- Explain that, at first, people may react to bandages, scars, or slurred speech, but this dissipates. If the child is disfigured or now has a speech or hearing impediment, take as much time as necessary to deal with feelings. The child fears peer rejection the most.
- Explore feelings about any aspect of being in the hospital. Each child will adjust in his or her own way. Don't make comparisons with the kid in the next bed by saying, "Why can't you smile like he does?" This won't cheer up someone who is sad or terrified. Be as positive as you can, minimizing criticisms of food service or the attitudes or availability of the staff.
- When appropriate, describe the recovery of others who have had similar accidents, such as burns, broken bones, or loss of limbs. Call on hospital personnel and specialists to spend time with you and your child. The child needs to know, from experts, how bones heal or how skin grafts work. The angry child may not accept such information from a parent, thinking that you are only saying optimistic things in order to cheer him or her up.
- If the child becomes grouchy about shots and tests, remain businesslike. Nobody likes shots, but inappropriate sympathy won't help. The child may need a great number of shots in the months to come.
- Consult the doctor and see if your child needs help to work through the trauma of the accident. It may take months, even years, for some children to talk about being hit by a car or being thrown off a bike. On the other hand, some children stay on the topic and go into great detail about it, again and again. Talking about the accident is an effective way to diminish stress. Prepare family members to be listeners.
- In preparing the child to go home, discuss what may be expected. Some siblings may be resentful of all the time that parents have

to spend with the accident victim, and they may need and want more attention now. Others will be delighted to have the sibling home, anxious to be helpful, ready to bring water, flowers, and medicines, to play games or watch TV together.

Homeschooling may be necessary for some period of time. When the child returns to school, arrange for shortened days at first. This may mean that you have to play chauffeur or ask an older brother or sister to pick the child up. Some school districts have helpful, adjustable bus schedules. Negotiate with your child as to which subjects he or she would like to concentrate on. Consider getting a tutor. Just remember that, to a child, grades are not as important as resuming a normal social life.

If your child runs into problems with teasing, take responsibility and ask a teacher to deal with student insensitivity. If it is necessary for the child to give up a favorite sport, go to school and confer with the teacher to find alternative, challenging activities.

Finally, if you feel guilty because of the accident or the treatment your child has received, get help for yourself. Otherwise there may be a tendency to give exaggerated attention to that child.

After a crisis there are unknowns and serious adjustments to be confronted. Any adult or child may exhibit posttraumatic stress syndrome (PTSS), a combination of physical and emotional responses that reveal the effects of the shock, fear, anguish, disbelief, and perhaps anger resulting from the trauma. Since becoming aware of PTSS, many psychologists and counselors are trained to give support to victims and their families. Such support should start almost immediately and can help reestablish stability in the family and abet the emotional recovery of everyone involved— although the process still may take months.

Near-death Experiences

After an accident, a child may reveal the details of a near-death experience. Be open and accepting of these reports. Research has established their validity and frequency. They are not a figment of the child's imagination but a revelation of a highly significant event that the child has experienced. Such revelations may actually speed up or affect the child's recovery in a positive way. A book entitled *Closer to the Light,* by Melvin

Morse, M.D., contains interesting, true stories on this subject. I have selected one of the stories for you to read.

> Chris, age ten, related, "I woke up from surgery and there was my mom. I just couldn't wait to tell her what happened while I was on the operating table. I said, 'I have a wonderful secret to tell you, Mother. I've been climbing a staircase to heaven.'
>
> "It was such a good and peaceful feeling. I felt wonderful. I was on a staircase, and it was dark, and I started climbing upward. I got about halfway up the staircase and decided not to go any higher. I wanted to go on up, but I knew I wouldn't come back if I went too high. That would hurt my mom and dad; since my little brother had already died, they wouldn't have anyone to take care of."*

27.
Learning Disabilities and Attention Deficit Disorder

In 1950, one might have read this brief scenario. Jimmy, a nine-year-old third grader, is a problem at school. Teachers lament that his parents have been too permissive and too critical—that they have created a monster—a hyperactive, unsuccessful, inattentive, attention-demanding, and unpopular child.

We've come a long way in the past forty-three years. In 1993, educators and parents have become aware of two significant learning difficulties, and *parents are not to blame.* I refer to learning disabilities (LD) and attention deficit disorder (ADD).

Genetic, internal, neurological, and physical difficulties cause the problems. Parents have an ongoing, difficult job to remain stable, optimistic, and supportive when *involuntary instability* is the core of the difficulties. Parenting does affect the child's progress and his self-esteem. There is no need to feel discouraged. Early diagnosis, well-trained professionals in schools and clinics, established medications, and books and materials for parents are essential. Learning disabled kids and kids with ADD can be helped—can achieve in school, become

---

* © Morse, Melvin, M.D. with Paul Perry. *Closer to the Light.* New York: Ivy Books, 1990.

most successful, and be stable thanks to important improvements. Hard work on the part of everyone involved pays off.

Attention Deficit Disorder and Learning Disabilities Described

Definitions are important. Children and adults with ADD have two characteristic traits. First, they have trouble deliberately *focusing* their attention on any one thing for more than a short time; and second, once they do focus, they have trouble *switching* focus to a new task. These people may or may not be hyperactive or have learning disabilities, though there is much overlap between the two.

LD covers a number of difficulties (see the following list), but the master symptom for educators is *reading two years below normal grade level.* Technically a child would have to be in third grade and reading at only first-grade level before a diagnosis could be made, in spite of a history of other difficulties. LD includes a variety of malfunctions or deficits that can be differentiated into verbal, motor, visual, auditory, and psychosocial. ADD symptoms are frequently noted in LD children.

ADD—Clues that reflect attention problems

Inattention:
• Has difficulty sustaining attention in tasks or play activities.
• Often shifts from one uncompleted activity to another.
• Has difficulty playing quietly.
• Often talks excessively.
• Often does not seem to listen to what is being said to him or her.
• Often loses things necessary for tasks or activities at school or at home (e.g., toys, pencils, books, assignments).

Impulsiveness:
• Often blurts out answers to questions before they have been completed.
• Often interrupts or intrudes on others (e.g., butts into other children's games).
• Often engages in physically dangerous activities without considering possible consequences (not for the purpose of thrill-seeking), e.g., runs into the street without looking.

Hyperactivity:

- Often fidgets with hands or feet or squirms on seat (in adolescents, may be limited to subjective feelings of restlessness).
- Has difficulty remaining seated when required to do so.
- Is easily distracted by extraneous stimuli.
- Has difficulty awaiting turn in games or group situations.

Learning Disabilities

Verbal disabilities:

- Cannot understand what is said.
- Has small vocabulary, recognizing one meaning only for each word.
- Repeats many questions.
- May refuse to speak or speech may be halting, slow, or slurred.
- Tends to be forgetful of what he or she is saying.
- May use large words but not comprehend them.
- May be two or more grades below grade placement in oral reading ability.

Motor disabilities:

- Walking may be clumsy with frequent tripping.
- Handwriting may be labored, illegible.
- Buttons, shoelaces, and zippers may give difficulty.
- Onset of fatigue is rapid.
- Child may become disoriented in large, open space.
- May have difficulty participating in games that involve running, jumping, skipping, and hopping.

Visual disabilities:

- Cannot put pictures or letters in proper order.
- Cannot copy letters or numbers accurately.
- Cannot write a list of words, numbers, or letters in a column.
- Reverses or rotates all or part of written letters or numbers.
- Cannot maintain eye contact.
- Has difficulty copying from chalkboard or book.
- Cannot remember words from sight vocabulary after many presentations.
- May complain of tired eyes.

Auditory disabilities:
- Cannot locate sounds.
- Cannot follow oral direction.
- Cannot remember a series of three directions.
- May cover ears when room is noisy.
- Cannot attend to a story when it is read aloud.
- May attend to part of a spoken assignment.
- Tends to forget what he or she has heard.
- Cannot use context clues to correct wrong discrimination.

Emotional problems:
- Exaggerated anxiety.
- Mood swings.
- Depression.
- Anger and hostility or extreme docility.
- Inability to take teasing, jokes.
- Use of drugs or alcohol.

Indicators of instability abound because of developing self-doubt, social problems, and ongoing, difficult struggles at school. The problems compound. Over 90 percent of all boys who are sent to reform schools, detention centers, or jails have significant learning disabilities. The affected youngsters act out against society and are consequently often punished by the society they offend. Such children come from all walks of life and all kinds of schools.

> *Over 10 million kids have learning disabilities and ADD— many of them never diagnosed or given any help. One out of every ten boys (a ten-to-one ratio more than girls) suffers from some significant learning problem. They display instability the only way they know how—with anger and impulsive or inappropriate behavior. Some take drugs as an escape. Many get very depressed—even suicidal.*

PARENTS—PROCEDURES FOR YOU

Recognize that your responsibilities are three-fold. First, *take care of yourself.* Join parent groups, get guidance, counseling, and time off. Second, *learn as much as you can about the difficulties.* This will provide much-needed predictability—even though, at first, some of the predictions may be discouraging or frightening. Surprises may be even more disturbing. Use the best resources you can find in the schools and community. And third, *be your child's advocate.* Speak up for what your child needs, and consistently note and applaud all strengths and improvements that your child displays. This builds optimism and stability.

Call (1985) estimates that a developmentally appropriate length of attention for a sustained attention activity, such as viewing television, is as follows:

2 years old—7 minutes
3 years old—9 minutes
4 years old—13 minutes
5 years old—15 minutes
6 to 7 years old—60 minutes

These times are presented as guidelines only; all children vary greatly in their attention spans. However, children with attention disorders will find it challenging to maintain attention on a structured task for these lengths of time. Many factors will affect how well a child attends: the type of activity, what has preceded the activity throughout the child's day, and the child's level of interest in the task. *

PROCEDURES: WITH YOUNG TODDLERS

These children are often extremely irritable and have unexplained outbursts. The outbursts are described as a breakdown in all the controls the child has acquired. They are frequently confused with the tantrums of the spoiled or willful child. They are signs of the child's internal disorganization. Try these useful management ideas:

---

*J. D. Call, *Practice of Pediatrics*, Philadelphia: Harper and Row, 1985.

- Require orderliness and regularity to fix habits; routines are essential.
- Limit assortment of foods to the familiar. For example, hamburgers, peanut butter sandwiches, and cereal may be the only foods the child will eat. Limit sugar intake.
- Provide quiet, avoid stimulation from TV, radio, or loud stereo. A child may respond well to soft music.
- Keep tensions to a minimum; perhaps allow the child to eat alone or before the others and to play in his or her own room at times.
- Put away fragile items such as easily tipped lamps because the child may be clumsy and awkward.
- Choose clothing that closes easily.
- Repeat explanations of limits and consequences as often as necessary.
- Follow through with medication as prescribed.

PROCEDURES: WITH SCHOOL-AGED CHILDREN

The major thrust for ADD and LD children is to provide structure, variety, brevity, omission of unnecessary detail, and small chunks of required work or home responsibilities. Above all, consistently encourage children to slow down, control their movements, finish their tasks, and remember things as best they can.

These children need constant reinforcement. They need parents to ease off from expressions of disappointment and disapproval, because they invariably become very self-critical and feel defeated. Too many learn to live with failure and may become afraid of success.

Make certain that your children's eyes have been examined for visual-motor function difficulties (usually performed by an optometrist who specializes in the field). If perception is skewed, a child cannot visualize how relationships work, how letters or numbers will look or combine, how words will sound, or the outcome of decisions. In my experience as a therapist, I noted that over eighty percent of adult male patients had adjustment and emotional problems due to visualization difficulties that were not diagnosed and remediated. Even adults can benefit from visual training. Frequently, visual problems are hereditary.

PROCEDURES: WITH THE YOUNG CHILD
WITH LEARNING DISABILITIES

- Be predictable.
- Offer a consistent approach to all situations. Television viewing must be regulated.
- Give one-step instructions; too many words are confusing.
- Offer protection from being teased or ways to manage cruelties.
- Arrange for special considerations at school, perhaps special placement. Learning problems become progressively worse unless effectively remediated.
- Limit special events such as birthday parties or the circus because there are too many stimuli.

PROCEDURES: WITH THE ADOLESCENT
WITH LEARNING DISABILITIES

These strategies are intended to overcome fear of school and to maintain good feelings about family and friends.

- The school program must not isolate the student. If the child is placed in a special program, vocational training center, or the like, contact with nondisabled learners must be provided.
- School programming must be geared to future survival in the community, offering preparation in the social and work skills areas.
- Money management merits the special attention of parents and teachers. The learning-disabled student may be ripped off, cheated, or conned out of money by others who take advantage of his or her vulnerability.
- Parents must help the adolescent maintain realistic goals. The teenager may be very aware of the successes of others and make comparisons. He or she may become very depressed. Parental understanding of the child's moods, inconsistencies, demands, and changes is essential. This may be difficult because parents also are often worried and depressed.
- If your teenager gets unusually depressed, urge him or her to participate in a group of other persons with similar problems. There are a number of such groups around, in schools and in some community mental health centers, for example. It is necessary to explain the facts about learning problems. Re-

mind him or her of those things that he or she can do well—such as drive a car or use a computer.

- A predictable home environment with clear rules and equally clear enforcements offers stability.
- If a brain-damaged child has siblings who are callous or unkind, the parent must be assertive and not let uncaring habits persist.

Special Needs of the Learning Disabled Child of a Family in Turmoil

This is a very difficult struggle. Give repeated explanations of the problems, couched in words and simple concepts that he or she can grasp. One can predict many questions from the child for a long time to come. You are asking the child to see the nuances and comprehend consequences and feelings that he or she may not be able to visualize at all (such as the concept of ambivalence).

These difficulties are especially true when trying to help a child understand abuse. More and more studies show that it is often the difficult or disabled child who is singled out for child abuse by a battering parent. The healthiest child needs an enormous amount of help to understand complex family problems. Realistically the disabled child will need even more. If, for example, it becomes necessary to remove the child from the home, this must be handled with immeasurable skill and caring and requires repeated explanations. The trauma may be overwhelming even to a child who is not an impaired learner.

28.
The Gifted Child

The 1980s heralded a vast number of new exciting programs for gifted and talented children, both in schools and in the community. Parents, educators, artisans, coaches, and others accepted the responsibility of identifying these children and providing for the maximum development of their potential.

Twenty percent of school dropouts are gifted children.

When a gifted child is identified, family stability may be threatened or undermined for a number of reasons. The needs of this child may demand special transportation, a place to practice, a musical instrument, travel money, special tutoring, uniforms, and so forth. In order to meet these needs, the parents may overextend themselves, resulting in fatigue, tensions, worries, and other problems that promote misunderstandings, misconceptions, confusion, and difficult decisions. If parents cannot afford the extras for the gifted child, they may feel guilty or resentful. These negative feelings undermine stability. Jealousy of the other siblings may be a second problem. On the other hand, an entire family may become involved in a gifted child's programs, performances, and games, and share a sense of pride.

INDICATORS OF INSTABILITY

The gifted child is invariably under stress. Personal expectations may include the need to excel and to be perfect. No one can be perfect all the time, and this may cause depression, frustration, and loss of self-esteem.

Predictably the indicators of instability may be similar to those of any anxious child, including nervous habits, inappropriate responses to persons and situations, neediness, attention-seeking, or unusual isolation. However, most gifted children are outgoing, delightful, well-disciplined, and friendly, albeit, they may be very selective about companions.

The stability of the gifted child may be a direct reflection of the pressure that parents exert, but as the child strives to achieve personal goals, it is internal, rather than external, pressure that may result in instability.

Most gifted children have an incredible sense of humor, and many are inordinately sensitive to others and display unusual understanding and empathy.

PROCEDURES FOR PARENTS

There are many ways to help the gifted child feel competent, secure, and stable. Above all, enjoy their companionship, and become excited and committed to their pursuits. In addition:

- Explain about perfectionism and expectations completely and carefully.
- Anticipate some variable motivation even though the gifted child becomes absorbed and dedicated to their interests. If motivation varies, avoid being harsh or too critical, and be cautious about threatening to take away lessons, dancing classes, or the like. These are just children, vulnerable to peer pressure and anxious to have friends. Most of their friends are among those who do what they do—computer whizzes, teammates, comembers of an acting group, dance class, or orchestra.
- Accept mistakes, and ease the children into a variety of situations—some where they excel and others where they may not be outstanding.
- Don't anticipate unusual control of emotions even though a child is very verbal. The child may still be impulsive or unusually emotional.
- Anticipate that some gifted children will stay with a task, such as practicing a musical instrument, for hours and hours. This can be regarded as a sign of stability. Express your admiration.
- Involve the child in as many family decisions as possible.
- Allow the child privacy.
- Encourage creativity—an established way for a child to deal with death, in particular. Let creative expressions be judgment free.

School can be a major source of stress for gifted children. Be aware of the school program provided for your gifted child. Be assertive. Make certain the child isn't bored with redundant busywork. The regular classroom has some advantages. Children participate in some competitive activities that satisfy school mandates and parents' realizations of the child's potential and that reaffirm for the child the superior quality of the learning of which he or she is capable. The democratic basis of the regular classroom is invaluable if the needs of the gifted are being met.

> *Giftedness is 10 percent inspiration and 90 percent perspiration.*

In a school class of gifted children, to the exclusion of others, a great deal of stress may result for some. *They may be brilliant and in some ways very mature, but they are still children.* They need to understand that there are individual differences among the members of the select group. This avoids the unnecessary pressure of trying to emulate the giftedness of others. For example, some children have far better fine muscle control than others, enabling them to excel with instruments and tools. The advantages of the class are inherent when the learning is geared to originality, problem solving, scientific methods, and the processes of analyzing, synthesizing, and evaluating. Furthermore, many of the special programs for the gifted and talented do not require grading. The kids can be free to use and expand their minds without the pressure that comes from unnecessary competition, though many love to compete in games. They are usually very selective about what and who they like and dislike.

A disadvantage of gifted-with-gifted groupings on a full-time, exclusive basis is that the groups become stratified on unique levels, and the stratifications inhibit or unwittingly diminish the self-esteem of some. This is particularly evident in the social skills. Some gifted leaders may become overbearing, while their gifted classmates assess the situation and may choose to be tolerant and passive—to their own detriment. If the more reticent ones were in a class with nongifted learners, their own leadership capabilities would stand a better chance of being nurtured and developed. One frequently sees the gifted at home as very bossy. If the child has learned well, but has poor work habits and is consistently sloppy, tardy, and disorganized, these undesirable habits must be confronted. The remediation of such deficiencies is preparation for the career world ahead, where genius is judged and respected, but responsibility and account-ability are equally important.

The Gifted Child in Family Turmoil

Gifted children seem to be particularly vulnerable to family turmoil. They are usually acutely aware of what is happening and want to fix problems such as parental fighting, separa-tions—even divorce. When unable to effect changes, they feel impotent and incompetent, which undermines stability. In order to help, consider these suggestions:

- Encourage expression of feelings. The gifted child may deny feelings and focus on intellectual understanding of a situation instead.
- Look for signs of depression and guilt and guide them to see that the adults make the decisions—even if there have been family discussions.
- Let the gifted regress as you do the nongifted. Accept that they may be uncooperative, hostile, and unforgiving—especially teenagers. The gifted are usually problem-solvers and can be intolerant when others cannot solve their problems in a peaceful way.
- If a death has occurred, anticipate loss of concentration and unusual distractibility. Assure the child that this is an appropriate, short-lived reaction to important loss.

Above all, when serious family problems arise, don't fall into the trap of a ready explanation such as, "Harry is gifted. He understands. He can figure it out on his own and will know what to do." Gifted children need support too—perhaps even professional counseling. The most important *reassurance* that parents can provide is an honest declaration of their struggles and what they are doing to regain their strength and stability.

7

Family Lifestyle Affects Stability

HAVE YOU HEARD a friend say, "Our family is just a bunch of individuals living under the same roof"? Or have you listened when someone exclaimed, "We are a close, loving family"? Another person may comment, "We know Dad's the captain and we kids have to tow the mark." Each is describing the lifestyle of a family—not who makes up the group but *the characteristic way the people interact.* The lifestyle includes the way the members treat each other. Some are expressive, others reserved—some distant, others intimate. Family holiday traditions and patterns are important in one household while another family may be casual, even helter-skelter. A lifestyle encompasses a style of parenting and the varying activities of all family members. "All" may extend to in-laws, cousins, and close friends.

Rituals of a family contribute to stability. The kids may protest, "Do we always have to go to grandma's on Thanksgiving? Why can't she come here?", but traditions add to family definition.

Some lifestyles may cause uneasiness, and this may create difficulties that infringe on the stability of certain members of the family. Amy is embarrassed to invite her friends to her house because it is a mess. The dishes aren't washed and dirty clothes are deposited in piles on the floor. Although embarrassed, Amy's stability is not threatened. In fact, there are times when she can joke about being a *hang-loose* family.

Amelia, on the other hand, cannot handle the lifestyle at her house without feeling insecure. She has never been able to accept the ongoing arguments, name-calling, and assorted temper tantrums of her mother and her two older sisters. The tensions and threats of violence, although it's the family lifestyle, keeps Amelia unsettled and ashamed. There is no way she would invite her friends to come to study together after school. She doesn't want to be home herself. When the lifestyle of a family must adjust to living with an alcoholic parent, certain predictable roles will be played. (See *Living with an Alcoholic Parent*, page 148.)

The family is a social system. Each person is affected by the others. There is always some connectedness. When the needs of one member are unsatisfied or when there is a lack of respect, stability is at risk.

At various times every person within a family will experience problems. Both adults and children contribute. Some ride out the storms more easily than others. "We can handle it—all except Becky. She's so hot tempered," or "Paul needs everything planned—the rest of us are spontaneous," may typify a family. Relationships and alliances shift. "This year, Laura and Megan seem to be ganging up on Gwenna. Last year, it was Gwenna and Laura against Megan." Shifts delineate underlying loyalties and love even though certain relationships are stressful at times. The family lifestyle is important because it is describable and familiar.

29.
Examples of Lifestyles

The Musical Family

The Martin family life centers around music. The father, Len, plays the clarinet and the oboe and sings in the church choir. The mom, Nan, plays the piano and accompanies the others. Both girls, Penny and Pam, have become competent violinists, while young Danny enjoys the cello. Sunday evenings are concerts at home. Everyone practices hard and, up to now, looked forward to Sundays.

This family's lifestyle is characterized by common interests, similar routines for the kids, and intense competition. Father and mother still insist on the concerts even though Penny is fifteen and wants to spend more time on studies and with her newly acquired boyfriend. She says she's done her "music things," and wishes she'd taken up a wind instrument so she could play with the school band. Already, Dan, at age ten, dreams of being a drum major and complains that dad is too bossy when they all play together.

The stability of the family is not threatened, but tensions are building due to several factors: the father's authoritarianism, the ages of the children, "too much of a good thing," the competition within the family, the increasing rebelliousness of one child, and the growing appeal of other interests outside the family. The kids now complain of headaches, are irritable, and refuse to cooperate. The sisters criticize each other more and more.

Suggestions may seem obvious to the outsider, but both Mr. and Mrs. Martin want to hang on to the family lifestyle. They are quick to say that they have the right to establish patterns and insist that the children stick with them. "It's the least they can do for us. A few hours a week is not asking too much. When they get older, they'll be grateful." It would be appropriate for the parents to try to negotiate. Perhaps the musical evening should be reduced to every other week, or Pam should be allowed to quit for a time, or the parents could remain determined that the Sunday events shall continue and plead for the children to be "good sports"—pleasant, enthusiastic, and appreciative. There is no guarantee that the children will cooperate. Nonetheless, there is the need for family negotiations.

The Martin family's lifestyle provides benefits for all:

- They pride themselves on their knowledge of music and their ability to play well.
- The children feel that their family is very special and tell their friends and acquaintances about their musical way of life.
- The parents have helped the children establish patterns of self-discipline and practice.
- Their proficiency as musicians has prepared the children to participate in fun, rewarding activities such as the band, orchestra, concert bands, or private musical groups.
- They have all learned to love music.

The Angry Family

Everybody in the Swan family is angry. Making sarcastic, biting remarks is their lifestyle. Underneath there is loyalty, but all conversations have a sting to them. Outsiders feel uncomfortable. Jeff and Debbie admit that they are embarrassed to bring their friends home. Mother and father are very close. Jeff, the oldest, has had privileges and consideration way beyond what Debbie and Carl have had. The younger two feel as if they are unimportant except to build up Jeff. Jeff monopolizes the conversation. Jeff gets everything he wants. Debbie and Carl have asked, "Why did you bother having us anyway?" If the family is going out for supper, Jeff gets to choose where they go. Every menu at home is planned around Jeff's allergies. Debbie and Carl lean on each other, but most of their conversations are critical and sarcastic too. There are problems with privacy too. When Debbie, now thirteen, wants to tell her mother about "girl things," she knows that her mother will tell her dad, and she'll be embarrassed. One day, Debbie told her friend, "I guess Jeff's happy—and mom and dad have a great thing going—but being at home is a drag."

Swan family members are all good workers. Both parents like their jobs and all three kids do well in school, but the younger children feel unstable for several reasons. Parental closeness represents the ideal couple but creates a marked distance from the kids; Jeff, the oldest, appears to be in an alliance with the parents much of the time; the family lifestyle is not open to compliments or loving remarks because of the sarcasm and criticism; the younger children can't discuss their problems with their parents—there is no privacy with either parent; and finally, the younger two, who are constantly compared to Jeff, don't like their brother at all.

Various symptoms of instability show up in the Swan family. Jeff plays up his allergies. He has few friends because he is dominating, callous, and obnoxious. His biting remarks are considered cute by his parents but alienate him from others. Debbie has headaches. She is very nervous, tense, and whiny. Carl, now eleven, is withdrawn and unhappy. No one seems to notice him. He excels in school and hides out in his room to study and be alone. He occasionally has trouble with his bowels and has to take mineral oil. He is secretive. He feels it's the only way he can escape the biting remarks. Once in a while he explodes and throws his books around or slams doors.

Siblings usually have problems, don't they?, you may ask. True. However, the lifestyle of the Swan family derives from favoritism and adult exclusiveness, which damage the self-esteem of the younger children. The positive spin-offs are that the children are learning that a husband-wife relationship can be fulfilling and happy, the younger children learn to look to each other for support, the importance of doing well in school has been established (perhaps as compensation for little acclaim or praise at home), and the younger children wisely reach out to other people outside the family for support.

The Fishing Family

This family enjoys trips, loves the outdoors, and the whole fishing experience—tying flies, studying water conditions, and operating boats.

Negative attributes	Positive attributes
Too competitive	Fosters togetherness
Boring for some	Unpretentious
Takes away time from other activities	Expands interests in ecology, environmental concerns, water rights
	Encourages children to earn money for equipment, thus establishing goal-setting patterns

The Athletic Family

This family takes sports seriously, goes on team trips, is interested in health, exercise, and fun, and makes friends with families of other team members.

Negative attributes	Positive attributes
Competition may be too intense	Child-parent participation
	Children self-disciplined

Burnout possible
Family overly critical of
   coaching, refereeing
Children compelled to
   live up to parental
   expectations
Other interests crowded
   out of their lives

High standards of
   sportsmanship
Learning lifelong skills, such
   as tennis, skiing, bowling
Basic for friendships

The Funny Family

The funny family enjoys jokes, tricks, laughter, high-spirited get-togethers, and family traditions.

Negative attributes	Positive attributes
Competition	Fun quality of life, a great reprieve from stress
Cover-up for real feelings	
Intolerance for people who are somber	As performers, feel confident, poised
Inappropriate humor—wrong subject, wrong place	Creativity encouraged
	Learn to applaud each other
	Improve vocabulary
Victims—some jokes are brutal, hurtful	Extend humor to reading, writing
May be the only level on which family members relate	Enhances social skills
	Volunteer as clowns, performers, entertainers in hospitals, nursing homes, and so forth

The Studious Family

This family enjoys books, classical music, fine art, museums, lectures, exhibits, a home studio, intellectual conversation, stimulating friends, and school activities such as debate, foreign exchange groups, and service organizations.

Negative attributes	Positive attributes
Intolerance of less intellectual families	Lifelong interests, pursuits
	Enriching activities

Too much criticism of teachers

Too serious, too introspective

Scorn for nonintellectual activities such as rodeos, some athletic events

Vocabulary tends to alienate neighbors, classmates

Feelings covered up

Isolation

Snobbish values

Parents giving children worthwhile values

Stimulating discussions at home

The Food Fanatic Family

SlimFast for breakfast for mom, grapefruit and bran for dad, well-balanced vitamins, protein, and fat for the kids; that takes planning. It may become an obsession, the lifestyle of a family. Dinner discussions, over and over again, focus on who has lost or gained weight, Ellie's latest allergies, Jim's blemishes from eating chocolate, and toddler Tim's refusal to try vegetables— and how much exercise did you get today? This gets boring, even counterproductive. Health- and body-conscious parents pro- duce health- and body-conscious kids, and this may have positive or adverse effects.

Negative attributes

Children rebel, express disdain for parents' obsession, rush through meals

Children use food selection and intake to attract attention

Discussion of other perhaps equally important subjects is sacrificed

No one enjoys the food— eating becomes an

Positive attributes

Everyone learns important information, becomes health conscious

Parents and children participate together

Exercise becomes routine

May discourage children from smoking

May encourage other good habits: brushing teeth, shampooing, exercising

May stimulate discussion of mind, body, spiritual

obligation. In extreme cases, attitudes may contribute to bulimia and anorexia

Children become too figure-conscious or focused on looks and lose sight of other interests or talents, e.g., good school work

Obese children, in particular, may become deeply depressed—their self-esteem shattered

interconnections

May limit intake of "unhealthy" snacks, fast foods, and treats

Family Lifestyle: A Recap

The lifestyle, in effect, demonstrates how parents' personalities, values, and philosophies mesh into patterns and habits.

INDICATORS OF INSTABILITY

It is difficult to determine if the behavior of a child is a direct message that family lifestyle is not meeting his or her needs. However, you may want to listen to some statements.

- "Kids won't come to our house. We are too snobbish."
- "My mom would worry."
- "We have no money."
- "My dad might lose his job."
- "We never do anything different."
- "We'd never be allowed to do that."
- "Our household is too disorganized."
- "My brother is on drugs."
- "We're supposed to be home all the time."
- "It would take us too long to get ready."
- "My parents don't understand kids."

Then consider your own statements:

- "I believe the children should earn whatever money they need."
- "I use grounding to punish the kids. Nothing else seems to work."

- "I watch TV all the time."
- "I can talk about anything."
- "I am not an affectionate person."
- "I never miss church on Sundays."
- "I urge the children to bring their friends to the house."

   You might want to hear how your children react to your statements. Then, together, discuss the following. Does our family:
- Welcome changes? "We like it when mom introduces new treats for us to eat." "We're going to have family meetings to negotiate jobs. That's new for us. Our parents give us orders about everything and that's going to change."
- Resist changes? "Why do we have to do things the way we have always done them? Eating dinner at the table is stupid. We like to eat in front of the TV." "No, I don't want to share my room with Lillian. I like having my own room. Let the others double up."
- Encourage expression of feelings? "I like it when mom and dad tell us how they feel. We're learning to talk about emotions. Seems like every family should be like ours."
- Encourage talking about needs? "We're learning to be sensitive about each others' needs. Now I can understand what dad means when he says he needs quiet or when Jane says she's got to have extra time to fix her hair."
- Handle painful situations such as a death by supporting each other or roughing it out alone? "I notice that dad pulled away when his father died, but mom seems to like to talk over her feelings with everyone. Dad really got upset when we asked if we could help."
- Confront each other when we are indirect rather than outspoken? "The little guy still tries to whine or beg his way into whatever he wants, but the rest of us have learned to be open. We use the question, 'What's the issue?' a lot because then we don't have to guess about things. We like that."
- Encourage each other to feel comfortable with our different personalities and interests? "Mom always tells us, 'Each one of you is different—be proud.' She never makes comparisons. She keeps telling us, 'We don't have any carbon copies around here.'"
- Resist traditions, belittle sentiments? "We make a big deal out of Christmas but we don't celebrate birthdays. I'd like to change

that around, so I'm going to buy some balloons and decorate the house for dad's birthday. Maybe I can talk mom into baking a cake." "We celebrate everything at our house—even the dog's birthday!"

- Seem split or disloyal? "I hate it when the family seems split. Even when mom and dad come at us as the grownups, I feel bad," or "There are so many kids at our house that the big ones hardly know the little ones. They're like strangers."

Parents and children together may select one or two areas that need improvement. "Let's cut down the sarcastic remarks," or "For every sarcastic remark, you will say something nice." Then plan once-a-week, a half-hour meeting to find out what's happening and how everyone feels about the changes you are working on. Praise the kids and save some for yourself as well.

———

You are urged to express your pride in the family—its heritage and traditions. Keep telling yourself that you want your family life to be happy. You know that there may be personality conflicts, that you will hurt when your children are openly hostile to each other. You know each individual will find things to complain about and things to love. Encourage family members to communicate, to share their feelings. It is one good way to enhance stability. Make sure that everyone gets the message that in order for a family to run smoothly, each member must assume responsibility.

Every family is unique. There is no such thing as an abnormal family—but some families are more stable than others. Every family wants love and mutual respect for all.

8

Family Arrangements that Affect Stability

ARE YOU TIRED OF HEARING about the idealized, blissful family life of your great-grandparents? I am. Are you suspicious when you read that your grandparents worked out their problems, their children prospered, and everyone was stable—even happy? I am.

Family problems are not new. Let's stop pretending that everybody was loving and giving, brave and adventuresome. They weren't! Instability wasn't publicized as much, but it was rife. Parents did drink too much, did get divorced, did abuse kids, and did cause dissension as they ventured toward self-awareness, self-fulfillment, and financial security. You know that. Your own parents introduced you to happy times and troubled times too. Many of you were victims of instability and it wasn't easy. Many of you felt unimportant and still have problems with your self-esteem. Others of you were blessed with stability, and your energy and optimism are delightful.

The stable family is attainable; that's the message in this book. It is important to examine how the family arrangement affects children, parents, and family stability.

30.
Working Parents:
Multiple Caretakes Help Raise the Kids

The traditional family is now atypical. Mother has helpers, and child care extends beyond the parents. More than fifty percent of mothers of children under one year of age work outside the home; some estimates are as high as seventy percent. The typical school-aged child has a mother who is outside the home a number of hours a day.

Work may be necessary, especially for the single parent (and almost one-half of American families are single-parent households headed by a woman). Leaving the children with someone else does not forecast instability unless the caretakers are not caring, or there are marked inconsistencies among the caretakers. Inconsistencies cause children to feel unimportant, unloved, and insecure.

A child cannot bond to a moving target.

INDICATORS OF INSTABILITY

Research shows that infants under six months tend to handle multiple caretakers more readily than older babies. After six months of age, indicators of instability include:
- Prolonged, exaggerated expressions of despair at time of separation
- Listlessness, failure to show warmth and responsiveness to anyone
- Agitation, a sense of continuous discomfort in any setting
- Physical rejection of any adult; the child doesn't want to be held or kissed

For older children the same symptoms apply plus:
- Demonstrations of lack of trust of adults, outbursts such as, "You don't care where I am," or "You never come when you say you will."
- "Sometimes I don't know who my mom is, and sometimes I

really don't care," is a sign that the child may feel unimportant to all of his or her caretakers.
- Exaggerated fear of strangers.

If such comments or problems occur frequently or consistently, it is essential to find out why your child is so unhappy. You may have to take time to closely observe the interactions between the caretaker and the child, as well as to evaluate how much attention *you* give.

Before reviewing ways to minimize or prevent stress, consider these benefits of a multiple-caretaker way of life.
- The multiple-caretaker approach can enrich a child's life. Children learn that they can be loved by lots of people. They adjust to various styles of handling and assorted environments.
- In daycare centers, children are introduced to routines and materials that may abet their future school adjustment. Routines provide security.
- For parents, work time, time alone to pursue personal goals, to join friends, travel, or accompany a spouse are important.
- The traditional pattern involving "leaving the children with grandmother" is rare. A business arrangement has benefits. Though caretakers really love children, they may feel free to discipline or manage them with greater objectivity than a grandmother might. Also there may be continuity of care. Some children go to the same sitter for years. This provides security. When grandmother, from far away, arrives to baby-sit, as a visitor, or for emergency relief, the children may feel uneasy at first. A grandparent from afar may be more of a stranger than a familiar baby-sitter.
- Many older baby-sitters today are surrogate grandparents. They may be free of a lot of pressures that younger sitters face. They may offer tranquillity and a mellowed-with-age outlook. They provide a grandparent's approach combined with a businesslike manner. Some, however, may be a bit short-tempered or impatient.

PROCEDURES FOR PARENTS

Introduce your children, with great care, to the sitter before you leave them for the first time. Welcome their questions. "Why is Mrs. Jones so fat?" "Will I call her Mrs. Jones or Martha?" "Does she like to fix spaghetti?" "Will she make me take a nap?" "Will her kids always be there?" "What if I don't like them?" Answer these questions and remain optimistic.

- Inform the sitter about your child. Go beyond name, food dislikes, and when to take naps. Talk about ways your child responds to scoldings and affection. Tell about favorite TV shows, books, activities, and responsibilities. "Patty loves to help set the table, and Patrick loves to run errands." This will help to create a sense of comfort and serve as a bridge from home, which may help keep anxiety at a minimum.

- Be sure that your children understand that Mrs. Jones knows *what is okay and what is not okay at home.* Write down important items such as what you do when Patty hits Patrick and when Patrick refuses to eat. You cannot remodel the way Mrs. Jones takes care of children, especially if she has her own children and a number of others, but the differences in your styles of caretaking are understood. *Children modify their behavior according to what is expected of them and adjust to different ways of adult handling.* There are many successful ways to manage kids in order to foster stability.

- Don't make comparisons or compete with other caretakers. Children can relate on many different levels and find different loving qualities. There is no need for you to feel insecure because your child loves his or her sitter or teacher.

- Don't overinterrogate on a daily basis. Your child may sense that you are too critical or looking for something with which to find fault. This is unfair to the sitter and your child.

- Don't overreact to a child's complaints. Many children find fault with almost everything. This can be a symptom of unhappiness or an attention-getting technique. If complaints are real and consistent and you perceive that the child is really unhappy, you should investigate. But bear in mind that children are great manipulators, and complaints are common and predictable. It can be the child's way of saying, "I miss you, mommy."

- Don't continually threaten to "find a better sitter"—one closer to home, less expensive, younger, older, or with fewer kids in the home. Children are entitled to a meaningful attachment to sitters and this may be undermined if they hear that the relationship may be cut off shortly.

Other Reminders

- Infant care needs careful planning, too. Depending on age, it involves a daily shift from breast feeding at home to bottles at the sitters. Allow enough time. Tell the child that you will be back—even if the child is too young to talk.
- Be on time. A child is not clock-conscious but can become very insecure if he or she experiences your absence as unduly long. With toddlers, try to say, "When the sun goes down, I will be back," or "When you get up from your nap, I'll be back." Some children take many weeks to adjust to a pattern of being left and then picked up.
- Let children take familiar clothes and objects with them, or leave some at the sitters. Do not chide if an older youngster wants to bring along a blanket or stuffed animal or doll.

REASSURANCES

You will feel better if you:
- Take time to evaluate the persons or institutions that help bring up your children. Evaluations give you a sense of comfort.
- Get comfortable with the fact that Mrs. Jones handles Patty differently from the way you do. She may be more firm or more permissive. This will not damage your relationship with Patty or Patty's self-esteem.
- Accept that your child may be closer to Mrs. Jones than to you. As Patty bursts in the door, she may spontaneously tell Mrs. Jones all about what happened in school today. She may be excited or cry. Mrs. Jones may have the time to listen to every detail. Patty is aware that you have many things to do at home—the mail, phone calls, dinner, dogs and cats, house-cleaning, all the other kids, homework, bathing, planning, and spouse time. Patty gets answers, questions, sympathy, or encouragement from Mrs. Jones. Is it reasonable to expect her to take time to repeat it with you when you have so little time together?
- Relinquish or share responsibilities that you think a mom or dad *should* have. For example, Patty may enjoy doing her homework with Mrs. Jones.

• Consider letting caretakers go in your place—or with you—to school conferences and school performances, for instance.

Multiple caretakers are part of the new look in the contemporary family. The relationships can enhance your well-being and, at the same time, meet the needs of your children.

31.
The Single-Parent Family

By the year 2000, more than two-thirds of all new jobs will be held by women—many of them single parents. One million children each year are added to the web of the single-parent home as a result of divorce. One of every twenty high school seniors knows life in a single-parent family due to the death of a mom or a dad.

Single parenting is a hard job for the parent and the kids. Some days are easier than others. If single parents are to feel confident about childraising, they need respect and encouragement. In years gone by, many were condemned, scolded, and cast aside. The 1990s herald a more accepting attitude though bubbles of doubt and disrespect occasionally surface. *Single parents, for the most part, do the best that they can do.*

Single fathers are no more or no less stress-free than single mothers. Handling parenting responsibilities and striving for harmony and stability is as important to dads as is it to moms.

If you are a single parent by choice, let someone else fret about you and your decisions. Quote to them, "Kids from single-parent families can be just as well-adjusted, successful, and stable as kids from a two-parent family."

Rather than dwell on the downside of single parenting (which gets a generous amount of press), this discussion will present additional facts to those listed above and strategies to support single parents.

Single parents represent the single largest subgroup of the

population that lives below the poverty level. As yet, single parents have not mobilized into as potent a political force as their potential might suggest. Organizations such as Parents Without Partners need to combine with other groups to push for daycare money, corporate child care facilities and staff, and more extensive well-baby services, including evening clinics for working parents.

Take Care of Yourself

Single parents want to take control of their lives by providing proper care for their children. This represents stability. Many also want a chance to grow up without a sense of discouragement or self-flagellation. Whether single by choice or not, as a single parent, you should ask yourself these questions:

- Do I have a support person? If I do, am I hesitant to call when I'm tired, worried, or discouraged?
- Do I use community helpers or facilities? I know that groups in centers, for example, can be worthwhile and entertaining—also a place to meet people.
- Do I make arrangements so that I can do things for me—away from the children?
- Have I had a recent physical exam?
- Have I learned to share magazines, newspapers, and videotapes with neighbors or friends, and do I visit the public library?
- Do I take advantage of free concerts, art shows, park fairs, and the like?
- If I'm dating, am I comfortable with a Dutch treat plan, given my financial status?
- Do I listen to my favorite music?
- Do I exercise enough?
- When was the last time I had a good laugh?

These questions do not focus on child care. They do not zero in on "old stuff," leftover problems with an ex-spouse or disapproving family. The focus is on you—your well-being—knowing that the better you feel about you, the easier it is to build a stable home for the children.

Although first printed in 1979 in the *Whole Single Person's Catalog*, you may find this box interesting.

**Here are ten tips about increasing
your chances to meet new people***

1. Divest yourself of any antiquated ideas you have about what are proper and improper ways of meeting people. The single world is fluid, casual, busy, interactive. Within reason, whatever works is okay.

2. You are not unique or alone in your needs. The desire to make contacts is common to almost all single men and women. Furthermore, this can be an automatic assumption on your part if you find people at a singles-only activity.

3. Assertiveness is not a dirty word. You can break the ice, be the one who opens a conversation, searches for and uses some common ground for communication,

4. Not everyone is going to like you. If that's "rejection," so be it. Just think about all the people you decide you don't want to know; if you have a right to be discriminating, so do they. It's not the end of the world nor does it mean you are a rotten, unlovable person.

5. Be receptive to conversation, overtures, openers. Be alert, aware of glances, tune in to people, flirt a bit.

6. If you have trouble carrying on a conversation, practice with the people you already know, like relatives, friends, and salespeople, until you get better.

7. Read. At the very least, you'll have something to say after you say hello.

8. Pursue your private interests, because they'll make you happy, and also because it is while doing them that you'll be the most relaxed and will have common interests to chat about with others.

9. Remember that success breeds success and raises self-esteem. Reward yourself when you courageously interact in ways you've never tried before, even if it's only a mental pat on the back.

10. Get where the action is. The fish can't bite if you're not casting where they are.

*Emily Collins, *The Whole Single Person's Catalog*, San Diego: 5737 Adelaide Ave., San Diego, CA 92115.

Some practical advice on other matters may be helpful. (See *Separation and Divorce: Parents Are Parents Forever*, page 223, and *The Child Born to a Single-by-Choice Parent*, page 84.)

Some serious thoughts: If a child does not know one of his or her natural parents, questions will come up. Don't equate questions with rudeness or a personal attack. Children want answers to unknowns. Kids want clarity about their heritage. Clarity contributes to a sense of completeness and well-being. Your honesty enhances your relationship. The unknowns are stressors. The stress comes from very basic questions. "Who am I? Who is my dad (or mom)? Why don't I know him (or her)? What if I get some disease that I've inherited?" (See *Adopted Children*, page 78.)

Repeat the statement, "A child from a single-parent family can be just as happy and successful as a child from a two-parent home." Many single parents are happy, run a smooth ship, and feel quite complete and stable. However, some have serious, disquieting moments, pierced with sustained doubts about their role as a parent. In particular, I refer to *the noncustodial parent—the majority of the fathers of divorced families.*

Noncustodial Parents, Shared Custody, and the Custodial Parent

There is no dress rehearsal for being out of the home and still connected to the lives of everyone there. This connection needs continuous definition in order not to cause problems exhibited as instability.

The noncustodial parent must respond to his or her self-generated questions: How much contact is enough? Should there be a time-out, a reprieve from the tug-of-war, a chance to heal before visits start, or is a break unwise? How do I take care of a toddler, much less an infant? How do I entertain the older children away from home? What about gifts? Now that I'm dating, how much do I tell the kids? Is it time for an introduction and time together?

There are no pat answers. Each person needs to bear in mind two issues: *trust* (Can my kids depend on me?) and *mutual respect* (Is the time we spend together enhancing our relationship?). Single, noncustodial parents must accept the possibility of the children's vacillating enthusiasm for visits. It may not reflect the quality of the relationship at all—rather, that kids are selfish, want to do their own thing, and may consider the visits a burden.

Joint custody or shared custody is an attempt to keep the parent-child relationships as stable as possible. (See *Separation and Divorce: Seldom a Surprise, Always a Loss*, page 226.) In effect, it avoids labeling one parent as "noncustodial." This conveys an important message to the children—that they are important to *both* parents.

The *single, custodial parent* has the jumbo job of the management of kids, home, self, and all the rest. Sometimes it's overwhelming; other times it seems relatively easy because the parent can make his or her own decisions. "I feel free to make my own mistakes without somebody telling me that I'm wrong. The kids accept the way we do things around here, and, by the way, they help a lot," one mother told me. Another mom says, "I miss the coparenting, but I don't miss the tension of the past five years."

All single parents must keep track of the age-appropriate developmental behaviors of their children. If not, they may needlessly blame themselves when two-year-old Ben has a temper tantrum, five-year-old Philip wants to run, bike, and bounce, or ten-year-old Mary Sue demands quiet time alone and is a bit moody. Ups and downs are part of growing up. They are not deliberate behaviors intended to scold mom because she and dad got a divorce, or because she didn't provide a daddy, or to punish dad for leaving.

REASSURANCES

There are some reassurances that may be useful for you:
- Remember that divorced persons recover at different rates. Translate "recover" into "feel more stable." The children may make comparisons. "How come you're still so crabby and daddy is more fun?" or "You are sad all the time. Why don't you smile like mommy does?" Such questions are not intended to hurt you. Kids will be kids; they pop up with spontaneous questions.
- Remember that all parents have misgivings and at some point are self-critical of their parenting. Some adults handle babies smoothly but have difficulties with older children who have temper tantrums or who tend to be smart alecks.

- If you are in the process of rebuilding or remodeling your relationship with your children, your kids may be resistant or mistrusting. Be patient!
- Learning to parent without the help of a spouse isn't easy. Learning to parent isn't easy for anyone. Each of you will discover and develop your own style of living and child rearing. Never lose sight of the fact that you are the adult in the family—residential or not—and there will be power struggles and lack of appreciation. As mentioned before, parenting is not a popularity contest.

A grandparents' rights movement has resulted in grandparent visitation statutes in all fifty states. Although considered controversial, many lawyers, judges, child advocates, and other professionals are working to safeguard the relationship between grandparents and grandchildren. Visitation and access problems develop following parental separation and divorce, death, interventional custody fights, and when grandparents report suspicions of child abuse. There is a need for continuity and measures to protect the emotional and physical health of the child and the child's preferences.

32.
Grandparents as Parents

Grandparenthood is supposedly a separate stage of family life, unfettered by childcare obligations. When grandparents become primary caretakers, they are taking "five giant steps backward."

Today, grandparents are increasingly necessary as a stabilizing force in the American family because the family system is changing. Some children need to be placed with grandparents due to divorce, remarriage, drugs, desertions, parental neglect or abuse of the children, death of a parent(s), incarceration, or mental illness. In 1988, it was estimated that 2.3 million children (or five percent of all American families) live in their grandparent's home.

Grandparents as parents is an alternative to foster home placement with nonrelatives. When placement is mandated by the courts, relatives and grandparents are historically the placement of choice. It is assumed that this is in the best interest of the child.

Four of the many issues that impact grandparents as parents are: (1) age of the kids and the grandparents, (2) health, (3) economic status, and (4) legal stipulations. Regarding age, *because of early marriages and early childbirths, grandparenthood is more recently being considered a middle-aged phenomena rather than one of old age.* A growing number of grandparents are in their mid-forties, whereas, in the past, grandparenthood traditionally began in the fifties and sixties. The median age at the birth of the first grandchild is now forty-five years.

The health of grandparents can be a major problem—especially if older, infirm grandparents are required to handle small children or be active with older grandchildren. If one grandparent becomes ill or disabled, the well spouse is caught between the needs of the ill spouse and the needs and demands of the grandchildren.

If one of the grandparents should die, the children will be faced with turmoil and grief. This adds yet another loss to the lives of these children. It takes a lot of energy and fortitude to keep up with kids—whether pushing a stroller or chasing a child on a bike or roller blades. If the children are upset, as well they may be, it is to be expected that they will have sleep problems which will disturb the grandparent's rest as well. It's hard to be stable when very tired.

Grandparents as parents are required to be disciplinarians and this may be distasteful—a contrast to the way they had visualized traditional grandparenting; a more fun-loving, relaxed relationship.

Build Your Grandparent-Grandchild Relationship

- Know what's going on in your grandchild's life. What are the favorite books, TV shows, best friends?
- Spend time, one-on-one, with each grandchild, when possible.
- Tell the children about you—as a child, a teenager, young married, a mom or dad, your work, your interests and hobbies.
- Send pictures.
- Write letters—supply self-addressed, stamped envelopes—an occasional dollar bill, or stickers add to the fun.

- Record bedtime stories or books for children to enjoy over and over again.
- If you have any health concerns that they need to know about, explain carefully. "I have a bad back and cannot pick you up as much as I'd like to. But you can sit on my lap or rest by me on the couch." Grandchildren usually harbor worries about the health of their grandparents and some unexpressed anxiety about their dying. They may personalize these fears into the poignant question, "What would happen to me then?"
- "If I can't trust my mother to want me or keep me, how do I know that I can trust you?" Joshua, age seven, asked his grandmother. Josh's mother lives with an alcoholic and he has been badly neglected. Don't assume that grandma's house will be considered a haven for abused children. Many are accustomed to violence—even abuse—and being separated from the familiar is traumatic. It takes time to adjust to a new place— even grandma's.
- Don't look for older children to express appreciation. They need time to recover from whatever determined that they are with you. They may need time *and* counseling. Entire families may benefit from professional help. Remember that foster parents and many adoptive parents receive a lot of support at the time of placements. Even though you are a relative, blood or in-law, you also are entitled to help. The children's problems are similar in many ways. Give children time to get acquainted. To many, you are almost an unknown, especially if you've lived far away or there hasn't been a close relationship with the parents.
- Research establishes that grandchildren benefit from contact with their biological parents. In some circumstances, this may be difficult. If physical reunions are impossible, be instrumental in the sending of letters, cards, phone calls, and so forth. If the biological parent does not respond, help the children understand parental problems. Even young children can understand, "Mom is sick." "Daddy had to go away." Don't make any promises or promote unrealistic hope.

The multigenerational family, where the parent is present, complicates the picture. Role clarification for all the adults is imperative. It is asking a great deal of grandparents to maintain a stable home twenty-four hours a day.

Economic considerations range from how to subsist to managing work schedules to the loss or necessary use of savings and resources. Money issues relate to legal stipulations. Custody arrangements provide certain guidelines regarding financial support and some important decision making. Regarding legal stipulations, when the parents of the grandchildren are still living, the grandparents may have either informal or formal custody. With informal, in which no state agency is involved, the grandparents receive no financial support for the kids. Whether formal or informal, court-ordered custody implies that the child is a dependent of the court. With formal placement, the grandparents become legal guardians and can obtain welfare and medical insurance benefits for the grandchildren. With informal custody, the court retains guardianship, and this precludes the grandparents from making some decisions regarding the kids. The biological parents or the courts may retain the decision-making authority. This affects everyone's stability. In some instances a grandparent cannot proceed with important medical procedures until a court order is available. This can be delayed (a judge may be on vacation or the courts can be overloaded) and the recommendations of the grandparents disallowed or discounted. This results in an emotional tug-of-war for the grandparents and children.

In other legal matters, there can be painful conflicts if there are hearings or a trial regarding child abuse or sexual assault in which the children are involved. The grandparents may initially be called on as witnesses and have to testify against their own children—on behalf of the grandchildren. You can imagine the conflicts.

PROCEDURES AND REASSURANCES FOR GRANDPARENTS AS PARENTS

- *Be kind to yourself.* Accept that in assuming the parenting role, you will have mixed feelings. Given the reasons described above, rest assured that everyone can understand your ambivalence or feelings of being overwhelmed. Perhaps there is resentment and confusion too.
- Your attitude toward the parents (your children) will depend on why the grandchildren have been placed with you. Prioritize the children's adjustment. There is plenty of time ahead to deal

with your relationship with your children. There is an urgency to establish as much stability for the grandchildren as rapidly as you can. You know that losing a parent, uprooting from the home, and moving in with you is very upsetting. Even though the grandchildren may love you a great deal, it will take time for them to see you as the authority person in their lives. A great deal depends on your age and the age of the children. It goes without saying that infants and toddlers may adjust more readily than older children who may have had to change schools, leave friends, or be separated from siblings who were placed elsewhere.

- From the beginning, tell the children how you plan to manage the household—what responsibilities they will have, specific schedules or plans you have for yourself: "I go to choir practice on Thursday nights; Grandpa will put you to bed," and other routines. "I expect you to put your dirty clothes in the hamper." "I want you to set the table every night." "My friends come to play bridge every other Wednesday."

In summary, grandparents as surrogate parents must deal with a myriad of problems. These range from their having to deal with personal health, economic problems, emotional needs, marital obligations, and the anxieties of aging to the complicated relationships with their children who have put them in this situation. Add the responsibilities of raising young children. This task is far more intricate and demanding than twenty or thirty years ago because of problems beyond your control—schools, neighborhood changes, material demands, violence in society, the prevalence of drugs, and so forth.

The children have to work through unique problems. They may develop divided loyalties between their biological parents and their grandparents. This creates stress for everyone. When grandparents have legal guardianship, the children need to know this because it offers a sense of orderliness that supports stability. Teenagers may want to strike out on their own—resisting authority from anyone—in spite of court orders.

You may feel isolated from your friends because of your grandparenting responsibilities. You may yearn for the times when you and your spouse were alone, enjoying yourselves and prospering in your empty nest. Your financial obligations may become oppressive, and though you may receive benefits from Aid for Families with Dependent Children or Social Security Disability Insurance, this is far from adequate. You may be using your own savings and resources to support this extended family and feel reluctant to do so.

If your daughter or son is a drug addict, you may have a very difficult time reconciling your devotion to them with your anger at what they have done to your grandchildren. Drug-infected cocaine infants suffer immeasurably and many have neurological and adjustment problems. Raising them can be frustrating and unrewarding to you. Older drug victims may have problems in school and with peer relationships. It is suggested that, as grandparent-parents, you let go of the dream of an old-fashioned home and concede that the drug culture has infected your family too. Such acceptance can promote stability.

If you long for the role of grandparent, not parent, to these children, it may be of some comfort to know that many, many others share the same longing. It's natural. Your compensation may be the smiles on the faces of the kids when they say, "I love you," or fall asleep in your arms.

"I want to do a better job with my grandbabies than I did with my own kids. Every day I think that I must have failed as a parent. Otherwise I wouldn't be in this situation. Maybe I should see this as a second chance and be grateful," a fifty-five-year-old woman said. Her husband added, *"If our kids went bad, they didn't learn it from us. I think my wife is foolish to blame herself."*

9

The Quest for Stability
Ongoing Family Problems

CERTAIN ONGOING, difficult situations may never improve or change dramatically. They corrode stability unless parents adapt well and help their children do the same. This section deals with what is termed "chronic" problems.

33.
Living with an Alcoholic Parent

More than 25 million children live with one adult who has a serious drinking problem. In only twenty percent of alcoholics' homes in America are *both* parents abusers. Accurate statistics for drug addicts are not available, but their problems are similar. Parental addiction results in damaged relationships, repressed feelings, fragmented bonding, and anxiety. Tragically, it is estimated that over fifty percent of violence and battering is associated with alcohol abuse.

Characteristics of the Alcoholic Family

Deception and unreliability are perhaps the two most easily recognized characteristics of the alcoholic family. Some parents may hide their drinking, while others may pass out on the living room couch. Children are deprived of honesty and consistency. Unanswered questions and unexplained behavior add to the problems. Irresponsible behavior frightens children. It's scary to feel, "I don't know where mom or dad is," or "I can't understand why dad is so mean today when he was so nice yesterday."

On a deeper level, these children invariably face *parental detachment, role changes, repressed feelings, or denial.* A parent who is absorbed in his or her own gratification cannot be expected to develop or maintain a normal bonding situation with the children. (See *Bond to the Children,* page 17.) Sometimes the child will feel cared for and other times the child will feel neglected. A feeling of worthlessness and abandonment can result. When role reversals are necessary and the child takes care of the parent, the child's dependency needs are neglected and mistrust infects the family. At the same time, the child learns to stop asking questions. It is not difficult to visualize that, when asked too many questions, a parent gets angry and ends up consuming more drinks. Children, seeing cause and effect, back off. They don't want to make their parents mad, but more importantly, they do not tell their parents how they feel. If they admit to being scared or embarrassed, it may simply start another scene and mom or dad will hit the bottle again.

Portrait of a female drinker

Six out of ten adult Americans drink. Ninety-five percent are light (three drinks a week) to moderate drinkers (one drink a day).

Women tend to use alcohol to relax or feel better. Men take a drink to become more sociable.

Women, who have multiple roles, wife, mother, worker outside the home, have fewer alcohol problems than women with fewer demands.

—National Council on Alcohol Abuse and Alcoholism, 1992

Secrets undermine stability. Children are naturally social persons who freely share almost all their thoughts. They learn quickly that talking about a parent's drinking is a family taboo. It is a lesson that can affect all of the child's relationships. The message kids get is to stay businesslike with teachers and have fun with friends, but do not talk about family to outsiders or discuss feelings with the other members of the family. Even brothers and sisters remain remote from each other; communication may become superficial or hostile.

Being a child of an addicted parent may force a child to take on different roles. Betty, a daughter, becomes a rescuer. If mom is drunk, Betty fixes dinner, does the laundry, or looks after the other kids. Matt, a son, takes on the role of hero: he tries to make things better for the family and works diligently to improve the situation. Because a parent who drinks needs to drink more and more, the hero is always losing ground and feels consistently inadequate. This feeling of inadequacy is well hidden by the obvious, visible success of the family achiever. The role of the hero is to provide self-worth for the family. He pays a very high price in terms of nonstop anxiety.

Louise, another daughter, has become a scapegoat. She chooses to pull away from the mess and stress in the family. She attracts attention by doing things that are self-defeating. She runs away, uses drugs, or provokes significant problems at school. She may become sexually promiscuous—even get pregnant. In providing distraction away from the alcoholic parent, she protects those she loves. The roles the children assume abet survival and may even provide a scenario of predictability, but this is not stability.

INDICATORS OF INSTABILITY

Some are easy to observe, while others are more subtle:
- Lack of positive self-image. "I don't like me."
- Inconsistent feelings about parents. "Sometimes I love my mom and sometimes I hate her."
- Uncertainties about who they are. "Am I a kid or a grownup?"
- Adult-child confusion. "Sometimes I have to take care of them."
- Lack of respect for parents. "I can't respect my parents. They tell lies."

- Feelings of helplessness, incompetence, pity, fear, anger, despair, and embarrassment that may not be openly expressed. "I can't do anything when my dad screams at us or when my mom blacks out." "I've learned I'd better not tell anyone how I feel."
- Need to be a self-reliant perfectionist. "No one takes care of me so I have to take care of myself and be the best I can be all the time."
- Depression, signs similar to anyone who suffers loss.
- Withdrawal, reluctance to ask for help. "I am the one who is supposed to be a helper. I shouldn't have to ask for help."
- Lack of self-esteem. "I feel guilty when I stand up for myself. I don't deserve all this attention."
- Uncommunicativeness. "I learned the best thing to do is to say nothing. I'm not going to be the one to tell. Maybe if I don't talk about it, it won't hurt so much."

The Characteristics of an Alcoholic

This list may help identify someone addicted to booze.
- You drink more and more because you really enjoy it. Actually, there is something wrong, but you can't pinpoint it; you are powerless against it, but you think you have it under control.
- You need "one or two" drinks nearly every day.
- You get drunk almost every weekend.
- You keep "going on the wagon."
- You think about booze a lot.
- You arrive at parties and social affairs already "well oiled."
- You begin to lose friends quickly even if you make them easily.
- You have blackouts—that is, the next day you can't remember what happened while you were drinking.
- You drink to get rid of a hangover.
- Once you take a drink, you find it hard to refuse another. In fact, you hardly think about it.
- You make excuses about your drinking.
- Your family makes excuses about your drinking.
- You get into trouble because of your drinking.
- Once you start drinking, you can't stop. You go on long binges that you can't help.

PROCEDURES FOR PARENTS

Parents *must* take two important steps. The first is to solve his or her own drinking problem. *This means to stop!* A commitment to a therapy or support program is imperative—detoxification if necessary! Therapy in an inpatient or outpatient facility can be intensive and hastens recovery. Alcoholics Anonymous is one of the most effective programs. Related programs like Ala-Teen and Al-Anon are designed to help children and mates of alcoholics.

The second step is to repair significant relationships as much as possible. Help the children with feelings and adjustment problems. Be open and communicative. Help each child learn that he or she can cope with life *without the use of alcohol.* This is important. Today too many boys and girls of eight, nine, and ten years of age are already addicts.

Note: If parents are still having addiction problems, another adult may have to be the support person for the children.

In addition, consider the following suggestions.
- Help children understand that they are not responsible for the fact that their parents cannot show love. Addictions distort emotions.
- Help children understand that parents who drink have impaired memories. They don't show up for conferences at school or for birthday parties; that is part of the addiction. Parents do not intentionally hurt their kids. The parents are victims of their disease.
- Let children know that they can confide in responsible adults, such as other family members or school counselors.
- Help the child learn to play. Many children from an alcoholic family have had to be caretakers since five years of age, and this meant playtime was gone. They have an overdeveloped sense of responsibility and approach life in a serious, sad way.
- Expect that the expression of feelings may be very, very difficult. Be patient. This may be a problem for many years to

come. Experts in the field of alcohol treatment state that crises from childhood experiences may be acted out in the late twenties by angry fights or sexual promiscuity, for instance. Acting out may precede verbal expressions of feelings.

- Encourage the kids to get involved with other kids from similar backgrounds. High school students might want to join SADD— Students Against Drunk Driving. This group was founded because kids suffered so much grief when their friends and siblings were killed in alcohol-related car accidents. Ten thousand people between the ages of sixteen and twenty-four die in alcohol-related motor vehicle crashes each year.
- Tell kids about fetal alcohol syndrome—the effect that alcohol has on an unborn child. Tell them about impaired development and mental retardation. Show them pictures of victims.
- If your family has broken up because of drinking or other addictions, make sure that the youngsters understand what happened. This is consistent with one theme of this book: that children are entitled to know the facts in order to have stability. *The alcoholic family has a higher rate of divorce, incest, death, money problems, violence, and neglect than any other.*

34.
Living with a Disabled Parent

A parent's disability may be a very private matter. Some kids are embarrassed by it. Very young children might believe that, "all moms can't hear," and "most daddies are in wheelchairs." Learning to take care of a parent, to help on a daily and often very personal basis, is a way of life for millions of youngsters. Situations vary dramatically. So much depends on the other helpers available, the degree of the handicap, and the attitude and expectations for all. There is no typical pattern, but all children accept that:

- Their home life is different from that of families where no one is disabled. Although children adjust to life with a disabled parent and learn what is expected of them without fanfare, there may be an undertone of resentment. "It's not fair that *my mom* is blind. Sometimes I think it's not fair that I have to take care of her so much."
- Older brothers and sisters can become unusually protective of

younger siblings to make up for what a parent can't do. In turn, they may put aside their own responsibilities, including school or outside interests such as music, scouts, or athletics. Marital problems are common. These affect everyone. The children become confused about dependency and helplessness. If Rose, a fourteen-year-old girl, helps to bathe her partially mobile mother every day, she knows that she is important to her mom. When Rose, herself, wants help with homework, she is reluctant to ask.

INDICATORS OF INSTABILITY

- The child appears too serious, depressed, or worried all the time.
- The child is afraid to leave the house for fear the parent will not be properly cared for. It is difficult to concentrate at school.
- The child has disturbed sleep patterns, fearful that the parent's middle-of-the-night plea for help might not be heard.
- The child gets embroiled in disturbing fantasies, imagines the worst, and can't seem to control such feelings. Children as young as age five may become obsessed with death and dying.
- The child is angry a lot, flies off the handle, or is moody— displaying how difficult it is to be controlled when involved with a disabled parent. There may be times when the child is jealous of the attention that the parent receives.
- The child withdraws, feels as if he or she cannot ask for anything (attention, help, or money) because this might deprive the disabled parent. I remember a child who appeared neglected. He refused any new clothes and protested against Christmas presents because, "Mom needs a new wheelchair."

A child who displays any of these symptoms needs someone to talk to. Most children who are unusually unstable are not given enough pertinent information such as who will be there with mom or dad—who will fix lunch, help with bathroom matters, bathe, or change clothes. Once they are made aware of such details, they feel more stable. Sometimes a vacation or visit away from home will help.

Sometimes a child will overreact to a parent's statement such as, "I love to have you here with me." Conflict ensues when the child interprets this as, "Don't leave me." The child needs to be told about the predictable emotional ups and downs of a seriously disabled person—especially conflicts about dependency.

PROCEDURES FOR PARENTS

Give the children support:
- They need thanks, compliments, and appreciation. Taking care of a handicapped parent becomes routine—like brushing your teeth—but children need to be thanked.
- They need to understand that everyone depends on others to some extent and that circumstances change. Remind them that they were babies once and their parents took care of them. Now it has to be turned around.
- Children need to be helped to see the "wellness" the parent displays—efforts to be independent, cheerful, helpful with school work, and ways the parent attempts to compensate for one deficiency by being proficient in something else. The kids need to be reminded that mom is a person first—a person with a handicap—deserving of their respect.
- Beyond the wellness, children want to admire a parent. In some instances, this may require looking back on what a parent accomplished in the past. This is important. In a handicapping situation such as that of a post-accident quadriplegic or progressive multiple sclerosis, where change is gradual, children will seldom ask questions about what's ahead. They need honest answers to whatever questions they may pose.
- Kids need to be allowed to be kids. Family routines should provide as much time as possible for kids to enjoy their own friends and activities.
- If possible provide a chance for your children to talk with other kids who help take care of a parent. Peer exchanges can be great.
- Give the kids an opportunity to tell their peers of the patterns in the home. Make it a learning experience for others. Most children do not have a "poor me" attitude. This mature, "accept life as it is" attitude is a fine example for other children and adults.
- Get materials from organizations and share them. Many are

written for children. Read them together and share ideas, feelings, and fears.

REASSURANCES

I'm certain that you have already pictured a number of ways you can help these children. Remember that children:
- Learn that life can be a struggle. The struggle will mean that you have to learn to be strong, unselfish, and adaptable.
- Learn that living in a home where there is a problem doesn't have to be a problem. Patterns are worked out. People do adjust. "That's just how it is at my house." Parents work hard to keep things as "normal" as possible.
- Learn that you cannot run away from some problems.
- May adapt a spiritual attitude about life and help to maintain as much stability as possible.

Remember that most children adapt readily or seem only moderately or appropriately caught up in the ups and downs of a parent's disability. However, some children become unduly upset and may overreact, especially if the disability results from some traumatic event such as an accident or a fire.

35.
Living with a Chronically Ill Parent

Congruent with living with a disabled parent (previous section), a child who lives with a chronically ill parent has similar and different issues to face. The most dramatic differences rest in these questions: Will my mother (or father) die? Does my mother know that she may be dying? If she dies, who will take care of me?

The fact that the disease may be longstanding does not negate these questions, although the children may not verbalize them frequently. As in any other situation, children are entitled to the facts—to know what you know about diabetes, emphysema, multiple sclerosis, AIDS, kidney failure (dialysis treatments), and so forth.

Usually a parent adapts to a chronic illness and makes few, if any, demands on the children. Marie's father has diabetes. His daily insulin shots and occasional urine tests are private matters. An occasional blackout is a vivid reminder of dad's condition, plus mother makes frequent comments about why certain foods or treats must be avoided. Marie doesn't dwell on her dad's condition. However, she was shocked when his foot had to be amputated. No one had told her about circulation problems. She was ten years old—old enough to understand. Her parents explained that they just didn't want her to worry.

Other common concerns that may affect the child's adjustment include:

- Will my father get worse and have to go to a nursing home?
- Will my family run out of money? If this happens, how will we get medicine for mom or pay for an operation?
- Will I be taken away if she gets any sicker? Children in a single-parent home may dwell on this and become very frightened. Some children in this situation refuse to go to school, wanting to make certain that they are not separated from the ailing parent.

INDICATORS OF INSTABILITY

This list is similar to those of *Living with a Disabled Parent*, page 153.

PROCEDURES FOR PARENTS

Children need to be given a realistic picture of what is ahead, in terms that they can understand. No one can predict the course a disease will take. But children want people to "get well and live happily ever after." When this will not be the case, help them to accept reality. One doesn't have to be morbid. The thrust is, "Let's make the best of every day we have."

If a parent becomes terminally ill and death is near, the child may need special support. (See Appendix B for the steps to follow to help a child deal with the anticipated loss of a loved one.) Hospice personnel give excellent information, advice, and support.

If the family anticipates that the ill parent may die at home, prepare the children as best you can. Reassure them that this may be the parent's choice—decision—to be surrounded by people he or she loves. Talk about pending peace and rest, sadness and loss. It is possible that children can be helped through a death without great trauma—*especially if they have been permitted to say good-bye in their own way.*

REASSURANCES

The terminally ill parent may be unresponsive. Reassure the children this is not rejection but what happens as the person becomes weaker.

Some older boys or girls learn that they cannot run away from some problems. Some become committed to doing something meaningful in the field of their parent's illness. Daniel's father had multiple sclerosis, and, as a young boy, Danny decided to become a doctor to "find out about my dad's illness." It may lead to a career choice or participation in an organization as a volunteer.

Many adopt a spiritual attitude about life and use this to maintain as much stability as possible. Some become philosophical and adaptable. "Oh, dad's back in the hospital getting some tests," is announced with a degree of nonchalance and comfort. Younger children may be more prone to become hysterical—perhaps reflecting great fear that the parent may die. Children of a chronically ill parent seldom exhibit bitterness. Almost always, they contribute a sense of liveliness or serenity to the family.

If you become aware that a child feels guilty because he or she has been inattentive or impatient with an ill parent, reassure the child that there is no ideal way to be a bystander or caregiver. Everyone has feelings of inadequacy. Little Billy may say, "I wanted to give my daddy my truck, but there was no place for it on his bed. Now I feel bad."

36.
Living with a Mentally Ill Parent

No discussion of living with a chronically ill parent would be complete without mention of the mentally ill. Since the 1960s, disturbed patients are released from state hospitals as rapidly as possible. Most are sent home or left to survive in public or private facilities, or they end up on the streets. The deinstitutionalization of the mentally ill has been called one of the new "shames of the cities."

Can a family attain stability when a parent suffers from mental illness? Some disturbed people bring a tyrannical presence into the family, some are significantly depressed and their intermittent suicide threats frighten everyone involved. Some are medicated, zombie-like, unable to take care of their own needs, much less attend to the children. The anxiety about the future is ongoing, whether expressed as money worries or serious doubts about the effectiveness of various therapies. It is safe to say that a goal of family stability is unfair, but shared concerns and feelings can create good communication and interdependency among the "well" members of the family. Outside support is a must.

The unpredictable and vivid emotional ups and downs of many mentally ill persons are particularly disturbing to children. Docile days followed by screaming evenings are hard to explain.

Irene is six years old. In the past few months, her mother has been hospitalized twice—once a suicide crisis and once a three-week stay to establish a new medication regime. Mom is now able to fix dinner and read to her before she goes to bed. Irene is elated. As an angel in the Christmas play at school, Irene was thrilled to see her mother in the audience. She waved to her mother and couldn't help whispering loudly to her best friend, "That's my mom!" much to the dismay of her teacher. The audience was delighted.

Medicines can help, but many mentally ill persons are indigent and cannot afford costly medicines on an ongoing basis.

INDICATORS OF INSTABILITY

To care for the children, the functioning parent or grandparent should be aware of signs of instability. These include:
- Signs of embarrassment, confusion, anger, and hurt brought on by the behavior of the mentally ill parent.
- Stays away from home as much as possible.
- Insists on taking responsibilities, sacrificing own needs.
- Defensiveness when questioned about the parent. Defensiveness can damage peer relationships.

- Drinks or uses medication to make the situation more tolerable.
- Ongoing sleep or eating problems—at times, severe nightmares.
- Signs of anxiety and grief similar to those evidenced when children experience separation, divorce, or other important loss.

PROCEDURES FOR THE "WELL" PARENT

Your job is enormous. First, deal with your own feelings and responsibilities. Second, make important decisions on behalf of the ill spouse, and third, provide support for the children. The needs of the children will vary depending on age, maturity, and understanding of the ill parent's problem. All children will benefit from:

- Knowing the facts about the parent's condition including the prognosis. One child told me, "I never imagined a person could look so blank so much of the time."
- Freedom from guilt, "You didn't drive your mother 'crazy'!"
- Encouragement to attend school and continue own activities.
- A loving, competent, and consistent mother-substitute for babies and young children if the mother is ill.
- Preparation for setbacks. The kids need to be told the truth and not be led to believe in miracles. Some medications and hospitalizations help dramatically, but unfortunately, these marked improvements do not always hold up. Use terms they can understand, such as, "Mommy isn't well and she gets very emotional." "Daddy gets upset very easily and he says and does things that he really doesn't mean to say or do." "When Bill gets violent, it's because he is emotionally sick."
- A description of some of your conflicts and emotions without any expectation that the children should try to comfort you or "fix" problems.

Provide the children with individual or family support, which can help children understand the stigma attached to mental illness. Whether in individual or group counseling, the child will learn how to answer difficult questions that someone may ask. This is both reassuring and can help the individual feel somewhat stable. Encourage siblings to give each other support. They all feel cheated.

REASSURANCES

Reassure the children that you will not abandon them—that you will do the best you can to be available, attend school conferences, help with homework, occasionally play games together, go to the movies, or take a trip.

Reassure the children, as best you can, that the chances of their becoming mentally ill "just like daddy" are very slight. If the illness is the result of drug abuse, reassure the children that they have the power to stay drug free.

37.
Living with a Mentally Retarded Sibling

Thousands of families have retarded children. One out of every 650 babies is a Down's syndrome child. There are many adjustments to make and they keep changing.

Enjoy every step forward, every achievement, every hug.

Most retarded children are happy and sociable. They enjoy certain foods and music, and some become hooked on TV, crafts, or other activities. In conversations they can be very direct and occasionally perceptive. "I'm going to stand here. The birds are pretty. That's what I'm going to do." Some are antisocial, fearing unfamiliar situations and meeting new people. Most become close to the members of the family even though communication is restricted and much goes on that they are unable to understand. Any age retarded persons may be prone to cry easily. This can upset caretakers.

Living with a mentally retarded sibling does not have to undermine family stability. The extent of the problem depends on the degree of the impairment, size of the family, birth order, and parental management. Parental management adds up to attitude, distribution of responsibilities, and how the needs of everyone are met. If the retarded child receives a disproportionate amount of adult time or family money (for example, for private education), siblings may feel displaced, ignored, or unimportant, although outbursts of anger or expressions of disgust are rare. These feelings may be expressed in various ways which replicate indicators of instability. Most siblings understand and accept that their impaired brother or sister cannot learn what they learn, cannot handle some machines, or cannot understand abstract ideas such as appreciation, consideration, anticipation, patience, or appropriateness.

From the point of view of siblings, the impaired brother or sister often just gets in the way. "She won't get out of my room," or "Why can't she keep her hands out of my goldfish bowl?" a young child may ask. If a retarded child is unduly stubborn, as many are, the others may complain, "She won't move away from in front of the TV and I can't see." Again, parental management is the key to harmony. Will the parent be assertive and move the child away from the TV, or will the other children hear, "But she doesn't understand and she likes to look at TV. You go find something else to do."?

All children will display weaknesses and limitations, and will disappoint you at some time by not becoming the child of your dreams: As parents we have to accept this sooner or later. A retarded child, a limited child, presents disappointments sooner, rather than later. Your acceptance starts early. Allow your retarded youngster to come to life, for real, like your mother and father allowed you to do— to be, grow, and develop into what he or she really is. Let the child of your mind die. Let the real child live.

Peske, 1973

It is hard to parent a mixed family. Yes, all families are mixed because each person is unique. The mixture that contains a retarded child is very complex. Many difficult decisions must be made which relate to the degree of impairment. *Mild* retardation means that the child is educable and, as an adult, can be surprisingly self-supportive though guidance and supervision may be needed. In contrast, the *profoundly* retarded may require institutional placement or nursing care. In between these extremes, retarded youngsters can communicate in limited ways. Habit training may be slow but most acquire adequate— even gracious—social skills. Some support themselves and live independently.

With the introduction of amniocentesis as an elective pre- natal diagnostic procedure, it is possible to find out if a developing fetus may be born with Down's syndrome. Couples can then elect to terminate the pregnancy or not. In situations where parents first become aware that the new baby is re- tarded, they may be angry, sad, frightened, and in denial. Predictably both parents may run the gamut of those feelings. They may vow to be supportive of each other and do the best they can for the child. Unfortunately, parenting a retarded child is a difficult task and resultant instability leads to separation and divorce in many situations. It is estimated that between forty-five and fifty-five percent of parents of mentally retarded children get divorced. This adds further instability with which everyone must contend. Retarded children become accus- tomed to routines and certain family patterns and interactions. They can become very upset if the family breaks up. Nonretarded siblings may do their best to help, or they may become absorbed in their own pain and needs.

REASSURANCES

As the child matures, certain *positive* patterns fall into place that can benefit everyone who lives with the child. These include:
- The opportunity to show love, empathy, compassion, and understanding.
- The opportunity to be unselfish, to accept and adapt to the needs of an impaired person, including their idiosyncrasies, immaturity, and naivete.
- The opportunity to be supportive of parents and other nonimpaired brothers and sisters.
- The opportunity to enrich their lives by learning "signing" and other methods of helping or teaching.

- The chance to become involved in organizations that provide services to the mentally retarded.
- The chance to be a spokesperson for the disabled, helping others overcome prejudices and fears.

The siblings of a retarded person are usually more mature and knowledgeable about disabling conditions and can model positive attitudes for extended family, neighbors, and friends.

PART III

THE QUEST FOR STABILITY
SOCIETAL PROBLEMS

FAMILIES CAN BECOME so absorbed in personality squabbles and Aunt Regina's arthritis that they ignore social and economic problems that may be corroding their stability. Nevertheless, societal, global, and environmental issues insidiously affect everyone. If you live in a congested, filthy city and contend with miserable traffic twice a day, you are affected by population, pollution, materialism, and are perhaps a victim of someone else's stress and frustrations as well as your own. Living in a rural area may mean that you are isolated or unduly concerned about inadequate services or the availability of medical care.

This section deals with social problems that disturb family equilibrium, or contemporary issues that impact everyone. These include schools and schooling, money—from homelessness to affluence—racism and discrimination, alternative lifestyles, environmental issues—from local drought conditions to concern about the rain forests in South America—and the future as major worries.

10

Schools and Schooling

38.
Homeschooling:
A Growing Trend

Why are more than 1.5 million children in America being educated entirely by their own parents? Is homeschooling a fad or simply an alternative to placing kids in situations that can demolish their self-esteem?

Is homeschooling a safeguard against introducing children to the regular school world of assorted activities for which they may not be physically, emotionally, or developmentally ready? The various answers to these questions reveal that parents are deeply concerned about their children's education and are, accordingly, making important, rational decisions to proceed with homeschooling. Homeschooling is not necessarily an enrichment of other schools—it is an alternative, and at times, a vastly superior educational program for some children.

> *In 1990, it was reported that children schooled at home seem to be five or even ten years ahead of their formally trained peers in their ability to think.*

Homeschooling permits parents to maintain control. It can be convenient, exceptionally productive, and rewarding. Homeschooling is not a panacea for all. Some parents want their kids to be Superkids under their tutelage—free to move as rapidly as possible in diverse ways, with diverse interests. Other homeschooling parents are motivated for exactly the opposite reason; they want kids to move gently through childhood—acquiring skills and knowledge at a pace that is in harmony with age-appropriate interests and excitement.

Children at home can be *free of burdening competition* and free to set and achieve their own goals without diminishing someone else—free to progress without feeling incompetent or inferior to someone else. As a consequence, the self-esteem of the child may be well-tended and nourished.

> *Homeschooling is legal in every state. Most homeschooling parents find that two hours a day at home teaches their children more than six hours a day at school.*

Homeschooling is not a free-wheeling opportunity for parents to choose what they will or will not teach. Inasmuch as children are obligated by law to attend school, the basic content and curriculum of homeschooling is supervised or regulated by the state department of education. The supervision is not strict; the curriculum is very open to enrichment and experimentation, but there are guidelines to follow and achievement measures that must satisfy state requirements. The goal of homeschooling is to provide learning experiences that build and support a child's self-esteem, and take advantage of parental talents and interests as well as their fervent desire that their children be successful, happy students.

Homeschooling requires the discipline inherent in scheduling. This in itself provides a measure of stability for parents and children. Most parents avail themselves of TV programs and prepackaged curriculum tapes, library books, magazines, and texts as teaching materials. Home computers and innumerable hands-on tools and instruments are used creatively, as well as motivating experiences and experiments with plants, animals, and assorted science supplies, games, and toys.

Homeschooled children sometimes yearn for more companionship—even team or group activities. Some report that parents are bossy as parents and bossy as teachers too.

This is not a pitch for homeschooling. This brief description serves as a backdrop for evaluating your child's experiences in public or private schools—experiences that can result in instability and unhappiness or stability, success, and satisfaction.

39.
Prekindergarten "School" Experiences that May Undermine Stability

I recently attended a preschool "graduation" replete with mortar boards and diplomas. I was miserable. The children were confused and excited—to them it was a party. Their parents were proud and confused. To the adults it was an ominous symbol of what lies ahead: school pressures and problems.

> *One dollar spent on preschool education will save $475 in remedial education, welfare, and crime control.*
>
> *Family background matters far more in determining student achievement than any attributes of the formal education system.*

In his book, *Miseducation: Preschoolers at Risk*, David Elkind deplores early instruction because, in attempts to "teach the wrong things at the wrong time," it usurps the children's natural explorations of their world; it "miseducates." I agree.

Parents of kindergarten-aged children too often concentrate on what a child can do, what he has learned, rather than on behaviors such as spontaneity, curiosity, and joyfulness. For many reasons, parents have been seduced into endorsing the educator's motto, "The younger they learn, the better off they will be as they march through school." Unfortunately for many children, such learning is not possible or is achieved by paying a high price—their happiness, self-esteem, and childhood.

Parents beware! Let the children be children. They will learn in time. The British Infant School has had hundreds of years to convince us that youngsters don't need formal reading instruction until six years of age when most eyes, hands, brains, and the nervous system are ready to learn.

> *The theory that the earlier a child begins to learn, the better off he or she will be, does not hold true. By the third grade, there is little difference between a child who entered kindergarten able to read and the child who learned to read in school.*
>
> —David Elkind

40.
Kindergarten Experiences Can Undermine Stability

Unfortunately for some children, the kindergarten experience imbues significant self-doubt that can cause instability for years to come. Originally kindergarten was intended to give children early childhood experiences in independence; teach them how to get along with others; let them learn about games, toys, school routines, and perhaps numbers or letters. Nowadays kindergarten, in most places, has become a junior first grade with an emphasis on academic skills and competition. Inattentive and immature children are penalized. They are totally unprepared for comparisons such as star charts that tell them that they are not as good as others. For many reasons they have a short attention span, perhaps an impoverished vocabulary or undeveloped language skills, and may also be ill-prepared to separate from the home or another caretaking situation. For some, the socialization in a room full of other kids is frightening. This is the scenario for some children—others do well and have a wonderful time.

INDICATORS OF INSTABILITY

The unstable kindergarten-aged child usually appears immature. In observing your child in school, look for babyish behaviors you may not see at home or an exaggeration of these behaviors—wetting pants, thumb sucking, crying, clinging, unwillingness to talk, withdrawal from adults, stuttering, disruptive or aggressive acts—and also inattentiveness and constant pleas for attention.

PROCEDURES FOR PARENTS

To help your kindergarten child, answer these questions:
1. Is my child immature? (Perhaps all he needs is the gift of more time.)
2. Is my child given too much freedom at home, to a point where he or she cannot adjust to the way this teacher manages this group?
3. Is my child bored at school?
4. Is my child feeling well?

If your answer to the second question is yes, your child requires more discipline or more responsibilities. It is not difficult to start such a regime. Begin by asking your child to perform a single task, such as putting his or her dirty socks in the laundry and build from there. (For suggestions regarding discipline, see *Build Mutual Respect to Support Stability*, page 20.)

Regarding question three, bear in mind that many children have benefited from "Sesame Street," Head Start programs, preschool, parental stimulation, books, and trips, and they may be overprepared for some kindergartens. They may be bored and, as a result, become disruptive. Gifted children may have taught themselves how to read or to handle computers or calculators and may seek sophisticated answers to many questions. Take time to talk to the teacher. Find out what he or she considers important for your child and what the plans are to fill his or her needs. Unless these needs are met, boredom may lead to unacceptable social behaviors, and this may interfere with friendships for years to come—not to mention how it will affect the child's attitude toward school.

Regarding question four, some children pick up all kinds of "bugs" when they first go to school. They are exposed to illnesses they have never had. Be on the lookout for chicken pox, for instance. Also look for the first signs of learning disabilities, hearing problems, or visual problems, which may never have been apparent before. Eye strain, hyperactivity, or inability to follow instructions may indicate perceptual problems. They can be handled. It is important to get professional help at this early stage before your child begins to see himself or herself as a poor student or failure. (See *Learning Disabilities and Attention Deficit Disorder*, page 110.)

Kindergarten should and can be a happy experience. Almost all children are eager to go to school and to make friends. The benefits of these school days are immeasurable for those children who respond to a stimulating and caring situation. For most children at this level, there is very little stress after the initial adjustment period.

41.
Elementary School Experiences Can Undermine Stability (Grades One through Five or Six)

There are endless sources of potential problems in school. They derive from grading and competition, classroom management (grouping practices), methods of discipline, child-teacher relationships, peer relationships, special problems, and teacher personalities. I suggest you read the following table because they apply to both early and late elementary grades.

INDICATORS OF INSTABILITY/IMMATURITY

In some instances, *unhappiness* is the most noteworthy. Others include:

Academic

Cannot concentrate

Has trouble remembering

Refuses to study

Is apathetic, disinterested

Constantly complains that it
is too easy or too hard

Displays test anxiety, gets ill,
has headaches, stomach-
aches

**Classroom, school
management**

Embarrassed by grouping
(always in the slow reading
group, for example)

Never gets to be in a group
with class leaders

Resents hearing test scores
announced in front of the
whole class

Never has a chance to be alone

Feels teacher doesn't trust the
class

Feels discipline, punishments
consistently unfair

Complains that the teacher
never tells anything about
himself or herself; feels
estranged and unimportant
to him or her

Tired of being asked to help
others

Feels teacher doesn't grade
fairly

Child-teacher relationship

Too dependent

Repeatedly says the teacher
doesn't like him or her

Feels teacher enjoys
embarrassing him or her

Shows anger when compared
to older siblings

Says teacher is impersonal,
callous

Peer relationships

Has no close friends

Never invited to parties
or to play

Oversensitive to peer
remarks

Unduly bossy with peers

Criticizes others, quotes
criticisms of himself or herself

Intolerant

Feels too good for others,
appears to be a snob

Personal behaviors

Persistently unhappy or
depressed

Uses drugs, alcohol

Threatens to run away

Refuses to go to school

Destroys personal or school
property

When your child has problems in school, you can expect problems at home. If at all possible, find time to observe classes; drop in unexpectedly, also casually converse with your child's classmates or friends when you have a chance. Kids are spontaneous. They report accurately what's happening. After evaluating the situation, you may want to confer with the teacher. Tell the child ahead of time what you plan to do. Imply that you want to validate his or her reports—not that you are collecting negative or critical information about him or her.

In grades four, five, and six, girls, in particular, may be more concerned about getting a smile from the cutest boy in the class than they are about doing well on a test. Bear in mind:

- Girls are more aggressive than boys and everyone may end up feeling uncomfortable.
- Girls may lose interest in academics, causing school work to suffer.
- Peer relationships become increasingly fragile because some students are ready for dating and going steady while others are not.
- The more sophisticated kids may belittle or embarrass the less mature children.
- Serious students, athletic kids, and "straight" kids may pull away from the less sophisticated kids, thus splitting the class into factions.
- A minority person in the class—disabled or disadvantaged, foreign student, member of a racial minority, or even the "new kid in the school"—may feel unwelcome and display instability at home. (See *Religion: Stress or Solace?*, page 208.)

PROCEDURES FOR PARENTS

If there are any difficulties, these procedures may help:

- Avoid being too critical of how teachers conduct a class or how a principal runs a school. In most instances, there is little you can do. Instead, help your child get a realistic picture of his or her own behavior, attitudes, expectations, and interactions.
- Make suggestions about how your child can change his or her behavior for the better. If Charlie feels that Mrs. French really hates him, he has undoubtedly begun to react to this. Find out what he does. Ask him. Talk to the teacher. Then suggest alternatives. Let's suppose he is now talking to his seatmate as a way of getting back at Mrs. French. He already knows that she will get angry and scold him again. Help him find something about Mrs. French to like. Sometimes kids have to be more flexible and controlled than the teacher. Don't scold.

Maybe Mrs. French really is a pill. Charlie has to learn to cope with the friendly and the unfriendly. He may have a great relationship with some or all of his other teachers.

- If a situation has become destructive and your child feels totally rejected by a teacher, I think it is appropriate for a parent to go to the school and try to make alternative arrangements. This isn't always possible, but at least your efforts on his behalf will impress Charlie. As your child's advocate, you must be the one to challenge teachers and administrators. *If you do not take risks on behalf of your child, who will?*
- If your child is locked into an unhappy situation for 180 school days, make every effort to find enjoyable activities at home and out of school. He needs to feel successful and happy somewhere.
- Look back on the year you spent in a class with a teacher you didn't like. What did you do? What do you wish your parents would have done on your behalf? Develop a plan based in part on your answer to those questions. Some teachers appreciate your input. Some changes may occur. Your child will appreciate your concern.
- If all else fails, consider changing schools or homeschooling. In some instances, tutoring can prepare a child to step up a grade, thereby avoiding a difficult teacher and introducing new peers as potential friends.

———

Few, if any, children go through school without experiencing some rough spots. Whether in a private school, public school, boarding school, or parochial school setting, there are predictable times when the coping style of a child is put to the test.

Realistically, a problem isn't always the teacher's fault and it isn't always the child's fault. There can be a teacher-child mismatch or there can be unfair practices. Some groups of kids can be mighty cruel to others. In my experience, kids are surprisingly accurate reporters on what is going on and who is doing what to whom. Listen to what they tell you and remain as objective as you can. Take time to question your child about being pushed too fast, being bored, having a grouchy teacher, getting into too many fights on the playground, the presence of gangs, and those sorts of things. *If your child, from kindergarten* on, gets in the habit of telling you about almost everything that happens in school, you can readily spot the source of a problem. The child's report on his or her day should be given time equal to the five o'clock news. Second-hand reports from sitters need your attention too.

42.
Middle School Experiences Can Undermine Stability (Middle School May Include Fifth Grade in Some Districts)

When sixth, seventh, and eighth graders are asked to talk about their concerns, four major subjects come up: school, friends, parents, and family problems. Most preadolescents love school. Many blossom academically. School is a friendly place to be. They like the responsibility they have been given and the freedom. They enjoy moving from class to class and having study halls. There are more sports and more activities.

POSSIBLE CAUSES OF INSTABILITY OR UNHAPPINESS

- Concern about grades
- Parental expectations
- Impersonal teachers
- Poor study habits from the past
- Problems with peers; scorn, jealousy, prejudices or abusive, unsuccessful social skills, and rivalries

INDICATORS OF INSTABILITY

Indicators of instability for the middle or junior high school child approximate those described for younger children. Some have never had academic grades before and symptoms of anxiety will begin. The majority of the children are determined to continue to do well or to do better than they have in the past. Those who need special help may reach out for special classes or tutoring labs. Middle-school-aged students sense an urgency to master skills before they head into high school. Their internal goal setting may offset emotional outbursts or other indicators of instability.

With the opportunity to select classes on different ability levels such as basic math versus geometry, social cliques may form. Separation from old friends may provide opportunities to develop new friendships. Until new friendships are made, a child may appear unstable, become agitated, depressed, or show a lot of anger. A few may get discouraged and need a lot of support and attention from teachers and counselors. Unstable kids may even start to experiment with drugs and alcohol or sex, which will distract from academics and school life.

PROCEDURES FOR PARENTS

- *Be available.* Kids need to be reminded that their school life is important to you. Read homework, ask quiz questions, share computer experiences; follow up on long-term assignments. "How are you doing on that report about Jamaica? Do you need any help?"
- *Negotiate grades.* Discuss which subjects are easy and which are hard. Decide, together, which subjects will be most important and what would be an appropriate grade to work toward. The push for straight A's or to always do better creates stress. Perfect grades may be easy for some children but hard for others. Grades are not worth nonstop sleeplessness, headaches, depression, or irritability. A child may get good grades and still have poor self-esteem. "I can study and do okay, but I'm still not important to anyone." *Too often, a parent knows more about the child's grades than he or she knows about the child.* The child is confused, thinking, "If I don't get great grades, I'm no good." Parents *must* guard against saying, "Debbie is a dear but she is certainly not a good student." The child hears only the comments that come *after* the word "but."
- *Don't pay for grades.* This penalizes the child who may put more energy into piano lessons or athletics than academics. The possibility of unnecessary sibling competition goes without saying.
- *Attend conferences.* Arrange to have your child present. Conferences should cover achievements and clarify where encouragement is needed. With Mary present, the possibility of misunderstanding is minimized. Teachers should encourage Mary to help prepare the conference and assure the child that

there will be no surprises. Unexpected comments such as, "Mary is one of the brightest kids in the class," may give Mary the impression that this is for mother's benefit and has no merit. If Mary knows ahead of time that her teacher plans to make that statement, she will have more confidence in all statements that are made. School-parent-child bonds are important and the conference is the most effective tool at all grade levels. Some disgruntled children may attempt to manipulate the home against the school and vice versa. Such maneuvers are fruitless when parent-teacher-child conferences confront the facts. No one benefits if the child is allowed to continue to badmouth the school at home to seek attention or make excuses for his or her own inappropriate behavior. A parent-school alliance is powerful—especially when all adults involved are supportive of the child.

- *Continue your habit of being open and honest about yourself and possible problems.* When you appear unhappy or detached without explanation, this distresses the child. Concentration in school is affected. Studying at home also becomes difficult if there are tensions or fights that the child does not clearly understand. At this age, children need explanations about such things as drinking problems or chronic illnesses. They are mature enough to want to help.

- *Above all, try to set a good example for your child.* Your commitment to education and school success needs to be expressed frequently. This does not mean setting unrealistic goals; it means you are there to help and encourage your child to do the best he or she can.

Benefits of Middle School Level Attendance

Preteen students have crushes on teachers (usually of the same sex) and will try in every way to please. This attachment may be much stronger than any teacher-child relationship that the child has known in the lower grades. The teacher involved has power—almost magical power—to inspire the child to do well and to build self-esteem. With a special teacher as encourager, friend, and mentor, the child can readily deal with problems at school.

Middle school years mark the beginning of self-searching.

Many kids become introspective. They want to feel secure in the daily ups and downs of relationships. The child at thirteen or fourteen may ponder, Will I ever have a boyfriend/girlfriend? How tall will I be? Will I get into a college? Will I ever be happy? What really is a friend? They try to cope in many new ways and benefit from developing self-awareness. In order to do this, they may typically talk over their problems with a friend for hours. (Ask all parents who have telephones!) Many are versatile and learn from their commitments—athletics, bike riding, jogging, team sports, musical pursuits (band, piano, choir), or one of many other activities. They may also decide to put a great deal of effort into schoolwork.

43.
High School Experiences Can Undermine Stability

In America today, there is such an assortment of high schools, such a collection of teachers, and such a variety of students that one cannot describe a typical school. Nevertheless, it is accepted that there are some stressful high school environments. This is the result of the way the high school is run, the teaching methods of some of the staff, and student attitudes. Frequently student attitudes and expectations reflect those of parents, who may be critical and nonsupportive.

Student stress in high school may reflect teacher apathy. The amount of violence against teachers is growing every day. Teacher concerns about their own safety have to affect the way they relate to their students, their jobs, and to the community in which they work.

Students want their high school experience to be *personal, relevant, and interesting.* Personal means the kids are asking for the school to be aware of their needs, skills, rate of learning, and special talents, and to provide a personalized program. They do not want to be shuffled from one class to another feeling unwanted, out of place, inadequate, bored, or like a number in a computer.

Relevant means the student wants school to help him or her adjust to the circumstances of his or her life today and the working world of the future. Many students look to their teachers and the content of classes to help them understand the intricacies of relationships, family disturbances, and such societal issues as racism, discrimination, political maneuvers, and economic scams.

Interesting means the student anticipates that classes will be conducted in such a way that he or she will want to attend. Kids want to admire their teachers. Teachers who are creative, personable, and knowledgeable motivate students to do well.

In September 1992, the National Dropout Prevention Center at Clemson University reported that eighty-three percent of all prison inmates are school dropouts.

Assuming that teachers do their part, there are still groups of students who may experience difficulties:

- Kids who consider themselves misfits
- Immature students who needlessly rebel against authority and are unduly critical
- Kids who consider school a waste of time
- Kids who experience too much pressure from home
- Kids with low self-esteem who express it with anger
- The slow learner or problem learner whose needs are not being met
- The gifted learner whose needs are not being met

You may ask if there are any kids who do not fall into one of those groups. Of course there are. Schools are full of kids who may fuss a bit but are into learning, sports, activities, school spirit, and the normal ups and downs of tests, grades, and reports. They have achieved a balance between good stress and possible debilitating stress. Expressed another way, they have developed a successful coping style.

Please note that in the past ten years, schools across the country have experimented with many new creative programs to meet a variety of student needs. Exemplary programs exist for pregnant teenagers, teen mothers, non-English-speaking students, former drug addicts, former juvenile delinquents, victims of child abuse, and so forth. Most schools are committed to student success, but unfortunately, some remain calcified in old-fashioned, traditional thinking and methods that devastate some students. In some districts, a school board made up of ultraconservative members may resist change and innovation.

As a parent, you are urged to do your homework—read student manuals, go to school board meetings, get involved in parent organizations, and make your feelings known. Teachers, school boards, and superintendents complain about parent apathy. Don't hesitate to ask the questions you want to ask. You may want to read *Secrets Parents Should Know About Public Schools: The parent's guide to getting the best possible education for their children in today's public elementary school system* (Frith, 1985). Ask a group of parents to join with you to adapt the suggestions to your middle or high schools. It would be a valuable contribution.

Your child has to know you care. You validate your concerns when you observe behaviors that worry you. Your next step is to confront your child. Don't pretend you don't see what you see. You are a support person—not an adversary. The child's indicators of instability are your cues to take action, at home and at school.

Many potential dropouts seem to be most vulnerable after eighth grade, between middle and high school.

Successful reentry programs build confidence, self-esteem, and skills that can lead to jobs.

Preventing kids from dropping out of school is a must. Funds for identification and prevention are limited.

INDICATORS OF INSTABILITY

The most dramatic indicators of instability are the child refuses to go to school; pretends to be ill; gets "high" in order to face school; will not study; can't sleep; is apathetic, surly, or depressed; is drinking or experimenting with drugs.

In order to provide support for a teenager, parents must be the great jugglers of the world. As described in *Parenting the Adolescent*, page 44, there will be times when kids are open to parental suggestions and support and times when they are not. Parents have to juggle their support between the blocks or barricades.

PROCEDURES FOR PARENTS

Do Not	Do
Ground kids for poor grades.	Remember that many classes today are boring. Accept the fact that kids will do better in some subjects than others.
Use clichés that kids consider unimportant. "When I was in school, I had to. ..."	Take time to help with homework and projects.
Make threats such as, "You won't get into college with those kinds of grades!" There are many alternative ways for kids to get into college, including GED tests, and many colleges that are stepping stones to more difficult programs.	Negotiate grades. Respect areas of strength and areas of weakness.
Ignore symptoms, assuming that, "all kids that age hate school."	Encourage extracurricular activities.
Ignore the attitudes of your child's friends about school. They have a strong influence.	Maintain limits—time to be home, and time for homework, sports, and other extracurricular activities.
Ignore the fact that if there are problems at home, the child's attitude about school will be affected.	Discuss facts—most employers require a high school diploma. New jobs demand new skills.
	If your child needs to go to a different school or work at a different pace, accept this.
	Consider alternative schools.

In many high schools, counselors will want to team up with you to help your child. Go for it. It may lead to a new approach that neither you nor the counselor would have arrived at independently. An alliance between counselor and parent tells the student that his success is important to you.

Seventy-five percent of U.S. public high school students spend one hour or less per school night doing homework. Twenty-five percent spend less than one hour per week.

Benefits of High School Attendance

- If friends are loving and teachers are supportive, a child believes that school is great. Many students are excited about what they learn and must put forth a lot of effort. While learning may be a struggle, they continue to feel good about themselves. For others, learning comes easily, and they set high goals for themselves and work hard to achieve them.
- In addition to academic effort, a student learns tolerance. Children learn to accept individual differences among the students and the staff. In turn, this helps them to accept personal strengths and weaknesses and begin some thoughtful introspection.
- Self-discipline is a benefit. "I have to study." "I've got to learn how to use that machine." "If I buckle down, I can make the honor roll."
- Self-control is another benefit that comes from being surrounded by many different people. "If I get mad, I'd better play it cool," or "Those big kids will push me around if I am a pest."
- An appreciation of one's special talents may result from pressure to excel. "I didn't think I played any better than anyone else, but when I had to do a solo, I began to see that I was pretty good. It was a lot of work, but it was worth it. I'm really grateful now."
- Peer relationships provide happiness, challenge, and comfort even when problems must be solved.

44.
The Parent-Teacher Alliance

Parents can make suggestions to teachers. Parents are obligated to provide teachers with information about their child and family to help the teacher make the best decisions possible on behalf of the kids.

Some suggestions to the teacher—voiced by parents—have a different ring and a stronger value than those presented in an article in a magazine or a sentence heard at an in-service.

Only one-quarter of parents ever visit their child's school. Put another way, three out of four parents are not involved. The average Japanese mother visits twice a month, and each day the child carries a notebook back and forth to school in which mother and teacher alternately write notes regarding child's health, mood, and activities both at home and at school.

You may want to consider the following. *Urge teachers to:*

- Tell your child about himself or herself. This is not an invasion of privacy nor is it unprofessional. Teachers are people—human, vulnerable, and strong. When they share with the kids, this enriches the student-teacher relationship. It is most important for a fatherless boy to know about the boyhood or life of a revered male teacher.
- Keep you informed of the indicators of instability that your child shows. Compare observations. Brainstorm solutions. Together you may decide to confer with the counselor, change classes or schedules, and so forth.
- Develop a plan for phone communication as opposed to an open-ended arrangement to "call at anytime." A plan denotes commitment and both parties can make notes or jot down questions in anticipation of the conversation "every Friday at 4:30 P.M." Communication can focus on accomplishments and improvements as well as problems.
- Make suggestions to you regarding home management: discipline, responsibilities, homework, and so forth. A teacher may be your only contact with a professional in the community.

- Visit in your home. This can mean a lot to a child, regardless of age. The message is, "My teacher cares enough about me to take time to come to my house."
- Utilize various ways to have your child discuss feelings or emotions in private or in an appropriate group activity. Students may be willing to express themselves to a teacher who cares while reluctant to say anything at home. Sharing feelings can support a progression toward stability.

Become an advocate. Insist that your school library be open beyond school hours. Let the school library become a family resource with books, media materials, programs, and resources for all. If possible, arrange your schedule so that you can be a volunteer. Read to kids. Help them select books. Show videotapes.

PARENTS VOLUNTEER

Schools need change and improvement as parents and the community have declared for generations. Now it is your opportunity to become involved and not leave the work to others because you are "too busy." Attend meetings, write notes and letters, and instruct your children to convey the ongoing message that you care about what is happening.

Beyond the Classroom
How Parents Can Help Kids Learn

To CONTRIBUTE to your child's intellectual growth, consider these as important steps to take.

- Provide a basic learning center composed of books, books, and more books.
- Make certain the children have ready access to a multivolume set of encyclopedias—attractive, informative and up-to-date with pictures that kids can tote around. Foster the habit of looking up answers to questions; kids abound with questions that even the TV won't answer.
- Add some standard reference books—dictionaries, *Bartlett's Familiar Quotation*, and specialized references that reflect a variety of interests—nature, art, music, sports, mechanics, space, and so forth.
- Surround all these with novels, how to, classics, best-sellers, and throwaways. Some comic books are fun and worthwhile. Search for library book sales.
- Enrich with learning center hardware—typewriters and computers when possible.
- Borrow, rent, or buy video and audio tapes.

You know your child's interests, talents and needs. Parental encouragement is not to create overachievers but to provide a *frame of confidence* from one happy, learning, exploring experience from which many, many others will grow.

Excerpted from Colfax article "Mothering,"
Fall, 1986, reported *Utne Reader*, October 1990.

11

Money
Homelessness to Affluence

THE AVAILABILITY OF A MYRIAD of things may destroy a family. Those who can afford to buy, buy, buy are intent on acquiring money to become the best shoppers on the block. Family stability and togetherness may be touch-and-go while everyone is programmed to herald the new toaster, new car, new house, or the new linens that grace the beds.

Those who cannot afford to buy, who are entrenched in marginal economic survival, are devastated by fear, bitterness, sorrow, and jealousy. TV commercials are daily reminders of what they do not have. This hurts parental self-esteem and such hurt is too often displayed in ways that destroy family togetherness, impair parent-child relationships, and, likewise, preclude stability.

In 1990 more than half the children seen in well-baby clinics were undernourished. Some parents reported they could only afford cat food, dog food, and dried skim milk. These parents were not being abusive—they were trying to survive.

Depending on the definition of poverty that you select, more than 18 million children do not have enough to eat, much less adequate medical or dental care, or a childhood that underwrites positive self-esteem. *Most are not minority children. Statis-*

tically, the majority of poor children are white. Some learn to cope surprisingly well. They find the energy to confront dangers and scarcities, and they come up with a positive drive. Others are withdrawn, passive, or callous. The all-pervasive anxiety that results from being poor cannot be readily erased. For some it becomes lifelong defeat.

45.
Poverty, Homelessness, and Marginal Families

This book touches on contemporary family problems—some of which will interest the reader and some of which will not. I urge you to read some of the details about the plight of homeless parents and their children. Homelessness may be considered a virulent boil in the matrix of American families—one that is infectious and enlarging. Why? Because the threat of homelessness is too pressing on marginal or poverty families and all citizens need to be aware of the struggles and efforts the homeless portray.

> *For most of us, parenthood is a life-long commitment to sustain and enhance the lives of our kids. For homeless parents, it's a grim battle to keep their children's bodies and spirits alive, a constant struggle to ward off illness, anger, and depression. Sharing the pain of homelessness sometimes creates a bond between parents that helps them stay together, but sometimes the pressures result in the breakup of the family.*
>
> —Jonathan Kozol
> Parenting, *March 1989*

Homelessness

In 1991 there were more than 330,000 children with no home, no address, and no way to visualize a puppy waiting at the front door. Some sleep on the street, some snuggle into bed in a shelter, and others attempt to keep warm in the back of a van, an abandoned car, or under a bridge. The adjustment of these children is a direct reflection of how their parents cope and how much support they receive from adults and fellow homeless.

The children are more like other children than different from them, but they have some special or pressing needs.

> *There are not enough shelters for all on some wintry nights. As many as 75 percent of applicants have to be turned away in places like Chicago, Denver, Detroit, and Washington, D.C.*

Because of other scarcities and deprivations, homeless children need:

- Love and affection and frequent reassurance that their parents will not abandon them. Many suffer from severe depression, anxiety, and severe separation problems. The young children are prone to panic attacks—hysterics, crying, and vomiting.
- Their pleas, needs, protests, and feelings to be heard. These children have significant sleep problems, are shy, withdrawn, or aggressive. Some preschool children are diagnosed as emotionally disturbed.
- Opportunity to go to school. Serious learning deprivation and difficulties abound.
- Diversions—materials for creativity—crayons, pencils, and paper. The children try to avoid napping and have short attention spans because of fear and sadness. Diversions are important.
- A possession of his or her own—a little car to tuck in a pocket or a special comb. Though minimal, this may enhance a child's sense of personal worth.
- Clothes similar to those of other children. Many feel unwanted, different, and ashamed. Similar clothing can mask some of those feelings.
- A sense of cleanliness.
- As much predictability or orderliness as possible. This may prevent violent mood swings and offer some temporary repose.
- Freedom from teasing, taunting, or embarrassment.
- Someone to express guarded hope, optimism, or faith in the future, in words the children can understand.

- Adults to accept their insecurities, mood swings, negativity, tantrums, anger, and depression. These behaviors indicate low self-esteem—often mirroring parental images. They also interfere with peer relationships and the formation of much-needed friendships.

Characteristics of homeless parents include a history of abuse as children and battering as adults, drug and alcohol abuse, psychiatric problems much greater than among mothers living in public or private subsidized housing, and lack of a long-term dependable support system.

Homeless parents vary dramatically in how they manage. Most of these parents sincerely want to provide for their children, but lack of money impacts a job search. Without funds, they don't have proper clothes to wear; they have no money for transportation or babysitting. They don't have addresses and, therefore, are precluded from filling out job applications. *It is important for persons with homes to understand that homeless parents are deeply aware of the serious problems their children face, their losses and shattered dreams.*

Marginal Families

Poverty must be considered a social issue. The key issues of prejudice, inequality, justice, brutality, and lack of opportunity must be mentioned. Families are inundated with fear and despair. The wasted human potential is indefensible. When teachers try to befriend and encourage the young victims, they frequently meet with disinterest or even a readiness to attack. Many poverty-stricken people do not trust teachers and other community helpers who represent an alien value system. Concern for the children is universal. Health, mental health, schooling, and safety issues are but a few of the ongoing, startling problems which increase daily.

> *Family poverty is predictably correlated with high rates of infant mortality, child neglect, school failure, teen pregnancy, and violent crime. Each day in the United States sixty-seven newborn babies die. Within one year, forty-thousand babies will be buried.*

INDICATORS OF INSTABILITY

- Children may show fear and signs of abuse. Domestic violence and child abuse frequently stem from money problems and parental frustrations.
- Children may acquire a defeatist attitude and become isolated and depressed.
- Children may feel alienated or angry. Most youngsters beset by poverty find it too painful to focus on the future.
- Antisocial behaviors, such as stealing, may begin. For middle-class children, stealing denotes emotional problems or the need to keep up with peers. For children of poverty, it may denote despair or immaturity—a child thinks he or she is contributing to the family. Little Jimmy takes a loaf of bread because his baby brother is hungry.

There are possible *benefits* to living in poverty, although few persons would choose such insecurity. Some benefits would be:
- Family ties may be strengthened.
- Children learn to tolerate or become less vulnerable to parental depression or despair.
- Children become more resourceful in finding ways to amuse themselves without toys and equipment.
- Children share responsibilities.
- Children may read a lot.
- Children learn to ask for help.
- It minimizes their attachment to *things* and strengthens interpersonal dependency and attachment.
- Children learn to care for other kids. They create ways to play together, share, and enjoy each other.

Finally, some children are motivated to take advantage of

every opportunity they can to better themselves and their families. Rags to riches will be more than just a story for some; the acquisition of material possessions can become a fervent prayer and a potent goal.

ABOUT REASSURANCES

Reassurances seem empty to parents who are unable to provide for their children. Political rhetoric and promises mean nothing. Parents want jobs that pay enough to partially restore their self-esteem. Parents almost always regard poverty as personal failure, and this is humiliating, especially in front of the children. Families crave independence but all too often must acquiesce to assistance. *Stability is the exception rather than the rule.* However, poverty does not preclude loving relationships and important families ties and spirited children.

46.
The Middle Class: The "Average" Family

From the viewpoint of children of poverty, middle class people— those with some security—are rich. The so-called middle class encompasses persons formerly known as "blue-collar workers," as well as nurses, paralegals, teachers, and many others who do not have abundant amounts of money. They may have a home, a steady job, a car to drive, and two or more TV sets. Children of middle-class families frequently benefit from many opportunities.

> *Who knows where the next layoffs may be? Make sure that children do not confuse unemployment with irresponsibility. Being out of work is embarrassing, especially when it is necessary to borrow money, depend on unemployment benefits, or other public assistance.*

The children have confused ideas about money—partly due to the current increase in unemployment and partly due to mixed messages from parents. This confusion tends to foster instability.

Because the newly unemployed have had jobs, shifting from security to insecurity can be earth-shattering. The injured self-esteem of the now jobless parent, accompanied by anxiety and a reduced standard of living, invariably creates interpersonal tensions. The children may have had a good start with stable family relationships, smooth school adjustment, and well-developed coping styles. The family money crisis disrupts everyone's sense of well-being. Survival may become the issue for which they are ill-prepared. Instability erupts.

Your kids may say, "Well, why didn't you save money so we would have some when we need it?" Remind them that the cost of living is high and saving, for many, many families, is impossible. Put this in terms and vocabulary that your children can understand. Tell the children about the pain, confusion, and strain of hard times. Many marriages cannot withstand such pressure, and then the children have to cope with even more loss and stress. Finally, urge them to choose friends on the basis of personality and companionability—not the status of family finances.

PROCEDURES FOR PARENTS

No matter the financial status of the family, parents must focus on the parent-child relationship. Parents should:
- Take time to be loving. Even though overwhelmed by important money concerns and responsibilities, take the time to be affectionate and to be a good listener.
- Talk about some of your worries and frustrations without creating guilt. Don't be unrealistically optimistic or pessimistic.
- Help prepare your child for his or her survival in the world of money. Discuss money. Children may not be able to picture what can be bought for twenty-five dollars, but they can learn about food prices, clothing, car expenses, housing matters, and much more. Read the ads to them. It is okay for older children to know how you plan and budget.
- Teach children to budget. Set firm limits on how much money they may have. Children will make mistakes in the way they handle money, just as adults do. If Bert spends all his allowance on video games at the store and has nothing left for school lunch, let him prepare a peanut butter sandwich and take an apple to school. Do not bail him out. It is especially important that both parents agree about this. If one parent

undermines the decision of the other, the child will not acquire a realistic understanding about budgeting.

- If your child works, permit him or her to contribute to the family if he or she insists. It may only be a token amount, but from the child's point of view, this may be very important.
- Saving is important to some children and not important to others. Some children will attempt to save every penny that they have. Look at this carefully. Is Mary Anne holding on to money as a way of feeling secure? Has she had many losses in her life so that now she only trusts what she can hold in her hand? This may indicate that she needs emotional reassurances or that she is a planner—has goals, wants to be able to buy new clothes, cosmetics, or even a present for someone else. If Bert spends all his money to please others or to buy friendships, help is needed to build his self-esteem and find other ways to make friends.
- Involve the children in as many decisions about money as you deem appropriate. This includes allowances, household expenses (including menus), buying furniture or clothing, or occasional treats—even luxuries.
- Encourage children to enjoy activities that don't cost anything, such as public library functions, museums, and band concerts in the park.

> *Money problems directly affect the self-esteem of a parent. In turn, self-esteem problems may lead to serious family disruptions. The parents may split; parent-child estrangement may result due to issues over money. On the other hand, when there are money problems, family ties may get stronger and everyone learns compassion and empathy.*

REASSURANCES

Reassurances should be focused on the parent-child relationship and some preparation for possible changes in the family's economic status, either up or down. Equipped with self-esteem, children will be stable enough to adapt to whatever may be forthcoming, although it may be a struggle. We are all familiar with the stories of suicides that took place in 1929 at the time of the Great Depression. Those people were not prepared for economic devastation. The stable family of today should not pretend that security is here to stay. There are too many unknowns, too many influences that could potentially explode at any time (such as the collapse of an economy of another country) that will affect *your* family, *your* job, and the future of *your* kids. As you talk with the children, you are also helping yourself understand what may happen and how to cope. The more everyone is prepared, the more stable each will feel.

Reassurances should include your commitment to help your children reaffirm their strengths and wellness, adaptability, and social skills. A sense of competency and optimism helps everyone.

47.
Affluent Families

Affluent families enjoy a luxurious lifestyle bestowed upon them by a generous, secure income. They are upscale—perhaps extravagant—and almost always free of the anxiety that stems from potential change of circumstance. Some children are unimpressed with family wealth—even deny it or are embarrassed to have so many things. They may be reluctant to talk about vacations, a boat, a plane, or servants. There may be great pressure on the children to succeed.

INDICATORS OF INSTABILITY

Children from affluent families may have some problems that denote or promote instability:

- They may have low self-esteem because their needs are secondary to the energy and efforts that parents put forth to earn or manage money. "My dad knows all about the stock market, but he doesn't know my best friend's name. He never looks at my report card or asks me about school. I am not important to him."
- Family lifestyle may include excessive drinking and/or parental absence for business or pleasure. Children feel abandoned and unimportant; rich children are as readily victimized by parental addictions as are children from low-income families.
- Children as young as eight may be placed in boarding schools because parents believe they will be happier or more success-

ful than if they stay at home. It also may be family tradition. That doesn't mean that the children are happy or don't resent being shipped away.

- A child in an affluent family may acquire the attitude, "Why try? I'll never be as successful as my dad anyway." Defeatism causes instability.
- Children's value systems may be tilted toward "more." One child was asked, "What do rich people want?" The answer: "To be richer."

PROCEDURES FOR PARENTS

Review the procedures listed on pages 194–195. They apply to you. In addition, your family lifestyle and values may need to be examined, perhaps revised, to meet the needs of the children and to build and maintain family stability. Stress the importance of family ties and loyalty above all else. Gift giving must be appropriate to the individual child and his or her interests, needs, and desires. Try to minimize competition among siblings. Just because one child demands and gets an expensive instrument (such as a clarinet) doesn't mean that a second child who only received new CDs is loved any less.

When you exercise good judgment and restraint, make sure the children are aware of this. They will benefit from knowing how you select what you buy and what you consider important. Also, your policies on lending money must be clarified. Discuss that all families have to work hard to develop and stick to spending habits that seem reasonable and fair to all. *Fairness is an essential part of stability.* Parents have the right to some indulgences without having to apologize to the kids. Reassure the children that having money is a convenience and comfort but not a substitute for mutual respect and good communication with family members.

12

Social Issues that Affect Stability

48.
Television as a Threat to Childhood Stability

Television, video games, and school have a profound effect on the developing stability of children. Parents must remain managerial and involved to minimize these effects.

Your influence as a parent may be preempted by a TV set. Programs have an enormous impact on viewers. They are vivid. Children watch anything and everything—good, bad, and indifferent. Parents often don't have the time to monitor and help children select worthwhile shows. They are simply grateful that the TV set distracts or absorbs the kids when dinner is being prepared or the phone must be answered. The TV has gotten out of hand. In the movie *Fantasia*, the Sorcerer's apprentice was amazed when the water got out of control. In many respects, TV content today is equally out of control.

The average child of five may watch TV for three to five hours a day. By the end of high school, a child will have seen 350,000 commercials. More important, children will have seen twenty thousand murders and countless rapes and other acts of violence.

Children are affected by watching violence. They may:

• *Imitate the violence they watch, may seek knives and guns.*
• *Identify with certain characters, victims, and/or victim-izers.*
• *Become immune to the horror of violence.*
• *Become anxious—anticipate that they or other family members, friends, or schoolmates may be hurt or killed.*

PARENTS: Be managerial! Turn off that TV set.

Certainly some children are more vulnerable and sensitive than others to realistic TV dramas they watch. Is it reasonable to ask a child to be impervious to the meaning that violence spells mastery? Can a child witness so many fights without thinking that somehow this is acceptable behavior? There are many reports that children explain their violent behaviors with the statement, "I learned it on TV."

Violent acts are performed by angry people. Violence on TV demonstrates ways to act out anger. The anger is not caused by the television.

Above all, TV shows ignore the feelings of victims or survivors. There is not time for these feelings. Viewers are left to guess how the victim felt or how the survivors were able to cope, or they may not give it any thought at all. Displays of compassion and support are ignored or cut short. A child may wonder, "What happened to the little girl after her mom was killed?" No answers are forthcoming.

As family manager, you have a right to control the TV set. Select what your kids watch. TURN OFF the set if you have to. Your children may get angry—better they should be angry than terrified.

It is recommended that young children not be allowed to have a TV set in the bedroom because there tends to be minimal parental supervision. Many kids are sneaky and secretive about what they watch, and this harms family communication and stability.

INDICATORS OF INSTABILITY

If you observe your child displaying nervous habits, becoming unduly tired, irritable, or fearful, and you are unaware of other current problems, take the time to ask:
• What have you been watching on TV?
• How did you feel when you saw_____?
• What do you think might have helped the people (or animals)?
• Have you had bad dreams since you saw that show?
• Do you realize that some shows (newscasts, documentaries) tell real stories but others are make-believe?
• Will you tell me about happy or interesting things you have watched?

Be patient. It may take a while or repeated questioning before a child may be able to respond. Reassurances from you are important. Your counsel and your interest in their reactions to scary TV is essential. Express your feelings. Tell what you experienced when you saw a sad or violent incident on the show.

Don't scold by saying, "Why do you watch such stuff?" It is impossible to preview all shows, even selected ones, and regular shows and newscasts will present unexpected, traumatic, and deeply frightening pictures.*

PROCEDURES FOR PARENTS

It is suggested that you remind all children:
• Even though you see awful things on TV, this does not mean that these things will happen to you or to us.
• Even though you see kids and parents argue, fight, and hurt each other, these are not "how-to" lessons for our family.

---

*TV has been singled out as a threat to stability. Similar statements would be true for the movies your children attend.

- All people have some problems; TV stories seem to point out unhappy problems because they are interesting.
- When you see things that upset or worry you, please come and tell me about them. If you don't, then your worries may grow and grow. You can become very upset and not even know why. You may have bad dreams or be unable to pay attention in school.

At what age should a child be approached? Any age. Nonverbal preschoolers may need to hear your reassurances even though they are unable to give you any answers. For example, if you have both watched a house burn down on TV, tell about your fears and fascination. School-aged children should know ways to escape or special precautions to take at home. Be certain that they know how to dial 911. If the frightening show has to do with kidnapping, violence, car accidents, or getting lost, express your feelings and be reassuring. "You are here with me now," and "We take good care of the cars. The brakes are fine." Stories about kidnappings, for example, should be followed by your comments and instructions. "Not all strangers are friendly. Never get in a car with a stranger," or "You can say NO! You can say 'I'll tell!'"

"Mom, are the people on TV real?" Billy asked when he finished watching reruns of Captain Kangaroo with Mr. Greenjeans. He asked the same question after "Sesame Street" was over. "Is there a real person behind Big Bird and why doesn't he come out so I can see him?" Mother explained carefully about make-believe and disguises. She talked about costumes and catsup as "blood." Billy, age four, seemed satisfied.

Ten minutes later, the news came on and Billy saw a blood-covered child on a stretcher being placed in an ambulance. "Why doesn't someone wipe off the catsup?"

Helping young children distinguish between reality and make-believe is difficult. It is the responsibility of parents to be as sensitive as possible, perhaps "covering up" some disturbing news or reports so that young children are not unduly upset.

Learning problems and stress from TV may be inevitable. Parents frequently discount it or ignore it. TV may impair memory, reduce problem-solving abilities, inhibit verbal expression, cause eye problems, and overload a child with contradictions. Too much TV stimulation contributes to problems at school. Video games can become addictive. The never-ending challenge of a better score—more people destroyed, more targets blown up—can motivate kids for hours. Parental selection and supervision is necessary. There are some great educational videos including science, nature, and biographies—the supply seems endless.

In many homes, moms and dads and the TV set contribute to a fractured family. Dad appears more concerned about the fate of the Denver Broncos than he does about the outcome of his son's tryouts for the team at the local high school. Mother may be a soap opera addict. *Parents: Don't let the TV usurp your attention away from your kids.*

REASSURANCES

How can anyone keep abreast of all that television offers when there are so many channels to select from? Can we expect immature kids to consistently select high IQ, intellectually stimulating programs when so many are intriguing, exciting, seductive, and fun? No, we can't! You, the parents, must express your opinions, set some guidelines, read reviews when possible and be definitive about your own selections. If you have a "lock-out" capability on your television set, you can use this method of keeping your children from watching certain TV shows when you are away from home.

Feel reassured that even if the kids are watching disturbing, inappropriate, violent, and disgusting shows, this does not mean that your parent-child relationship is in jeopardy or that family stability will crumble.

Kids are resilient. We've all had experiences that were nerve racking. And the influence of television violence may be somewhat counteracted by fruitful family discussions about anger, impulsivity, control, and the like.

49.
Racism and Discrimination

Since the early 1970s, millions of people have migrated to the United States. In 1990 alone, 1,536,483 immigrants arrived in the United States. Many from Asia have become economically secure due to self-sacrifice, diligence, and fortitude. They were determined to "make it." Then what happened? In many places they have become targets of discrimination, ridiculed for being uncommunicative or remote. In some instances, the attackers are jealous. Misunderstandings are rife. They have become victims of racism and discrimination—a familiar and sad fact of our society.

Racism and discrimination are underlying threats to everyone because the diversity of the population lends itself to the sad parceling of persons as "them, not us." Such splits become emotional, irrational excuses for threats and acting out. We are all enclosed in a violent, trigger-happy society and the job of raising stable children is difficult. Discrimination goes beyond one race versus another, one age versus another, one sex versus the other, or the wealthy versus the poor. It reflects the *basic insecurities* of every individual.

Parents are required to instill in their children the necessary self-esteem, in concert with teaching respect for others starting with members of the family, that the individual can withstand disrespect or differences, no matter what the threat or confrontation may be. That is an enormously difficult responsibility that takes time and consistent effort.

If love comes from the heart, where does hate come from? Children aren't born knowing how to hate. They must be taught. Therefore, the lesson is simple. Let's not teach our children hatred and prejudice. Because what they don't know won't hurt them. Or others.
        National Conference of Christians and Jews
        Learning to Live Together: The Unfinished Task

Racial issues, religious differences, sex discrimination, age biases, and economic discrepancies are universals. How do parents weave the resultant quivers into a stable, unwavering attitude for the family?

PROCEDURES FOR PARENTS

Some of these suggestions, albeit idealistic, may help. Insist that children:

- Learn to describe themselves. Be unrelenting. Have the child look in the mirror, draw self-portraits, tell about self to an audio- or videotape, write dreams, thoughts, feelings, and experiences in great detail. "I like chocolate." "I am loving." "I am afraid of snakes." "I cry when others cry." "My skin is white." "I am a Native American."
- From this self-portrait, lead the child into the consistent theme that all people are created equal in the sense of evolution. We are all the same species. Point out genetic differences: "You have these genes that produce black skin." "I have dimples." "He has a small head." "She has a deformed hand."
- Teach the child that differences are okay.
- Explain that the immediate family and the extended family can help children feel loved and secure. In the United States, the melting pot ideal did not work. It was hoped that there would be widespread, if not universal, mixing and blending of all races, nationalities, and ethnic groups. This was a democratic ideal, and, yes, there are numerous interracial, interethnic marriages and families, but for the most part, there remain racial and ethnic clusters. Clusters provide comfort and may also create potential problems such as discrimination. *Explain that this is okay until one group purposely excludes or harms others because of racial or ethnic differences. Your children may be victims of such exclusions and all its ramifications.* Help them learn to appreciate the stability that the immediate family and extended family strives to provide.
- Teach strong statements about *equal rights*. When the farmer throws corn into the chicken coop, every chicken has the right to snatch as much as it can. Each chicken has an equal right to the corn. This amounts to survival. The chickens eat the corn to live; they don't eat each other. People are not chickens, but they have equal rights. Other animals, when food is scarce, do attack each other. Humans also harm each other to acquire

land and food and for other reasons, too. The acting out of prejudice is one of these reasons.

- Extend the child's thinking about *self-determination*. Say to the children, "You will learn many things. You will choose what you want to do or say. You will decide if you want to be pleasant or nasty, as an example. As you make your choices, others will, too. You will choose different things. There is no law that says you must approve of what others choose or sit in judgment of their choices. Just because they choose differently does not make *you* or your choices *any better or worse—only different.* The same goes for their choices—not better or worse, only different." Teach the children to be proud of their choices—and when others criticize, belittle, or envy, to ignore their statements.

- Teach children simplistic phrases such as, "I'm proud to be me." "Everyone is unique." "In some ways, everyone is the same."

- Make certain children understand that when others hurt you, and discriminate against you, they are showing that they are not proud of themselves, *not secure enough* to accept differences. (They do not have good self-esteem.) Many need to be mean because that makes them feel powerful. You are not responsible for fixing them up. Your responsibility is to remain proud of yourself, accept the differences, and appreciate your inner stability. Understanding others abets stability.

To assist your children in adjusting to the many multicultural experiences of everyday life, push the words fair, fear, and facts. Make certain your child is certain that his or her judgment or criticism of someone else is fair. Explain that any child's fear of being different, being discriminated against, can cause him or her to do things that are not okay. Encourage your kids to notice how others show that they are afraid, how they try to be accepted or to go unnoticed. Facts are important. Be explicit. Talk about individual differences, male-female distinctions, cultural or ethnic heritage, and why, for some children, retreat to the family home and its customs is the only place they feel safe. Why? Because elsewhere prejudice abounds.

If your children are victimized, called names, insulted, excluded from situations, or such, *listen* to their reports. Don't discount them by saying, "That used to happen to me," or "You'll get used to it," or "You better learn to be tough-skinned and tough-minded." Instead consider, "When people do that, they are in trouble, just let them go. By showing them that you have self-respect, you show that their attacks are worthless."

Say, "You may want to fight back and call them dirty names, but you can't achieve much by that—though it may make you feel better. When someone attacks you, remember your statement, 'I'm proud to be me,' and walk away."

These statements are intended for school-aged children to build and support stability. Adult victims of discrimination, with stable self-esteem, have other viable options including political action.

Bias is learned behavior. Kids reflect parental prejudices. They also develop powerful prejudices from the media and other kids, especially other gang-members. *Parental influence is the most powerful deterrent to unacceptable behavior.*

If your child is subjected to name-calling, ostracizing, teasing, and the like, *take action.* When neighborhood children offended the daughters of a friend of mine, she proceeded to invite the parents of the offenders to her home, in a friendly, nonthreatening way. Because all the parents discussed, frankly, that the name-calling and threats were not acceptable, they were able to agree on some consequences if the offenses continued.

If your children experience racist attacks at school, empower your child to tell the teacher. If that is to no avail, have the child tell the principal. If neither of these people from the school will step in, you may have to call the parent. If you are not the spokesperson for your children, who will be?

Unhappily, racial slurs and other cruelties abound among children. Teachers report that, in some areas, the attacks on Hispanic children are merciless. Even when teachers and principals become involved, the offenses continue. In other areas, Afro-Americans, Jewish, and Asian children are victims. If the school or neighborhood is a scary or humiliating place to be, this undermines stability. Parents must try to compensate for this as best they can. *The indicators of instability* almost always include refusal to go out to play, reluctance to go to school, hiding, psychosomatic problems, tears, and other familiar signs of both fear and anger. If the child is threatened by a gang (and children as young as nine years old join gangs), this must be discussed at school, and it is hoped that school authorities can handle the situation effectively. There must be clear-cut, understandable consequences for offenses, which may extend to law enforcement.

———

Parents have no choice but to teach tolerance. It is one way to contribute to the stability of each individual and each family. All people want the same things—love, peace, joy, and security.

Many minority families are retreating from multicultural neighborhoods, if they can, because of community violence, teacher prejudice in the schools, gangs, riots, and inequitable job opportunities. Children hear about democracy and the American melting pot in schools. They become confused. Mounting economic hardship and vanishing manufacturing jobs lie at the heart of the resurgence of ethnic "ghettos" and tensions. Children need you to explain what is taking place.

Multiracial Families

Multiracial and multiethnic families have become part of today's American image. More people of diverse cultural and racial backgrounds are intermarrying. Publicity about successful multiracial, multiethnic marriages of movie stars, entertainers, and sports figures has strengthened a positive image. As the kids might ask, "So what's the *big deal* anyhow?" No longer are adoptions being restricted to any particular "matching" profile. More adoptive parents are reaching into other cultures and countries for children.

The scene has shifted away from dismay and disapproval to

a comfort zone that respects the family and parental selection. Some persons will always hold on to their prejudices, especially if surrounded by like-minded neighbors. Reports of racial tension bear witness to this. However, in most areas today, children are not nearly as harassed or singled out due to prejudice and racism as they were in years gone by.

Children are more at ease with classmates of diverse backgrounds. In a number of elementary schools, high schools, and colleges, the outstanding performance of a large percentage of Asian children is frequently the envy of others. Asian children benefit from the discipline and commitment of all their generations who want them to be successful.

Parents who adopt minority children—including disabled youngsters—tend to have poise and equanimity about racial issues. This can be labeled "stability."

50.
Religion: Stress or Solace?

Religion can bind family members together in a loving way or cause a serious rift that can undermine stability. Religious beliefs establish attitudes, prejudices, and practices that can result in misunderstanding and alienation among members of a family. As parents, you have every right to pronounce your ideas and direct your children into the religious arena of your choice. Children may not always follow your direction. They may seek other faiths or practices or seek none at all.

> *Children have a rich spiritual life that reveals itself in naive questions about nature, the meaning of life, and a personal path to learning about God, the "soul," and other wonderments.*

Current Status

Following a trend toward casual or informal religious practices, the 1980s hosted a wave of returns to traditional religious enthusiasm and church attendance. At the same time two important splinter groups became increasingly vested in America. The first is *new-age thinking*; the second is *Satanism, devil worship, and witchcraft,* which promote superstition and fear— even carnal abuse and torture. The acceleration of Satanism is believed to be due in part to a game called Dungeons and Dragons, which absorbed the minds of many young people applauding evil over good and the power of Satan. Regardless of the cause, many who are now caught up in devil worship are well respected and well educated. They may join cults. Some involuntary members of cults, especially children and girls, are reportedly brutally victimized by sadistic practices.

New age or spiritual parenting intends to provide children with a sense of the sacred in an age dominated by material and secular concerns. Among other things, it teaches love and reverence for all living things, meditation techniques, unselfish morals, values, and self-awareness.

Perhaps the most comprehensive understanding of the *spiritual life of children* is presented by the noted child psychiatrist, Robert Coles, in a book by the same name. You may find the pictures and interpretations worthwhile background as you lead your children into the world of religion.

Commonly recognized clusters or levels of religious involvement are:

- Disclaimers of any formal religion. May emphasize nature, natural forces, spiritualism, ancestor worship, focus on interpersonal relationships, man's inhumanity to man, or methods geared to personal search. Social issues may be paramount.
- Casual concern for the teachings of the prophets, the Bible, higher power, prayers, and mysticism. Does not prioritize religious practices or traditions. Tolerant of other groups, with emphasis on the family, interpersonal interactions—perhaps social issues.
- Commitment to regular religious observances. Strong identification with a specific religion. Bible or scriptures, basic teachings, or interpretations may be inspirational as well as repressive and frightening. Traditions are important. Some prejudice against other groups. Strong clerical leadership.
- Cults or fanatical devotion as a way of life, such as in Jonestown and Waco, Texas. All decisions build from the commitment to serve a religious cause. A total lifestyle encircles the religion;

every action taken is done so in the name of the religion. Situations may be strict and prohibitive with many constraints that require members to differentiate themselves from nonbelievers in clothing, nonreligious celebrations, and financial planning, for instance. Expression of emotions may be restricted. A judgmental attitude may exist.

In some situations, children learn to repress all feelings. They may or may not feel close to their parents. Teachings of a faith may obstruct social relationships with some children of other backgrounds although family stability is not threatened.

Family Stability May Be Threatened by Religious Practices

"The family that prays together stays together" is a familiar phrase. It implies stability and can be readily demonstrated to hold true for many families in a variety of faiths. Nevertheless, there can be problems when:

- Parent-child conflicts arise over idealistic or practical differences. For example, children hear about other beliefs or see disturbing programs on TV and find their parents unwilling or unable to discuss these differences. "They must think they're right and we think we're right. How come?" The young Jewish child wonders about Christmas and Santa Claus, neither of which is a part of the Jewish faith.
- Parents are so involved in religious or church work that children feel unimportant. "How come daddy has time to help paint the church, but he can never help me with my homework?"
- Rigid family practices conflict with children's desires or other commitments. For example, Louise wants to go camping with the scouts, but her parents will not let her miss Sunday school. Such rebellion may cause a serious rift between the generations. By giving in, the parents abdicate their power—give up their in-charge position. This is an appropriate situation in which to use negotiations as a means of solving a problem.

A child's spiritual experience may be his or her mind racing across a meadow or engulfed in the clouds overhead.

- There is a double standard about church or synagogue attendance. Children have to go, but both parents stay home; or children have to go, one parent stays home. Differences between parents may cause significant tension.
- Parents may disapprove if their children become too intensely involved in a religion. The upswing in conservative groups among young people is nationwide. Parents feel they have lost control; the children will adopt the values of an outside group, even though based on ethical values or a search for enlightenment.

In order to support stability, consider these five purposes of religion: to provide guidance, comfort, direction, spiritual enrichment, and security. For many, these offer a framework within which a person finds definitions of ethics, faith, morals, and life.

As a parent, you want your children to have those dimensions in their lives. You offer what you can, with or without religious intensity. If your children take a different spiritual direction from yours, try to assess their beliefs or practices. Your own life may be enriched in the process to the subsequent benefit of the child-parent relationship.

PROCEDURES FOR PARENTS

Congruent with open communication and basic to stability:
- Be honest about your own beliefs. Talk about your conflicts, tell about experiences you have had. Discuss self-awareness, fulfillment, humility, service, and such concepts in terms that children can understand.
- In order for a child to search for answers or for an identity, it may be important to search outside family structure. Accept their confusion—even their anger—if it is expressed. Don't misinterpret a child's search as a rejection of you.
- Make certain that you are not misusing religion. Have you frequently used the threat, *God will punish you if you are not good?* Children do misbehave. It is part of growing up. Children want approval and love when they are good. It is unreasonable to assume that children understand that misbehavior is a sign of immaturity or frustration. Therefore, if punishment is moralistic, they feel condemned without realizing that being

naughty is part of being a child. Continuous and unspoken threats result in ongoing anxiety.

- Do you perceive that your child is putting up a false front—being good to please you and God? If your child lacks spontaneity, reaffirm your love repeatedly. Show affection. Talk about your own strengths and weaknesses.
- If your child has a morbid fear of death or is obsessed with fear of the future, he or she may be reacting to threats of punishment in the hereafter. Johnny, an impulsive six-year-old boy, hears that a friend disobeyed his mother, climbed a ladder, fell off, and was killed. Johnny, who thinks God punished his friend for *being bad,* now refuses to participate in rough play, hesitates to let mom out of his sight, and fears that he too will be killed if he is bad. Take time to find out what Johnny is thinking and be as reassuring as possible.
- Emphasize the positive. Issues about right and wrong, morality, wisdom, prophecy, legend, caring, giving, and adventure are all part of the heritage of a faith. Children are entitled to a pride in their heritage and to be involved in the process of the many changes that are occurring today.
- Teach tolerance. With older children, be realistic about the strife that the world has known historically and continues to experience over religious differences. Ireland, India, and parts of the Middle East are examples. If your children have strong beliefs, they must be taught that it is okay for other kids to have different but equally strong beliefs. Otherwise religious upbringing may result in unnecessary social conflicts and peer rejection. Teach them to assess what prejudices they may have.
- If you are involved in self-awareness programs or human potential movements that have become important to you, tell your children. Explain how these activities enrich or dovetail with your religious convictions or your understanding of the purpose of religion. They do not have to conflict. They may reaffirm your commitment to your faith.
- If your financial commitment to the church appears to the children to be disproportionately high, this needs to be discussed. Although the children may protest, you are entitled to make such decisions without apology. You are demonstrating actions that support your commitments and this is an invaluable lesson.

• Be open to discussions of issues such as reincarnation, karma, Eastern philosophies, and extremist religious groups. Open discussion may help your children acquire attitudes that may prevent impulsive involvement in activities, some of which may be injurious to mental health. Such discussion enhances parent-child communication. Express your opinions, but remember that open-mindedness allows children to ask questions on all subjects. This supports a trusting relationship and enhances respect.

REASSURE THE CHILDREN

Religion enriches. Spirituality enriches. Reassure your children that any or all of their questions or fantasies are acceptable. Reassurances in the spiritual realm should reaffirm the benefits of faith. The other side of the statement implores parents to avoid phrases such as, "You are the Devil incarnate," or "God will punish you for that," or "God will strike you down if you talk like that."

When you tell your children about visions, biblical stories, heroes, heroines, and festivities, you fulfill some of their desire to know all about everything. Their questions about nature, death, and birth may be considered both scientific and spiritual—depending on your point of view.

Stability requires honesty. When children want concrete answers to delicate questions, be scrupulously clear. *Why did God choose Jimmy to get leukemia? If God is loving, why do we have wars? Why do men kill each other as a sacrifice to their religion? What about their kids?*

Be sensitive. Keep your explanations simple and reasonable. Reassure the children that you are troubled by these questions and that there are some things that no one can explain. Reassure them that many people are learning about levels of awareness—that we are conscious of some things and not conscious of others at the same time. You may want to introduce the idea that dreams are meaningful and share explanations about the mind, the spirit, and the body. Reassure them that many of these issues are very old and some are brand new because of all the new information available to us today.

51.
The Future Can Undermine the Stability of Today

When the map changes every day, when the media exposes hidden scams, intriguing scandals, and international plots, no one knows what to expect tomorrow. Add the reports of new discoveries, new medical miracles, the wonders of computers and the demise of our planet, and it is impossible to visualize the "future." It's too extensive, too diverse, and overwhelming. This is frustrating, frightening, and exciting.

As a retreat from these matters, most parents concentrate on the future of their family—their parents, their children, their grandchildren, and themselves. The American economy is unsettling and parents rightfully question the future: "What's going to happen to me?" "Will we have money in the future?" "What's ahead for my children and grandchildren?"

Children ask similar questions. They watch TV, discuss global and environmental issues at school or at 4-H Club meetings, become interested in politics and government, and they know about poverty and homelessness, child abuse, suicides, and related problems. When they ask piercing questions, they want three things: reassurances, to know how their lives will be affected, and some ideas for actions they can take. Your answers may be bleak, discouraging, and frankly realistic. They may also be positive and proclaim readily recognizable signs of stability such as, "We have laws. Our country is not going to fall apart like the Soviet Union did. Your school will be here for years to come. Our family works hard to care for each other."

The future belongs to those who believe in the beauty of their dreams.

—*Eleanor Roosevelt*

Reassurances about the economy, jobs, and personal money matters may be more difficult. Numerous jobs are in jeopardy—from the position of CEO of a large corporation to a laborer repairing roads who loses a job because tax monies are not available. There are few guarantees in the workplace and money world of today.

How can parents build and maintain stability and not let fear of the future render them helpless? Determine where you do have control; let this provide direction for you and your family. This fosters stability.

Under your control
Management of children
Contribution to the marriage, family (extended and nuclear)
Physical condition—your health
Pursuit of self-awareness, wellness
Acquisition of new skills
Management of available money
Some professional careers
Keep children aware of what they can do for conservation: recycling, protecting animal lives, and the planet

Subject to circumstances
Changes in the workplace
Caretaking responsibilities such as older parents, accident victims
Change due to aging and health problems
Demands and needs of others that involve you

Beyond the scope of your control, but you can be a contributor
Economic shifts and disasters
Global issues—pollution, rain forests, wildlife, waste disposal, and so forth
International problems, threats, dangers

Consider:
Personal matters
Confronting overload, overstimulation, overlapping conflicts and obligations, knowledge explosion, and personal stress
Career training including computer literacy
Sexual conflicts including safe sex, no sex, sexual preference, abortions, sex changes
Mind-body-spirit matters: choice of health care methods, religious practices and beliefs, intellectual

Family matters
Definitions of "family"
Contracts—prenuptial agreements, property distributions
Separation, divorce, visitation concerns, parental rights, joint custody, and other options
Genetic engineering, family planning
Surrogate mothers

and educational pursuits
Self-awareness, including
disclosure, therapies, self-help,
recovery programs
Right-to-die issue

Social issues

Child-care arrangements, facilities
Homelessness, poverty issues
Child health problems
Child abuse and neglect:
violence, incest, emotional
battering, sexual assault
Senior citizens, social security
Nursing homes
Disabled, mentally ill, displaced
persons
Education, homeschooling, cost
of higher education, vocational
training, standards, and quality
control

Medical issues

AIDS and other epidemics
Costs: government participa-
tion/responsibilities, insur-
ance matters, HMOs
Right-to-die, right-to-suicide,
organ donations
Holistic health, acupuncture,
alternative treatments
Drugs: research, control
Personnel: physician aides,
practitioners, new specialists
Home services: traveling clin-
ics, hospices
Transplant donors
Computer diagnosis, new ma-
chines, new therapies

Political issues

Unemployment
Immigration, integration
Military matters
Equal rights issues, sex and age
discrimination, racism, religious
conflicts

Global issues

Overpopulation
Endangered lands, species
Nuclear war, other conflicts
Third World countries, realigned
nations, struggling nations
Racial wars

INDICATORS OF INSTABILITY

Concerned teenagers may:
- Be critical or depressed most of the time.
- Be reckless, give up, adopt a "what's the use" approach to life.
- Deny the problems, pretend that they do not exist.
- Cover up worries by abusing alcohol and/or drugs.
- Become obsessed with issues, lose capacity for fun.
- Become overly attached to material objects. "I better enjoy these now. Who knows what we may have tomorrow."

Teenagers today face the complexities of the future with more pessimism than ever before. Even college graduates report that their optimism is short-lived. Good jobs are scarce, even in highly technical areas. A Ph.D. pumping gas is not an amusing picture. Many are refused jobs because they are "overqualified" or experience *reverse discrimination.* Noncollege persons are even more discouraged about what lies ahead, as are the kids who are high school dropouts.

> *Opportunities are usually disguised by hard work, so most people don't recognize them.*
>
> —Ann Landers

Many schools advocate vocational training, which no longer has a negative stigma. Students appreciate that job preparation is an important issue today. Parents should be supportive when their kids take such programs whether for work preparation or enrichment.

PROCEDURES FOR PARENTS

Helping children become stable is the greatest "procedure" that parents attempt. You may not determine what is ahead, but you do your best to provide your children with the attitudes and skills they will need. The following procedures support that challenge.

- Be an example that you are self-accepting of your own intellectual prowess. It is not possible to know everything. No one can be a Leonardo da Vinci today. The knowledge explosion is still exploding. Help your child feel reasonably confident that there are niches to be filled or problems ahead that await his or her solution. New tools and new information can be used to help give children direction.
- Encourage your children to attend workshops, exhibits, displays, classes, and public demonstrations in many fields. For example, numerous scout troops of ten- to twelve-year-old girls and boys go to health fairs. They see many exhibits of instruments, movies and slides about doctors, nurses, paramedics, nurse practitioners, sports medicine, medicines, re-

habilitation therapies and facilities, drug rehabilitation programs, and environmental issues such as pollution and sewer
management. They receive interesting booklets and handouts
that are explicit enough to provoke questions and possible
career selections.
- Take the time to tell your children about the work that you do.
Explain how your work has changed and what new problems
you may be having. Talk about machines, company mergers,
and company reorganization. Bring up the issues of robots.
Have you been replaced? How do you feel about that? There are
120,000 robots (and counting) in U.S. plants today.

> *Fifty percent of the jobs that will be available in the year
> 2000 do not exist today.*

- Explain *continuing education* and help children accept the
concept of lifelong learning. In many states, professionals have
to continue to go to school in order to be licensed doctors,
lawyers, social workers, nurses, and dentists. If your child
chooses to be a mechanic, this, too, requires continuing
schooling when engines are retooled and new electronic devices are added, for example. An endless assortment of new
machines are being introduced that impact all fields—computer networks, for example.
- Be reassuring. People provide instant communication worldwide. People make changes and people make decisions they
regret. The average person today makes five important job
changes in a lifetime. The high cost of college requires many
people to hold off or take one or two courses at a time rather
than plunge into a four-year or longer program. This means
that a job one holds in order to earn money and pay tuition may
have nothing to do with a choice of career. On the other hand,
the job-for-now may become interesting and challenging enough
to become the career choice. A boy may mark time as a waiter
but then develop a fondness for the food industry that will lead
to a managerial or ownership position.
- Don't present unrealistic pie-in-the-sky agendas about the
future. Urge your children to learn to ask the right questions,

read the right critiques, and take time to be experimental. Children hear about miracles: TV ads tell them that impossible spots will come out with this product, grass will grow, cars will be trouble free. Share your experiences. Explain why you select certain products and why you have discarded others. *Product explosion can create anxiety in a way similar to the knowledge explosion.* We tend to think that everyone has set ideas about what to buy. This isn't true—or so the advertising experts would have us believe.

- Take time to confront sensitive issues together. Sensitive issues do not have to jeopardize family relationships. Discuss old attitudes as you accept that values shift because circumstances dictate that they must. Suppose a gang of hoods has hurt your child; your values may switch from a liberal position to a conservative, prejudicial stance. Perhaps you have expressed opposition to interracial marriages, that you believe mixed marriages are too risky. Then your eighteen-year-old son announces that he has chosen a bride of another race. This requires you to look at the values you expressed. *Personal and societal values are in flux; flux represents uncertainty, and uncertainty can create instability.*

Doomsday prophets are popular. Nostradamus is widely read. You and your children should work hard to maintain a positive, yet realistic, attitude about the future. Family discussions must emphasize how to relate skills acquisition, training, and problem solving effectively. This amounts to mutual understanding, self-improvement, and goal setting, and it provides ways to cope with personal, interpersonal, and societal issues. It provides each individual with competencies and encouragement to face unknowns ahead with as much stability as possible.

Today is the tomorrow you worried about yesterday. *Help children become aware of the power of positive thinking. Get in the habit of acknowledging how they deal effectively with daily challenges. Each day is preparation for the next.*

REASSURANCES

Although difficult times may infect your family with strife or misunderstandings, remember that mutual respect remains the fulcrum of your parent-child relationship. Although the teeter-totter effect of family stability may cause worry, visualize that the balance of the past *is* attainable again in the future.

And wonderful times may happen—thanks to your dreams, schemes, luck, and the ongoing work of striving for stability in unstable times.

Part IV

MAJOR SOURCES OF INSTABILITY TO OVERCOME

13

Separation and Divorce
Parents Are Parents Forever

52.
The Predivorce Situation and
the Meaning of Ambivalence

There was an old, familiar refrain, "My parents stayed together for the sake of the children." It was an accurate statement. In the sixties, seventies, and eighties, this reasoning lost its power; divorces abounded and still do. Enter the 1990s and once again, "Stay together for the sake of the children" ripples through conversations and may be recommended.

Why? Because there is a growing body of research that establishes how badly children are damaged by divorce. New books are surfacing that urge couples to do everything possible to solve problems, change their relationship, and create a positive environment. *Divorce Busting: A Revolutionary and Rapid Program for Staying Together,* by Michele Weiner-Davis, is an example.

In all fairness, it must be noted that divorce can have positive effects on some children—and kids do survive. But most such children, at some time, display low self-esteem, depression, anger, loss of concentration, confusion, fear of commitment, and other indicators of instability. Many factors determine a child's adjustment. One point is well documented by research: A child's emotional health may be harmed more by the emotional tensions of the predivorce home than by the divorce itself.

The purpose of this chapter is to provide suggestions to a fighting couple or divorcing spouses to help each progress toward as much personal stability as possible. Parental stability fosters stability in the kids. No matter what decisions you make, it is imperative that you be aware of the needs of the children and how they are adjusting to the situation. Too frequently adults do battle or face major readjustments of their own and downplay the children's needs. You may hear the comment, "Oh they'll be fine once things are settled. Lots of kids get through a divorce with no problems." Not so! All kids suffer and that's why this chapter is focused on the child. Ultimately, it is the children who bear the brunt of parental incompatibility.

Divorce may not be considered an event. It is often the solution to a conflict that has been going on for years. It may take months for the children to accept the decision as final. Working through such a realization is difficult and, for some, visibly disturbing with immediate or greatly delayed signs of instability. Children have mixed feelings about a predivorce situation. Memories of good times and bad times can be upsetting and confusing.

The adjustment of the children requires that they understand *ambivalence* as the simultaneous, conflicting feelings (such as love and hate) that characterizes many relationships. Positive aspects of the ambivalent relationship should be acknowledged repeatedly, even if one parent is feeling rejected or bitter. This positive attitude helps diminish the children's anger and stress.

Prior to a divorce, family life may have been by turns full of anger, then free of tension, with occasional displays of displeasure, disappointment, or indifference—even violence. There were happy times too—birthday parties, trips, picnics, and ball games. From the children's point of view, that's the way it is in all families. The parents' decision to get a divorce is hard to understand. Knowing about ambivalence saves them from blaming one parent or the other. In cases where one parent has left due to a fight, the fight can be interpreted as an example of the negative side of the marriage.

Children can be far more charitable than grownups and want to be loving to both parents. "You guys are both okay some of the time so don't be unfair."

Even the child who has witnessed violence or has been abused will make an effort to excuse the abusive parent. "Daddy couldn't help it, mom," the child may explain.

Help children understand that relationships change. Do not underestimate what children want to know and what they can understand. Even the preschool-aged child is entitled to carefully worded explanations that safeguard respect for all. This is not an easy task.

Keep in mind that the *relationship between the parents does not end and never will*. They will always be the parents of the children and always have that tie. They will always have a relationship with each other whether it is based on anger, support, indifference, friendship, or disrespect.

How the parents manage their relationship is a vital key to the recovery of the children. Set this goal: Before, during, and after the divorce, provide a foundation whereby each child is free to develop a stable and mature relationship with each parent. That is the fervent desire of all children, whether verbalized or not. It requires the parents to stop any badmouthing and belittling.

Mention things that are admirable in the other parent; he or she is a good provider, has athletic ability, beauty, or talents. Parents must temper negative criticism. Even though children may have heard endless derogatory descriptions of a parent, they still harbor thoughts that this parent may change or that the unpleasant things that they have heard about one parent are just a reflection of the unhappiness of the other.

53.
Separation and Divorce:
Seldom a Surprise, Always a Loss

The adjustment of children to divorce is a direct reflection of how the parents handle the situation. Some parents may obtain a legal document declaring the marriage is over, but emotionally, the ambivalent tug-of-war interactions go on. The children invariably get caught in the middle, and this can be very disturbing. Other parents resolve the marriage with more clarity. While everyone will experience grief and loss, clarity can expedite recovery.

There is no time line for recovery, but there are signs that the breaking-up process and separation upsets the kids.

INDICATORS OF INSTABILITY

At the time of parental separation or divorce, young children may exhibit:
• Depression
• Temper tantrums
• Anger at both parents
• Disturbed sleep habits
• Nervous habits like thumb sucking or bedwetting
• Unusual pleas for dependency
• Demands to be held and cuddled, or to sleep with parent
• Agitation, even pacing

The age of the children may determine their reactions. For school-aged children, indicators of instability are displayed by:
• Lack of interest in school
• Bedwetting
• Inability to concentrate at school
• Signs of hyperactivity, physical problems
• Aggressive behavior toward siblings, friends, teachers, and the custodial parent
• Exaggerated, grown-up behaviors, bravado
• Aggression—especially boys

Middle school children may turn to:
- New or intensified interest in drugs, alcohol
- Sexual experimentation
- Prolonged visits with friends, grandparents, relatives
- Being either uncooperative or overly solicitous with the custodial parent
- Noncustodial parent for comfort—long telephone calls
- Threats to run away
- Extended periods of moroseness

High school students may:
- Depend increasingly on a clique or gang
- Quit school, run away
- Demand attention for immature behaviors
- Show exaggerated concern for younger siblings
- Express disgust at both parents
- Become very attached to a girlfriend or boyfriend and avoid family commitment
- Exhibit antisocial behaviors
- Show depression, express suicidal thought, act out self-destructive behaviors
- Withdraw, feign illness

The Needs of Children

Regardless of age, the child of divorce has important, ongoing needs. All children need:
- Affection and respect.
- Reassurance that the divorce or the decision to separate was not his or her fault.
- To know his or her legal rights.
- To be consulted regarding custody and visitation, commensurate with understanding. The feelings and wishes of the children are important; however, children must understand that the final decision will be up to the courts. Tell them that judges are professionals who have had a great deal of experience and make every effort to place the children in the best situation.
- To be allowed to be a child.

- Encouragement to express feelings, to be heard.
- To understand that even though the parents no longer love each other, this does not have to disturb their devotion to the children.
- To have their questions about the noncustodial parent answered. This is congruent with the consideration that children love both their parents. If a child is not permitted to ask questions about the absent parent, he or she may turn to fantasies, which can cause additional adjustment problems. Concern may be heightened at separation, around holidays, and at other special times.

Additional Needs of Teenagers

It is important to remember that adolescence is a time for self-searching, explorative social experiences, and intellectual broadening. These needs can be filled or become debilitating in any emotional climate, whether established by one parent or two. The teenagers of divorce need:

- Frequent reminders that school is an important priority.
- To be reminded that dwelling on the divorce can result in loss of interest in friends, school, activities, and learning. A self-pitying attitude can turn away much-needed friends.
- Help in understanding relationships, commitments, and working through conflicts, to understand that parents are not inadequate or bad persons simply because they no longer care for each other. Adolescents tend to make judgments and become close-minded. They need assistance to learn tolerance or perhaps forgiveness.
- Someone to acknowledge their feelings of powerlessness. Many try a myriad of things in order to keep the family together.
- To understand the family's economic situation and to make appropriate adjustments. Some may have been unreasonably demanding and may have to curtail requests.
- Peer support, both individually and in groups.
- Role models. This can be one person, such as a counselor or coach with admirable qualities to be observed and emulated, or the child can model different qualities from a number of persons.

Research reports that teenagers are more disturbed by parental divorce than any other age group. Many accounts quote teenagers as complaining about the secrecy that their parents displayed. Surprise announcements made them feel discounted and disrespected.

PROCEDURES FOR PARENTS

- Take charge. Be assertive even though it may be easier to take a passive, "this, too, shall pass" position. When your world seems to be coming apart, it is very hard to find the energy you need to deal with your own problems, much less those of the children. But children cannot cope alone and require parental guidance and strength. The young child who clings or whines or screams is not mature enough to know how much stress adults face. When mother pleads, "Leave me alone!" the child only begs for more attention. The adolescent may appear to be cool or relatively detached from the situation, but this may be only a facade. He may say, "That's mom's problem, let her deal with it!", but this does not alter the fact that teenagers need attention too. Remember, you will feel better when your children cope successfully.
- Listen to the children. Children feel unimportant when parents are fighting. They regain a sense of importance when mom or dad take time to listen to what they have to say. They have many questions that need to be answered. They gain a sense of importance when their emotional needs are met. Take the time to figure out what the child may be feeling or needing. Observe moods and demands. Little ones cannot express themselves in words; older ones may be afraid to do so. Some do not know what is worrying them. They need someone to talk to about what is happening.
- Be honest with the children. Reaffirm that the basic decisions were *adult* decisions.
- Talk about your feelings. This may be very difficult to do, but it is an important dimension of any coping style. You may have some grievances that you want to talk about. You may want to tell the children how much you appreciate their thoughtfulness or that you are aware that you have been irritable, withdrawn, or sulky. Children gain a lot from knowing that

parents experience the same feelings that they do. As mentioned earlier (*Bond to the Children*, page 17) trying to relate to a parent who is unreachable or who bounces around emotionally compounds the problems for the child. When you can sit down together and explain your unreachable or bouncing behavior, a sense of tolerance and understanding develops. Children love their parents. Parental power is immeasurable. Your honesty and humility are worthy lessons.

- Maintain the approach that a child must know as many of the facts as he or she can understand or handle. Facts support stability, even in difficult times. It enables them to proceed with problem solving. Without facts, the child's anxiety increases immeasurably. Try to share facts in a way that will let the child appreciate the problems and still feel compassionate toward all persons involved. *Children do not naturally hate other people.* Even if there have been terrible, cruel incidents, try to describe what has happened in a way that will give the child some insight into the problems and the pain felt by all.

- If possible, negotiate plans and decisions with the child. Take into account age, understanding, how upset the child is, and the realistic options. Do not make suggestions or hint at outcomes that could never happen. During times of turmoil, decision making may be very difficult. Ask the children for suggestions. They will learn that you welcome their input even though the recommendations may not be workable.

- Ease up on some pressures such as getting good grades or keeping a tidy room. Children need limits and guidelines. However, when a child is feeling overwhelmed, certain pressures should be set aside. Stop nagging and cajoling. And remind teachers that their commitment at this time is to the total child, not just to his or her math or writing skills. Such a recess may be of short duration, perhaps two or three weeks at most. Those things tentatively set aside will be placed in proper perspective in a short while.

- Establish your commitment that the children will see the absent parent as frequently as possible. A set schedule, respected by all, promotes stability. Boys are particularly eager to know when they will be with their fathers. Irregular schedules or no-show meetings are very painful.

- Seek help; it can be important. In family life, the symptoms are contagious. When adults become withdrawn, depressed, or angry, children react by feeling rejected or worthless. They become extremely anxious as they try to predict the future or grasp things beyond their understanding. Do not assume that immature and unusual behavior that a child exhibits will be permanent. The children do need help. Some children will ask for it. Seeking help is a healthy way to work through painful, complicated situations and ease their impact.

- Help can minimize disruption and anxiety for all.
- Help can promote problem solving and stability. It can demonstrate to parents how to communicate with the children.
- Help can produce marked improvements in relationships.
- Help may mean spending time and money that may prevent problems from starting or becoming increasingly serious. Divorce is a serious loss. Loss always impacts all members of the family.

Where to find help depends a great deal on where one lives. In some areas, few people have been trained to deal with children of divorce. The search itself may create additional stress, but it will be worth the effort. Often, within an organized group such as Parents Without Partners or a grief group, a member may be instrumental in suggesting an especially caring school social worker, clinician in a nearby hospital, or some other professional to whom to turn. You may discover that some professionals relate effectively to children and are less comfortable with adults, or vice versa. Nevertheless, goals for adults and children are the same: a repaired, healthy sense of personal worth and effective ways to cope that promote mutual respect and stability.

REASSURANCES

Everyone's recovery is helped when parents are reassured that:
- Living with one parent is *not* necessarily injurious to a child's development. A harmonious single-parent home has decided advantages. Children in a single-parent home learn responsibilities, become more aware of money matters, and frequently develop an appropriate role with the parent that teaches them to be sensitive to the needs of others. A *positive* attitude about single-parent families provides a constructive base for coping,

diminishing stress and promoting stability. (See *Grandparents as Parents*, page 142.)

- All children want their parents married. Before the divorce, school-aged children may make adjustments in hopes that they can effect parental compatibility. For example, they come home from school on time so that mom and dad won't quarrel about their being late. When separation and divorce occur, children feel incompetent, as if they have failed or perhaps even caused the split. This results in loss of self-esteem and adds to feelings of depression and anger.

- Children will plead for a reconciliation. Make certain that they do not construe reasonable communication between the parents as indications that a reconciliation is imminent. For example, take time to explain that just because daddy is invited to share a holiday does not mean that he will be moving back home. Without such an explanation, some young children may be confused and disappointed. The disappointment may trigger or reactivate certain indicators of instability that have begun to abate.

- Be assured that all children experience times of frustration, unfulfilled needs, and confusion, yet still manage to feel good about themselves. Even in many situations that are unpleasant, scary, disruptive, and bleak, children will not suffer permanent damage if their parents or others are available as helpers.

54.
Custody: Considerations and Changes

An abusive father gets custody of his daughter because the judge considers the protesting mother as "hysterical" and decides the child will be safer with the father. Does this make sense?

Most custody decisions have nothing to do with abuse—and in the majority of placements, the children remain with the mother. However, more fathers are asking for and being awarded custody. Since 1971 the trend for joint custody is increasing. Joint custody has several definitions. *Joint legal custody* is an arrangement whereby both parents share responsibility and major decisions about their children. *Joint physical custody* or shared custody parents share parenting in separate homes.

> *More fathers have become custodial parents following a divorce. They attend parent-teacher conferences, coach sports, and provide both physical and emotional care.*

Joint custody has pluses and minuses. In theory, it reflects the fervent desire of both parents to have equal access to the children to minimize the loss or trauma of a ruptured family. This requires appropriate planning and ongoing communication that benefits the children. It maximizes stability. Plans provide structure and shared decision making about the kids elevates their feelings of importance. Arrangements vary. Sometimes the children are shuffled back and forth like a commuter train; sometimes the children stay in the home and the parents take turns in the domicile. Problems occur when the kids have to switch schools or when the philosophy and methods of child management are vastly different: liberal dad versus conservative mom, or authoritarian mom versus hang-loose pop. Children do adjust to the lifestyle of each household because the differences are consistent and consistency is basic to stability.

Research has made it clear that both men and women can be sensitive, caring, and competent caregivers. An important conclusion is quoted in full:

> When both parents apply for custody, it is not the parents' sex but their individual circumstances that are of prime concern. Amongst these, the nature of the child's existing attachments and preferences are particularly important, though in establishing these, great care needs to be taken not to confront the child directly with the choice between the parents. The vast majority of children deplore the need for their parents' divorce and want to retain both mother and father: asking children to choose between their parents is likely to give rise to considerable feelings of guilt vis-à-vis the non-preferred parent that will haunt the child for years to come.
>
> The idea that children are better off with the same-sex parent, as suggested by some of the research, must as yet be treated with caution.*

---

*H. Rudolph Schaffer, *Making Decisions About Children*, Cambridge, MA: Basil Blackwood Ltd., 1990.

Any child may demand to live with the noncustodial parent. He or she wants a change and may make life miserable for everyone in an effort to make the point that things at home just aren't working. Let's suppose that Helen Blaine has custody of Jeff, fifteen years old, and Mary Anne, eleven. Jim Blaine lives in the same town and his visits with the children have been regular for more than four years. Both the children adore their father. As Helen struggles to manage with limited funds and juggles her social life and time with the kids, there is more and more friction—less stability. The kids spend a lot of time griping about their mother and fantasizing that living with dad would be great. Helen is distraught. She experiences headaches, insomnia, crying episodes, and depression. The more she pulls away from the children, the more they scream that they hate her and want to live with dad. Is this a real demand or just of way of saying that they are unhappy? Sit down and talk about it. The kids may be right. Sometimes a change of custody makes sense.

However, changes may take months in the courts and cost hundreds, even thousands of dollars. In the majority of cases, agreements between ex-spouses work very well and allow for future changes, thereby reducing legal fees.

Custody Kidnapping

It is estimated that 125,000 children are taken by noncustodial parents each year. Some of these children are never heard from again. Sometimes the children are not returned after a routine visit. From the child's vantage point, it is an accelerated custody fight with secretive qualities, fears for themselves and for the parent from whom they have been pulled away. Add loss and the problems inherent in fitting into a new home, and you can picture the trauma for the kids.

Realistically, some custody kidnappings result from court decisions that appear to penalize the noncustodial parent, or from problems that stem from an unfair visitation regime or unrecognized changes in circumstances. Sometimes court calendars are so jammed that an important, desirable change of custody is unnecessarily delayed. Regardless of explanations, the child is the victim. A change of custody may be in order, but forced or unexpected kidnappings are traumatic and harmful.

It may take months or years before the children understand what happened. Some will have adjusted to the new situation happily; some will not. The deception and ongoing conflict between parents will cause problems for all.

55.
Visitation

The purpose of visitation is to ensure the child and the noncustodial parent a chance to develop and maintain a stable, caring relationship. There must be a workable plan which takes into account many things. A plan is difficult because it is usually outlined shortly after separation while the feelings of both parents are still raw. Even when parents try to be fair, the situation is rife with uncertainty. In such an emotional time, and often under pressure from attorneys, it is not surprising that the plan agreed to does not work. It may start out smoothly but within a few weeks or months, it must be canceled or changed. It isn't necessary to figure out who is to blame but rather what can be done to keep the children's disappointments to a minimum.

How to Proceed

- Start with what is practical. There are at least three sets of schedules to consider: the children's, the custodial parent's, and the noncustodial parent's. Especially when things at home are shaky, it is important for children to keep up activities such as the scout troop, athletic team, or Sunday school class. The more a child is included in the planning, the more your relationship with the child is safeguarded. Hurt and distress are diminished.
- Be practical about expenses and travel time. Long-distance visitation is costly and often difficult to arrange around school or work schedules. In-town visitation can be expensive if the children demand and get restaurant meals, tickets to the movie, circus, ballgame, and so forth. The time together is for sharing, affection, and problem solving, not a "can you top this" spending orgy.
- Establish a pattern or schedule that considers the child's need for proper rest.

- Bear in mind that children feel secure when they have structure and predictable and consistent patterns and limits. Inconsistency and too much leniency during visits is confusing and detrimental.
- Consider the quality of communication concerning visitation. If visits are seen as a "payoff" for support payments, their purpose is undermined. If either parent asks inappropriate or endless questions of the child, the visits take on a painful dimension. If the noncustodial parent insists on giving material gifts while the custodial parent is having financial problems, children become confused and sometimes inappropriately demanding. If the visit to the noncustodial parent involves extended family members (grandparents, for instance) who maintain a bitter or critical attitude toward the custodial parent, the children will surely suffer. Such visits should reaffirm to the child that family members beyond the custodial parent love them and have accepted the divorce.
- Give the child an opportunity to express feelings. If the noncustodial parent has difficulty adjusting to separation from the nuclear family, children may become overwhelmed with sympathy and take it out in anger toward the custodial parent. Frequently, children react by wanting to move in with the noncustodial parent to be a companion or helper. Such an arrangement may not be feasible or desirable. The child will not understand this without some discussion and explanation.
- On long-distance visits, the time lapse between visits can create all kinds of questions and worries. As the noncustodial parent, be gentle. Don't look for enthusiasm. Anticipate that it may take several days or visits to reestablish patterns of affection and communication. When the children return to the custodial parent, they frequently show grief and conflict.

In my many years as a social worker, I have recommended a visitation plan which has worked well for families where school-aged children have been divided between two households. It is a rotation. (Obviously, with infants this may not be practical at all.) Let us assume that David (Child A) lives with daddy, and Louise (Child B) lives with her mother.

Weekend one: Child A at home (Home X) with father
                 Child B at home (Home Y) with mother
Weekend two: Child A + Child B (Home X) with father
Weekend three: Child A (Home Y) with mother
                 Child B (Home X) with father
Weekend four: Child A + Child B (Home Y) with mother

This provides opportunities for parents to have time free of any children. It provides time alone with the child from the other home and times with both children. Weekend one is a continuation of the weekday arrangement; no one is shifted around. Parents are urged to stay with this rotation because it enriches all relationships and maintains communication among all members of the family on a regular basis. It negates the subtle problem of territorial ownership. In time, the children may not want to move around so much because they want more unscheduled time. This can be negotiated.

Visitation Changes or Problems

In many situations visits from or to the noncustodial parent become less frequent. It is easy for others to be very critical. Criticisms only add to the stress that the children experience. Let the kids express their disappointment, concerns, or any feelings of detachment that may develop. Teenagers may rebel against any organized visitation plan that takes precedence over their own activities. Both parents should anticipate this.

56.
Fatherless Kids, Long-Distance Dads

Fourteen million children—about one-third of the kids in America—are growing up apart from their biological fathers. While the numbers soar, many persons are working diligently to provide services and compensations to the boys and girls who want to have a man to look up to, to enjoy, and to love.

Study after study show that the contact of an absent father matters most to young boys and that a father's absence is most disorienting and devastating for minority boys.

Procedures for custodial mothers should include making arrangements for the children to spend planned time with male mentors in the family, such as grandfathers, uncles, and male cousins—not spot visits, but scheduled times such as every other Saturday from 10:30 to 3:00, or supper together Tuesday nights to help with homework, read together, and talk.

Outside the family, mothers should request male teachers and male coaches, especially in the elementary schools. Seek out mentors—if possible, adults whom the children choose—Sunday school teachers, Big Brothers, and the like. Take time to urge parent-teacher groups or others to "adopt a family," arrange a sister-family program similar to Sister Cities in which one family with a father spends time with a fatherless family. This enriches the experiences of everyone involved.

> *The most successful mentor programs recruit neighbors, cousins, uncles, or brothers-in-law, rather than strangers.*

Long-distance dads who are noncustodial fathers report horror stories of how custodial mothers undermine visits, belittle them, and systematically try to negate their relationships with their children. This may be true or not, purposeful or not, but every man is urged to consider whether the children's mother has a need to punish or hurt the ex-husband because of her unfinished business with him. If this is the case, she is depriving her children of their much-needed entitlement—attention and care from their father. Immediate counseling may be necessary for all concerned.

Many absentee fathers are caught in a sad position with no job and not enough money to pay child support—therefore, no visitation. This should not be equated with not caring, but young children are not able to sort this out. Even if fathers deliberately do not pay, the children need their dad. At the present time, we see a wave of teenagers seeking a relationship with their long-lost dads and they disallow the financial history because they desire connectedness. This parallels adopted children's search for their biological parents.

> *Thirty-three percent of ten- to seventeen-year-old father-less boys said they turn to teachers and coaches for guidance, according to the National Commission on Children (1992).*

57.
The Fade-Away Parent

A word or two about the fade-away parent—the situation in which the child no longer sees the absent parent. Perhaps the most poignant questions a child may ask in the aftermath of divorce are: "Will daddy send me a birthday present?" "Will I see mom at Christmas?" "Do you think my dad will really write to me?" When confronted with questions like these:

- Never answer in a way that offers false hope.
- Take time to let the child express grief, anger, and despair.
- Point out that the situation is not the child's fault.
- Talk about ambivalence.

It may then be worth elaborating on one or more of the following explanations:

- Occasional visits followed by renewed separations became too painful for the parent to handle.
- The absent parent determined the necessity to start a new life for himself or herself, for reasons the child may not understand.
- The parent's plans may involve remarriage, precluding involvement with two families at the same time, at least for the present.
- The parent cannot handle ongoing problems and arguments that led to the divorce in the first place and opted to cut off all communication.
- A lawyer or judge may be responsible for the decision to disallow visitation, as in a restraining order or contingencies with regard to support payments, imprisonment, therapy, or matters related to child abuse.

The teenager who has not seen an absent parent for a number of years may become obsessed with this deprivation. Some run away from home to try to find the missing parent. These youngsters are not actually running *away* but rather running *to* the missing father or mother. Some organizations are currently developing programs to help children in their search. Reunions can be highly successful or can leave a child with a number of problems to resolve. If a child should run away from your home to search, don't feel rejected. See the positive side, even though you staunchly disagree and fear that a relationship with the long-absent parent will be unsuccessful. When the child returns, make the child feel welcome. Take the time to assess your own relationship with the child and try to determine if changes are in order.

> *Remember that children cannot have an ex-mother or an ex-father. The parent is present in thought, if not in person. Children may make unpleasant, unkind, or callous remarks about the absent parent, knowing that this is what the custodial parent wants to hear. But it may not reflect accurately how the child really feels. Therefore, try to develop a team approach with your ex-spouse. Children need to view their parents as allies, if not as husband and wife.*

REASSURANCES

- Children of divorce usually learn to be surprisingly self-reliant. When the custodial parent has overwhelming responsibilities, children learn to fend for themselves when they are told, "Please do your homework alone tonight," or "You don't have to have someone tuck you in every night. I love you, but I have to finish *my* work." Children acquire competence and a degree of independence. For some children, this represents a major shift from a time when mother may have been too solicitous or overprotective.

- A child may learn a number of self-protective measures to avoid being scapegoated. "Don't take it out on me because you are mad at daddy or because we don't have much money." If a parent becomes too dependent on the child, it doesn't hurt to hear, "Oh, mom, go by yourself. I want to stay home and watch TV."
- The child may learn the importance of a sense of humor.
- The child may discover that communication based on honesty and sharing can serve as a springboard for entering and surviving troubled times. Children are forthright and may often be the ones who confront adults who are indirect, dishonest, or unreasonable.
- The child may turn to friends, relatives, siblings, teachers, or to a parent for support. Healthy dependency and communication may develop that might not otherwise have happened. These relationships may have been initiated by a friend, parent, or teacher when symptoms of stress were noticed. Happily, the child was able to accept the help that was offered. It doesn't matter who took the first step. Benefits include the message, "I have someone to turn to." If a child's sense of trust is damaged when a family breaks up, it can be repaired as he or she turns to others for support.
- The child learns the importance of expressing emotions and respecting the emotional needs of others. When a child sees a parent cry or watches a sibling in a rage, he or she may be puzzled if this is a new experience. It is good to know that others have strong feelings, too. It is also beneficial to be reminded that we still must control ourselves at such a time even though we may want to hurt others.
- The child benefits from knowing that many others have had similar experiences and that things turned out okay. He or she may learn early on that self-pity is hard to stop and friends may get tired of hearing it.
- Children can benefit from a new understanding of the decision-making process. Decisions add up to taking responsibility for one's own behavior and that becomes a lifelong benefit. They may decide to do better in school. They may decide to stop whining or teasing.
- A sense of loneliness may prove to be a benefit. The child learns that others may not always be there to help. Although uncom-

fortable, it may be a step toward mature independence. It is not a "poor-me" position.

Inasmuch as teenagers seem to be unusually vulnerable when parents divorce, it is worth noting positive effects that they may derive. The adolescent of divorce frequently displays more maturity than peers. He or she is aware of this difference. It tends to influence, in a constructive way, choice of friends and career, goal setting, activities, general interests, and use of time and money.

Adolescents can learn to give support to the custodial parent, helping with companionship, transportation, babysitting, home responsibilities, and family income.

The teenager may be designated as the emergency contact for a younger sibling if it is not possible to reach a parent. A cheerful and cooperative adolescent may be an important role model for younger children.

58.
Parental Recovery:
Dating, Remarriage, Same-Sex Partners

Happy memories, dreams, or sentimental moments do not have to disrupt your recovery. They are indicators of the ambivalence of the marriage. Even though, in time, positive memories may outnumber unhappy or angry ones, this does not mean that a reconciliation is in order. If you now regret getting the divorce, force yourself to examine the faults and hurts that led to the separation. When divorced couples remarry each other, more than ninety percent of them divorce again. The ones that last have frequently had joint therapy for many months.

If the children go through periods of defiance or unruly acting out, keep in mind the normal rebelliousness of youth. For example, boys fourteen years of age can be argumentative and uncooperative. Do not blame the divorce for that. Talk to parents of others kids the same age to discover the universality of these kinds of behavior. This benefits your understanding and stability.

It takes courage to handle a divorce. Take time to be proud of the good decisions that you have made. Stress lays the foundation for insights and growth, painful as it may be. Recovery allows you to acknowledge progress and satisfactions.

The Parent Who Is Dating

When you start to date, the children will have mixed emotions. They may rejoice that mom or dad is no longer depressed and withdrawn. Or they may regard the dating as an infringement on their relationship with each parent. You should make it clear that blanket condemnation of your dating is unfair; you do not need their permission. Let the children learn to appreciate your conflict between time for dates and time with them. Help them understand your need for a loving adult relationship. Both sides must make certain adjustments. Young children can learn to stay with a sitter without fussing, and older boys and girls can stop griping. Children may be angry and push to be included or they may be rude to your dates. Share your feelings and acknowledge theirs. Let them talk about being jealous or ask why you are so nice to your date when you used to be so nasty to your ex-spouse. The basic parent-child relationship is not in jeopardy. Your dating is not a sign of rejection.

Depending upon the age of the children, discuss the situation as candidly as possible. They need to understand that not everyone you meet or whose company you enjoy is a prospective stepparent. Young children may implore you to "bring me a new daddy (or mommy)." In some situations children can cause bitter arguments and hard feelings. Time alone with you may help. It may take months before your children warm up to your friend or lover. Be patient! There are so many understandable reasons why they want to stay at arm's length. Don't take it to mean that they don't want you to be happy. See hesitations as the scars of earlier wounds that left the children fearful.

Live-in Arrangements

A live-in partner may be the facsimile of a stepparent or merely a visitor. This distinction needs to be made clear. It directly affects the answers to such questions as: How much authority does this person have? Does this person have the right to criticize how the parent handles the children? Are the children obligated to do as this person says? Clear answers help the children understand the roles and all the agreements. There will be rough times when demands or discipline cause problems, but roles become the foundation upon which everyone stands. Older boys and girls may rebel against a new authority person in the home. It is suggested that adults take the stand that as long as the child is living at home, the rules apply regardless of which adult may be carrying them out.

Children can become confused if a parade of sex partners stay in the home, either on a short-term or long-term basis. The confusion generally stems from unexpressed questions such as, Do I make friends or don't I? Do I try to get close, or will I have to say good-bye again? Such questions undermine stability. Children are basically focused on themselves and may be reluctant to reach out, especially since there are no guarantees about the future. In one way, this is self-preservation; in another way, it may obstruct the exchange of positive feelings and cause some misunderstandings. Help children confront this dilemma.

Same-Sex Partners

More people are choosing lovers of the same sex. If there are children involved, be certain to take time to deal with the uncertainties, prejudices, and misconceptions that the children may face. Children may feel bewildered, confused, embarrassed, or even ashamed. Their friends or members of the extended family or your ex-spouse's family may make disturbing, critical remarks. *Your goals should be to help the children accept the lifestyle you have selected and to become friends with your partner on the merits of the person himself or herself.* Most lesbian or gay households with children develop great loyalties and routines can run smoothly. The advantages and disadvantages of same-sex families are sometimes discussed on talk shows and in articles. One concern is the possible conflicts children may experience when working through their own male/female identifications. There are no available data to substantiate a fear that the children may prefer same-sex partners when they mature.

Your children may benefit from your broad-mindedness. Children of today must be helped to live comfortably in a world of diversified and controversial lifestyles. As they learn to confront the many options in life, the impact of parental honesty and sensitivity may far outweigh the impact of parental sexual preference.

The Custodial Parent Remarries

Bearing in mind that the goal for a child of divorce is a stable, mature relationship with each parent, the task becomes more difficult when one of the parents remarries. Former symptoms of instability may surface again. Even though the child may like the future stepparent, parental remarriage represents a return to unknowns. A child may perceive the stepparent as a rival. The child may not understand the bedroom arrangement. The child may not want to face a new disciplinarian. However, if workable patterns to reduce stress during the dating period were successful, the new marriage will enhance the experiences of everyone.

Your role must be to explain to your children that your needs are important and your love for your new spouse does not preclude a love for them. At the same time, do not make promises or paint rosy pictures that may not reflect reality. *A child does not have a new daddy but a new person with whom to develop a loving relationship.* Children fear that you may force them to be close to the new parent and cut off contact with the biological parent. Reassure them that is not your agenda.

Research points out that school-aged girls appear to have more difficulty accepting a stepfather than school-aged boys. The behavior of boys improves when a man is present in the home.

The Noncustodial Parent Remarries

When the noncustodial parent remarries, feelings of estrangement may increase, or there may be a strong awareness of a lack of involvement. Familiar and intense symptoms of grief and loss may be forthcoming. Other children may be casual or seem disinterested in the new marriage. This may hurt the parent's and new spouse's feelings. No one is to blame. It may reflect anxiety or loyalty to the custodial parent. It is usually temporary. Children may be expected to move cautiously or to make unexpected demands for attention and closeness. Do not personalize a lack of enthusiasm.

The question of custody is sometimes reopened following remarriage of the noncustodial parent. Such negotiations require the utmost tact and objectivity. When consulted, the very young (under seven years of age) may reason on the basis of something simplistic such as, "I get more candy at dad's," or "I get to watch more TV at mommy's." If the custodial parent has not remarried, the child may say, "But I want to live with two parents. That's why I want to go live with daddy." It is best not to rush into any change. Let the marriage stabilize. Give new relationships a chance to mature. Confer with professionals if a proposal to change is creating conflict or problems.

59.
Stepparenting, Stepbrothers, and Stepsisters

A stepparent, in cooperation with the natural parent, can make the child's adjustment easier by following these suggestions:
- Be honest about your feelings.
- Establish a level of communication with the stepchild that includes commendation and praise as well as expressions of disappointment, discouragement, and worries. The younger the child, and the more the custodial responsibilities, the easier it may be for some children to let go of a negative, "She's only my stepmother" attitude.
- When replacing a deceased parent, don't deliberately try to be different than you really are, or to emulate the idealized parent you are replacing. Be yourself.
- Don't expect stepchildren to love you. Maintain a realistic goal of a warm friendship built on respect. There is no time limit for winning over stepchildren. Most stepparent-stepchild relationships seem to harbor a marked ambivalence that dissipates slowly. Without the biological tie, it is difficult to establish the quality of a relationship that natural parents have except with young children.
- Expect complaints, gripes, testing by the child, offhand comparisons with the absent parent, and manipulative behavior

intended to separate you from your spouse. Also expect behaviors that signal insecurity and jealousy. Some children may be openly hostile and rejecting. Adolescents may be more accepting, depending on their maturity and understanding of adult needs.

- Be open to being called by your first name or a nickname; "mom" or "dad" may or may not be appropriate. So much depends on the child's age and ongoing relationship with the noncustodial parent.
- Come to terms with the child's feeling about the natural parent. Do not overreact to statements that begin, "I wish I were with my real mother (or father)." Such thoughts may be fleeting or may be a reaction to limits or discipline. If the child persists in this, set aside time to talk together and discuss whether changes in the visitation program, communication, or custody should be considered.

"I'm lucky enough to have a stepdad who loves me. Still, it took me a year to get over his 'taking away' part of the spotlight that mom gave me. But I thank him every chance I get for being there for me. And, most of all, for giving my mother the love she deserves."

—nineteen-year-old Kathy

Children of divorce need to participate in a family where the husband-wife relationship is a strong, respectful bond. Memories of the predivorce years or months of their parent's marriage often are selective—vivid scenes of arguments, tears, disrespect—even violence. As the stepparent in the new scenario, be pleased that you are contributing to positive messages about marriage which children want and need.

If things are stormy, tell the children, "I want to be accepted. I'm not here to take your daddy (or mommy) away." Declare, "You have big adjustments to make and I do, too."

"I'm doing the best I can. Your mom (or dad) is, too. Sometimes we get frustrated. At the beginning, I even considered walking away. I'm glad I didn't."

Stepbrothers and Stepsisters

When stepbrothers or stepsisters move into the home, there is instant competition. There are an infinite number of adjustments to make. Parents need to be sensitive to the fact that it takes months for some of these differences to work themselves out. Some never do. These strategies may help:

- Take time to be alone with *your* children. They need this time alone with you. You do not need to be defensive to your spouse or stepchildren about this decision. It is not showing favoritism. It nourishes the natural bonds between you. (You will also spend time with stepchildren alone to build those relationships.) This builds security and minimizes rivalries.
- Anticipate friction and misunderstanding and don't overreact. Relationships take time to develop.
- Don't push for your children and stepchildren to be best friends. It is okay if they do not like each other. The intensity of competition is far greater than with a classmate or fellow member of a scout troop. However, you do have to insist that all children involved are as polite and understanding to each other as they are to their friends, neighbors, and classmates.

Make certain that house rules are for *all* kids. It sometimes happens that a parent, in welcoming the stepchildren, becomes more strict with his or her own children and seems more flexible with the newcomers. "After all," you may say, "it takes time to get adjusted to a new home." True. But *all* the kids are feeling insecure and having to make adjustments. Sharing toys, a bedroom, and your mom or dad is a learning process for all and the rules must be fair. Fairness is in the eyes of the beholder. For example, older kids should know that the little ones need special considerations. The blended family is perhaps the most difficult of all to manage. As a couple, take time away from the kids whenever feasible.

The strength of the adult relationship will have a positive effect on all the children in the home and family management based on expressing emotions, maintaining limits, and adults taking an in-charge position will benefit everyone. As adults, discuss the situation, listen to the kids, be realistic, and project the pros and cons. Ask again and again, "Are we being manipulated? What is really the best arrangement at this time?" Make certain that there are fun times planned, and encourage both families to mix and match their traditions and some possessions.

Summary: Separation and Divorce

One of every six persons in the United States is a step-something: mother, father, sister, or brother. The future promises more of the same. In order to give children confidence, parents must help children. *The primary task for parents and stepparents is to help children to become self-accepting.* Feel reassured this is achievable and rewarding.

14

Violence and Abuse
There Is an Epidemic

WHY INCLUDE A DISCUSSION of abuse and neglect in a book that promotes stability? Isn't it safe to assume that the parents who read this book are knowledgeable about the problem and do not need the information about abuse and neglect? For the most part, that assumption seems warranted, but you may work with children or associate with them in church, scouts, classes, and so forth. Your own children may have classmates, neighbors, cousins, or other friends who are victims. Predictably, victims have difficulty in relationships and problems or friction may occur which include members of your family. In order for you to help children through difficult episodes, you need knowledge about victims and victimization. The alarming statistics and serious explanations of abuse and neglect are important information. Too many persons are trapped in denial and disclaimers.

This chapter is intended to promote involvement on behalf of child victims. Based on the information provided, readers can proceed to take responsibilities ranging from being a guardian *ad litum* to providing foster care, hospital companionship, volunteer committee work, or active political leadership. Becoming an aide in a classroom, residential setting, or a clinic is another worthy way to help. *The recognition that abusive behaviors do not occur in your home may, in itself, enhance stability for all.*

Conditions must change. Without the involvement of parents and committed help from the mental health, legal, and medical fields, the epidemic will not slow down. Another important reason for including extensive material is that the legal system is making changes regarding the status of people who report cases—expert witnesses, case workers, agency representatives, and so forth. It is recommended that every adult try to keep informed about the new rulings, revised laws, and new procedures because each of us may be involved sometime in the future—whether we choose it or not. Gather information now. Become an observer with an eye on problem behaviors that may denote that a child is a victim of any form of abuse. Develop your background facts and materials because they may be productive and useful to you some day.

A final reason for the identification checklist is that something tragic may happen to one of your children, one of the boys or girls in your Sunday school class, or a niece or nephew. A concise reference may expedite identification so that the victim can receive help as rapidly as possible.

60.
Definitions, Statistics, and Other Identification Information

What Is Emotional Abuse?

Two types of emotional maltreatment are generally recognized: emotional neglect and emotional abuse. Emotional neglect is the consistent failure of a parent or caregiver to provide a child with appropriate support, attention, and affection. Emotional abuse is a chronic pattern of behaviors, such as belittling, humiliating, and ridiculing a child. Both types of emotional abuse attack a child's emotional development and sense of self-worth. All physical abuse has an emotional abuse component.

What Is Child Physical Neglect?

Neglect is the chronic failure of a parent or caregiver to provide a child under eighteen with basic needs such as food, clothing, shelter, medical care, educational opportunity, protection, and supervision.

What Is Physical Abuse?

Physical abuse is any nonaccidental injury to a child under the age of eighteen by a parent or caregiver. Nonaccidental injuries may include beatings, shaking, burns, human bites, strangulation, immersion in scalding water with resulting burns, bruises, welts, broken bones, scars, internal injuries, or death. *Physical abuse is rarely a single physical attack, but rather a pattern of behavior that repeats over time.* It occurs when a parent or other person willfully or maliciously injures or causes a child to be injured, tortured, or maimed, or when unreasonable force is used upon a child. It may be the acceleration of discipline or punishment.

What Is Sexual Abuse?

Child sexual abuse is the *exploitation* of a child or adolescent for the sexual gratification of another person. It includes intercourse, sodomy, oral-genital stimulation, verbal stimulation, exhibitionism, voyeurism, fondling, and involving a child in prostitution or the production of pornography. *Incest* is sexual abuse that occurs within a family. The abuser may be a parent, stepparent, grandparent, sibling, cousin, or other family member. It is frequently ongoing and preplanned by the perpetrator.

Scope

The first early report of child abuse dates back to 1963. It was presented by the Children's Division of the American Humane Association. "The true dimensions of the problem cannot be accurately defined. Educated estimates place the number of abused children in the thousands ... some estimates running as high as ten thousand cases per year." Focusing on physical abuse, the battered child, they reported a total of 662 cases from stories in newspapers in all but two of the fifty states and the District of Columbia. Incest and sexual abuse were not investigated. The Federal Child Abuse Act of 1979 mandated the reporting of suspected child abuse. However, lack of federal funding has hampered the collection of data.

In 1991, 2.4 million children were reported as suspected victims of child abuse and neglect. The majority report neglect. Sexual abuse has the fewest reports. Nationwide, the child abuse death toll has gone as high as four thousand known cases a year. Yet no more than two to three percent of child abuse cases end in death. The average age of fatalities from child abuse is two and one-half years of age.

An abused child, returned to parents without intervention, has a 35 percent chance of being seriously reinjured; 1.7 percent will die.

A child is molested every two minutes. In 1990, it was reported that twenty-eight percent of girls and sixteen percent of boys under eighteen years of age have known some sexual abuse.

Approximately one hundred thousand cases of child sexual abuse are confirmed annually in the United States.

More children die of physical neglect than from physical abuse.

Is there a "system" in place to protect and support families and children? There is a hodgepodge of agencies, professionals, and judicial and political officials, as well as volunteers, committed to helping abused children and their families. At the present time, there is no comprehensive system and no federal leadership or funds to organize one. Children will continue to fall between the cracks until the public is sufficiently alarmed to demand a viable system, and the government is willing to be proactive.

It is true that many attorneys have learned to harass, trick, belittle, coach, bribe, threaten, and confuse child witnesses. They work hard to convince judges and juries—some inexperienced, some gullible—that children are, at best, too suggestible, fanciful, and immature to be credible witnesses. They decry the statement, "Believe the children," although there is a growing body of psychological and legal literature that indicates that *young children rarely lie intentionally.* According to experts, children cannot invent fantasies beyond the reach of their actual experiences.

A 1990 survey of the American Bar Association revealed that a majority of defendants sentenced for child sexual abuse receive probation, usually including mandated treatment.

Identifying Individual Victims

Most battered children are under the age of five, but reports of abuse, especially sexual molestation of junior high and high school students, are increasing. Older youngsters are more prone to deny violence upon direct questioning, and they make up excuses for problem behaviors or unusual bruises. Accordingly, abuse and molestation may be difficult to uncover. *If a child tells you about a beating or manhandling or asks questions, listen carefully.* The questions may reveal that the child has known such experiences. It takes a lot of courage for a child to talk about such things, and it is a great hardship when a child must repeat and repeat a story. Young children do not make up such content. The child's feelings are all mixed up. There have probably been many threats, such as, "If you tell ... ." Oftentimes a stepparent or a parent's boyfriend or girlfriend is involved and the child may tell about how he or she hates him or her, without going into detail. The word "hate" may be an important clue. Teenagers may be absent from school a lot or resort to drugs or alcohol to help handle their feelings. It is not unusual for teenagers to threaten to move away from home or to stay with a friend. This may be a hint that something is wrong at home and that they are frightened. Take time to piece together the things that you observe and hear. Again, "believe the children" is an urgent message.

INDICATORS OF ABUSE AND NEGLECT

Physical Indicators
Unexplained bruises and welts, clustered, forming regular patterns, often appearing after the weekend or vacation
Unexplained burns, immersion burns, patterns like electric range burner or iron, for instance
Unexplained fractures to skull, nose, facial structure in various stages of healing
Unexplained lacerations or abrasions

Sexual Indicators
Difficulty in walking or sitting
Torn, stained, or bloody underclothing
Pain or itching in genital area
Bruises or bleeding in genital, vaginal, or anal areas
Exaggerated use of sexual expressions

Behavioral Indicators
Wariness of adult contacts
Apprehension when other children cry
Extreme aggressiveness or withdrawal
Failure to grow, prosper
Inability to have fun
Fear of parents; fear of going home
Very infantile behavior
Excessive daydreaming
Bizarre, sophisticated, or unusual sexual behavior or knowledge
Poor peer relationships
Delinquency or running away
Reports of sexual assault by caretaker
Reports of sexual relations that friends are having, which are, in fact, reports of own

Other Clues

Major problems at school

Inability to conform with school regulations and policies

Obsession to hide in locker rooms, avoid gym classes if changing clothes is required, or failure to keep routine appointments in nurse's office

Occasional remarks about the situation at home that denote unusual anger, fear, or disrespect

Reports of conflict with stepparents

Unusual emotional outbursts such as crying, laughing

Expresses fear of beating by parents; refuses to go home; may express wish to beat up parents

Truancy

Sexual acting out, from excessive flirting to prostitution

Unexplained anger when adult mentions home situation or parent involvement at school, such as at conferences

Setting fires

Obsession with weapons—knives, guns

Bravado exclamations about not needing a family any more, yet appearing babyish or needy

Drug, alcohol abuse

Don't pretend you don't see what you see. Don't pretend you don't know that symptoms denote BIG problems at home.

This broad list includes "normal" or common reactions to many kinds of stress or trauma that children face. Child victims of neglect or abuse may be spotted because the symptoms are consistent, usually long-standing, and are markedly debilitating. Your next step may be reporting or counseling or both. But if you don't step forward, you may be enabling the child's denial or the threats of silence imposed by the victimizer.

Myths About Child Abuse and Neglect

1. "People that abuse their children are mentally ill."
   Only 10% of reported abusers are mentally ill.
2. "Abuse is only a lower class phenomenon."
   Abuse cuts across all socio-economic levels.
3. "Step-parents abuse more than natural parents."
   73% were natural parents in abuse cases.
4. "Black families abuse more than whites."
   Even distribution.
5. "There is more child abuse today than in the past."
   More are reported now and more people are aware of abuse now.
6. "Abusing parents should be beaten."
   Most abusing parents were beaten as children. That's where they learned how to do it.
7. "The kids asked for it."
   No child asks to be abused; in fact it's the child's right not to be.
8. "Abusing parents don't love their children."
   Most abusing parents love their children very much.
9. "They should know better."
   Of course they should. But, the question is, how do we teach them to know better.
10. "They can't help it."
    Maybe they can't while they are abusing, but they can learn to help it and to stop—many do!
    Source: Parent/Child Center—April 90.

61.
What Child Victims Need

You may be a scout leader or Sunday school teacher. You have heard rumors that Lucy is a battered child. You try very hard to get her to respond to you but she resists. She remains distant, almost disinterested. Nevertheless, you are intent on befriending her. Lucy probably needs some of the following:

• To be left alone, not to be touched

- Time to rest
- To be believed when she says something is wrong at home
- To be permitted to defend her parents
- To have fun if she can learn to trust you enough that she will
- Help to acknowledge successes and accomplishments and the fact that you care
- Time to express her feelings

    After she tells you about a problem, she needs:
- Recognition for being honest
- Appreciation for trying to help herself and others at home
- An understanding of what, if any, obligations you have to fill to get her some help

Victims join scouts, go to school, and join youth groups where persons such as yourself are sensitive to their needs. You may be the one person who can guide a "Lucy" and perhaps others, whom you identify, toward professional help. But you must not look for a bond or closeness. This child is impaired; self-esteem is damaged and the ability to trust adults has been smashed. Some children survive with a remarkable amount of self-esteem intact, yet, they need help, too. They need help to restore their trust in adults and faith in themselves. A guidebook detailing a nontherapy, short-term, step-by-step program to help children is presented in *Trust Building With Children Who Hurt*.* Some victims must have long-term therapy.

PROCEDURES FOR PARENTS

These abusive situations may seem foreign to you and your style of parenting, but your children know they exist. They watch TV, read, and listen to their peers. Your role is to talk to your child and monitor yourself.
- Help your children understand how differently others live and how differently parents parent.

---

*Ruth Arent. *Trust Building with Children Who Hurt, A One-to-One Support Program for Children Ages 5 to 14*, The Center for Applied Research in Education, West Nyack, NY: Simon & Schuster, 1992.

Children want to protect their parents even though they seek help, want out, or plead for a safe place to go. "My friend got beaten up the other day. Do you know some place she could go to get help?" Alice, a sophomore, asked the counselor. It didn't take long to discover Alice was talking about herself.

Comments such as "my friend" or "I know somebody who" or "I saw it on TV and I got to thinking about it ... " are approaches kids will use. Remarks such as these can be a ploy for you to ask questions, because they are afraid of personal revelations.

- Discuss violence in words children can understand. Use terms such as "temper tantrums," "out-of-control," "acted like a crazy person." Relate violent behavior to the effects of alcohol, drugs, and issues such as despair, loneliness, hopelessness, and a sense of feeling worthless.
- Take time to express yourself if you have been unduly harsh with your kids through unusual punishments, extended grounding, hitting, thrashing, or using abusive, derogatory expressions. You may feel that your behavior is justified. At the same time, you may want to explain that adults get frustrated and angry and that they sometimes overreact, too. Kids can understand and forgive. Give them credit for that. You can all benefit from such discussions.

The use of the word "stupid" can be lethal. "That was a stupid thing to do." "You must be stupid if you think ... " "Look, stupid, I've told you six times to do that."

62.
Who Abuses Children?

Most abused children live with both parents. Sex offenders are usually trusted family members, friends, neighbors, and babysitters. They appear to be responsible and respectable citizens.

Violent persons who attack, manhandle, torture, and kill children have learned violence. In *Save the Family, Save the Child*,* Vincent Fontana says, "It is the immature, unthinking or self-indulgent person—or the one so poisoned by his own upbringing—who makes a practice of physical punishment or automatically resorts to force." Most homicides are committed by mothers, followed by mothers' boyfriends, and then the biological fathers. Mothers' depression is the most predictable condition in assessing risk potential for children.

Detailed descriptions of violent persons are helpful because they provide information in an unemotional way. *When you recognize that a person has the problems or traits, urge that person to seek help now—as child abuse prevention.*

Facts About Abusers

- The parents are emotionally needy and look to their children to fill their needs.
- The parent misperceives the child's behaviors. The child may be accused of not loving the parent, of being willfully disrespectful or negligent, or of provoking the parent to hit, beat, or burn.
- The relationship between parent and child is characterized by a lack of warmth. Parents may not know how to show love, and children do not learn how to receive or give love.
- The parent's background almost always includes a history of battering. Consequently, the parent has not experienced close relationships or rewarding bonding. Fewer than ten percent, however, are psychotic or mentally ill, though all have suffered emotional stress or disturbance.
- A parent may expect adult behavior from a child, which is impossible at the child's age level. A toddler may be expected to understand and meet the parent's needs in addition to learning bowel and bladder control, perfect table manners, and the like. Children experience nonstop criticism no matter

---

*Dr. Vincent J. Fontana, *Save the Family, Save the Child*, New York: E.P. Dutton, 1991.

how hard they try to please. They end up feeling incompetent and unappreciated. They miss affection and approval.
- The parent, especially a stepparent, may be very jealous of other relationships in the family and act out this jealousy by beating the child, wishing to get rid of the rival.
- The incestuous parent has many other complicated problems involving sexual issues. Violence, as such, may not be the issue, as it is in rape. Nevertheless, the child is victimized.
- Many parents of middle- or upper-class backgrounds, not just of lower socioeconomic status, can display inadequate personalities, addictions, or unusual impulsivity.
- Therapy can help parents learn to stop the violence, call for help to prevent a crisis, be more self-accepting, and be more comfortable with the children.

There are successful programs conducted by professionals in prenatal clinics and mental health centers that identify *potential* batterers. Women are interviewed and their personalities checked out against a list, which includes the characteristics and items noted above. They are then helped to change attitudes, confront problems, and work through some unfinished struggles of their childhood. For some, this work may take a year or more. To support the women, the agency assigns a community volunteer as a surrogate, supportive "grandmother."

The family of violence must become better understood. This knowledge must be translated into *prevention* so that children and adults will be rescued before they are harmed, physically or emotionally. The circle of family violence that repeats its pattern, generation after generation, may be broken when victims get sufficient help. Sexist and power issues must be openly confronted. When people are helped to take responsibility for their behavior, they can find nonviolent ways to express anger and frustration.

Organized Exploitation

Become aware! Accept the fact that some child abuse in America is a well-organized, systematic crime and that the justice system has yet to prove to be a deterrent. There are organizations of pedophiles that advocate the sexual abuse of young children—North-American Man-Boy Love Association (NAMBLA) is an example. NAMBLA's motto is, "Sex before eight or else it's too late." It has worldwide connections, international conventions, computerized lists of child victims, and places to collect children for pornography and sex.

Help Is Available

No matter what your interest in abuse, neglect, or violence may be, bear in mind that parents do not abuse their children because they want to. More and more abusive persons are seeking help, and sometimes it is mandated by court orders. There are still too many who need help who refuse to go, or there is no service available.

A parent does not wake up in the morning and say, "Today I am going to kill my child."

Alarming as the statistics and stories may be, the problem of violence cannot be eradicated until many of the associated problems are confronted. Humanistic schools, expanded social services, increased job possibilities, and widespread promotion of professional help are all necessary. Federal support must be increased. Significant elimination of violence on TV is essential. Some of the vast increase in crime in the past ten years has been ascribed to TV. This cannot be ignored. The media must be encouraged to show empathy and compassion toward abusive persons as well as to report the ugly facts. Let it be pointed out that battering adults are needy. Like children who hurt, the violent adult hurts and cannot recover alone.

Adults who sexually molest children are very ill. Neverthe-less, they inflict serious damage and immeasurable pain on their victims. Every parent feels outraged when they read that children are raped, manhandled, or sodomized. It is essential that parents express their rage to the judicial system where the ultimate punishment must be pro-nounced. We must get molesters off the streets.

15

Death
The Transition from Tears to Tranquility

63.
The Reality of Death:
Working Toward Acceptance

When my son arrived back home after his father's funeral, he looked up at his grandfather and asked, "Grandpa, will you show me how to tie a tie?" Douglas was ten. He was making an effort to adjust to a fatherless world. Many people were aware that he would need help on various levels. His school principal and teachers found the time to talk to him—to stay involved in Doug's recovery, to go beyond the cursory comment, "I was sorry to hear about your dad." Doug was lucky. So many children lose a parent and get very little comfort and support. They suffer the loss, hide their feelings, and try to be brave.

Piece by piece, step by step, children can let go of intense grief. Reactions of disbelief and anger take a long while to dissipate. Many times children want to find someone to blame; too often they blame themselves. Young Paul's mother was killed in a car accident following a family argument about his grades. Paul was convinced that the accident was his fault because his mom was upset. Similarly, Jenny's father was killed instantly when his car skidded on ice. He had stormed out of the house, going to a bar to cool down from a family fight about the grubby ring in the bathtub. Jenny was the "guilty" one; over and over, she said, "If only I hadn't been so lazy. If only I had cleaned that tub." Children sometimes see death as punishment or rejection. It is essential for them to work through feelings that they might otherwise hang on to the rest of their lives.

Although it hurts to see a child suffer, there is no way to protect children all the time. Death is a part of the everyday world. We cannot protect children from death. But we can help them face and accept it.

One of every sixteen children will face the death of a parent during his or her childhood. Sometimes there are opportunities to say good-bye; more often, it is a sudden loss. No matter what the circumstances, it can undermine stability, temporarily in some cases, permanently in others. The most important question is, how does a child learn to accept that someone is really dead? For children, in particular, the reality of death has been confused by TV. They see a favorite hero killed on Monday and back up on his horse on Tuesday. Unless the reality of death is made clear, children may harbor anxiety for many years. The myth that, "Grandma is sleeping," or "We have lost mother," is no longer a satisfactory explanation. The child must know the truth—that there is no hope that the dead person will return. A year-old-child, though nonverbal, may be acutely aware of a loss, especially of a parent or sibling, and needs a meaningful explanation. Beyond that age, children express disbelief, anger, fear, or grief in what may appear to be babyish or inappropriate behavior. Adults may be looking for behavior similar to their own, whereas, young children express feelings briefly and go on to something else. A child becomes distracted by a butterfly at the cemetery; the parent scowls; the child is bewildered. Expect shifting emotions.

School-aged children, as well as teenagers, may turn to their friends. In Jill Krementz's book entitled *How It Feels When a Parent Dies*,* Stephen Jayne, age eleven, is quoted: "It helps if

---

*Jill Krementz, *How It Feels When a Parent Dies*. New York: Alfred A. Knopf, 1981.

your friends treat you the same way as before your parent died. When they start feeling sorry for you, it makes you feel sorry for yourself and then you start crying." Older kids may want to be surrounded by their friends so they can all cry together. Some children may not cry at all. You may have asked people to stay near or to talk with you through the night.

Children don't ask for help. When people offer comfort, they may feel uncomfortable. Some children may want to sleep beside you. Some run and hide. Others may scream, "I don't want to talk about it."

INDICATORS OF INSTABILITY AND NEEDS OF SURVIVORS

To a certain extent, *children mirror parental behaviors* and go through a similar series of stages.

Adults in Grief: Predictable Symptoms

Stage 1	Symptoms	Needs
Numbness	Shock	To be dependent on
	Sorrow	others
	Anger	To let others do tasks
	Guilt	To be permitted to be
	Automatic handling	self-pitying, remote,
	of routines	not responsible for
	Very focused on	others
	immediate decisions,	
	such as funeral	
	matters, insurance	

Stage 2	Symptoms	Needs
Disorganization	Need to talk about	To be intimate with
	deceased at length	friends, children,
	Acute loneliness	family
	Disorganization,	To be allowed to be
	irrational thoughts	distracted
	Deep depression	To express feelings
	Aimlessness	
	Apathy	
	Extreme fatigue	
	Anxiety	
	Greater anger	

Tightness in the
    throat
Loss of sleep
Clinging to deceased's
    possessions

Stage 3	Symptoms	Needs
Reorganization	Feelings less intense	To be encouraged to
	Appetite improves	do things—make new
	New interests, energy	friends, for instance
	Release from anxiety	To acknowledge the
	Greater acceptance of	growth that has
	the loss	resulted from the
		grief

The most recognizable differences between adults and children are:

- Children may deceptively appear to be less profoundly moved.
- Children may ask for facts that you, the adult, already know. Sometimes they will nag to have adults repeat and repeat every detail of what happened in an accident or in the hospital.
- Children will seek reassurances that important changes will not occur—they won't have to leave the house, change schools, or give away their pets.
- Children want reassurances that they will not have to fill the shoes of the deceased.
- Children may become very angry at the surviving parent.

ADDITIONAL INDICATORS OF INSTABILITY THAT A YOUNG CHILD MAY DISPLAY

- Demanding, attention-getting behavior
- Outbursts of anger directed toward surviving parent, siblings, friends, or animals
- Evidence of being distracted or confused—daydreaming
- Depression, disturbed sleep patterns—too much or too little
- Signs of school phobia, refusal to go to school
- Temper tantrums with some self-inflicted bodily harm
- A loss of interest in sports, friends, academics, and other people

- An attitude of feeling lost or bewildered
- Irritability

Children vary as to how they work through their grief. A lot depends on the adjustment of the other members of the family. If the surviving parent is still deeply depressed and maintaining a morose attitude in the home, the child's recovery may be stymied. Or the child may adjust well away from home and continue to have problems while under the influence of the parent. On the other hand, if the parent has progressed to the reorganization phase of recovery, the child may reflect this positive adjustment.

For those who are having difficulties after one year, these indicators of instability are common:

- Unexplained mood swings, including inappropriate laughter
- Persistent depression
- Unusual weight gain or loss
- Psychosomatic illnesses
- Feelings of unworthiness, incompleteness
- Violent or negative responses to changes and surprises
- Exaggerated fears of desertion
- A need to cling to material objects (blankets, toys) beyond traditional age expectations

These children need counseling. There are grief groups available for children in some schools and community service centers. They are frequently listed in newspapers.

The Adolescent and a Death in the Family

The reactions of a teenager to a death in the family depend on maturity, his or her relationship with the deceased, role in the family, understanding of the needs of others, and much more. It is fair to ask, "Will the teenager act more like the adults in the family or more like the younger children?" In general, in a crisis, the teenager shows maturity, reaches out to others, and puts aside personal needs. He or she may feel intense pain but appear strong and controlled, except around peers. Support from peers is crucial. After the crisis, indicators of instability may develop and persist. As with the younger children, counseling may be advisable.

Many teenagers were in the process of developing a mutually respectful relationship with the parent who died. The death represents unfinished, interrupted business, with appropriate regrets and a deep sense of loss.

Teen years provide opportunities to scrutinize the behaviors of the like-sex parent as a role model. After the death of that parent, fantasies and halo effects may evolve which interfere with accurate memories and interpretations of past actions. In time, the fantasies and the halo effect diminish. The surviving parent need not be overly concerned about the interruption in the role-modeling process. Realistically, young people today emulate one quality from one same-sex adult, such as integrity, and a second quality from another, such as sensitivity or generosity. *The incomplete same-sex role model experience does not forecast problems.* However, the loss remains profound. Men in their twenties or thirties may tear up as they say, "It was hard being raised as a fatherless boy." Women may do the same, "It's hard for me to picture what my mom would do in this situation. I'll never know. It makes me sad and sometimes bitter. I feel cheated."

Glenn's mother sat in the lunchroom at the office. Mary asked her, "How is Glenn getting along since his dad died? With two sisters and you, aren't you afraid he'll turn out to be a sissy?"

"Heavens no! He's fourteen now and I've learned that he admires his uncle's courage, his grandfather's manners, his coach's sense of humor, and the great work habits of our neighbor. I guess that's what all kids do. It certainly is working for Glenn."

"Kids learn to compensate, don't they?" Mary asked, not looking for any answer. "But they still feel sad and cheated when a parent dies."

Most teenagers are learning to express feelings of love and appreciation. The death of a loved one may elicit or inhibit such expression. The pain of grief can stifle emotional expressions.

Encourage teenagers to share their feelings because openness is invaluable to lifelong adjustment and healthy communication.

A parent is urged to watch for signs of brooding, distraction, and marked depression. If the boy or girl shuns all your attempts to comfort, don't overreact. Occasional days away from school may be in order—an escape from classroom pressure in favor of time spent with you. Consider introducing music lessons, assembling stereo speakers, or constructing intricate models, for example. Some teenagers may be attracted to groups or to unwholesome activities that never appealed to them before. Don't sit by and watch passively. Show that you care by taking charge. You do not want your child to get hooked into strange situations in a time of stress while searching for answers. Some may turn to alcohol or drugs to comfort themselves. If the depression doesn't let up within six months, counseling is recommended.

Discuss the details of the funeral before and after the fact. They may be confused about what they saw and heard. My fifteen-year-old daughter smiled at some family friends while attending her father's funeral. The friends did not smile back. Sally turned to me and asked, "Aren't you allowed to smile at a funeral?" Patient explanations put her at ease.

Needs of the Adolescent

- Time to be with friends.
- To be involved in some of the decisions about the funeral and burial, as well as decisions about family management and changes.
- Spiritual guidance.
- A listener—someone to hear regrets, guilty thoughts, memories.
- To be permitted to go through an extended period of wholesome dependency. This may begin months after the loss. It may reverse the movement toward independence that preceded the death.
- Guidance to express emotions, not to bury them in alcohol or drugs.
- Time to adjust to new family responsibilities.

An adolescent is still a child. Extend the same considerations to the older child as you do to younger siblings. Be affectionate. Be patient. Be understanding. Be available.

PROCEDURES FOR PARENTS

When it is necessary for you to handle your own recovery and meet the needs of bereaved children at the same time, it can be overwhelming. These procedures can help your child handle the death of a loved one. Your kids want:

- To be helped to understand that dying does not mean rejection.
- To be allowed to cry unashamedly. To understand there is no need to be embarrassed.
- To be helped to handle any guilt they may harbor. For example, if a parent or grandparent had been ill and unduly irritable or impatient, the child may have wished he or she would "hurry up and die." Such situations result in guilt.
- To be held; to hold others.
- To be encouraged to be creative.
- To express feelings, thoughts, and questions in any way that they can. To have all questions answered. Details can be filled in gradually. What and how much to tell depends on the child's maturity and the circumstances.
- To feel love around them. If separation from a surviving parent is necessary, reassure the child that a reunion is imminent. If both parents are deceased, adults in the decision-making capacity should listen to a child's pleas and input. The need for familiar people, pets, and things is important. If possible, the child should remain in the same class at school with a supportive teacher and friends.
- To learn that people handle the subject of death in many different ways, to understand that other children may not express sympathy or may show discomfort by giggling or silence. A child can learn that a friend really cares but does not know how to show sympathy.
- To be distracted, even to the point of going to the movies, because intense pain may be alleviated for a short time. This does not mean that experiencing intense pain can be avoided, but some distractions may be beneficial.
- Consider medication if the child cannot sleep or has a history of disturbed sleep. If the child is having nightmares about

accidents, death, corpses, and such, reassure him or her that this is natural and that these will become less frightening and less frequent.
- To hear or read books and stories that tell about similar experiences of other boys and girls. They will benefit from knowing that others have gone through what they are going through. (See *Bibliography*.)

Unlike other disturbing circumstances, there is nothing anyone can do to change the fact of a loss. One can only help the bereaved through the transition from tears to tranquillity. Feel reassured! *Children can and do adjust and regain their stability.*

64.
Violent Death: Anxiety for All

One out of every nine boys who dies is a victim of violence. Support groups for bereaved parents are more available than for families or surviving siblings. Many school psychologists, social workers, and counselors team up with community grief specialists and work in schools following the death of a student. Death on a playground or a murder in the classroom affects all children in one way or another. Very few can be callous, even though death is a way of life in some neighborhoods.

PROCEDURES FOR PARENTS

Suggestions for helping the child who has lost someone through violent death:
- Let the child ask endless questions. Your answers can be supportive even though you cannot always be reassuring.
- Provide repeated instruction for self-protection.
- Allow opportunities for release of anger as well as anxiety. Respect times for crying, wailing, praying, or silence.
- Specify certain times to attend to tasks at home, school, or elsewhere. Ease up on academic expectations.
- Help children sort out their values; make it important to fill each day with as much love as possible.
- Avoid dwelling on gory details that children may not understand or that do not serve a useful purpose.

- Expect nightmares.
- Express your fears.

REASSURANCES

It seems impossible to justify street violence, gang warfare, and careless gun accidents, especially when the victim is your child or someone you know. Unthinkable, inexcusable, unnecessary—these are among the words that describe the horror and shock of survivors. Violent deaths elicit rage and despair and reassurances may feel empty and useless when trying to comfort survivors or people outraged by unnecessary violent deaths.

65.
Surviving the Death of an Unborn, Newborn, or Baby Sibling

It has only been in the past ten years or so that parents who have experienced miscarriage, stillbirth, or death of an infant have been helped to grieve. Helped, yes, and urged to grieve, because the expression of grief is basic to recovery. Prior to that, the parents suffered from disinterest, callousness, and, above all, lack of understanding from family and friends, professionals, and the community at large.

Concern for the surviving siblings is still, in many instances, a secondary matter. Phrases such as, "Well, they never even knew each other," or "It was only a tiny baby, and Ellie had only held her twice," or "She'll forget about all this in a hurry. After all, the child was born dead" are ready excuses. Now, serious attention is directed to surviving siblings, especially because sudden infant death syndrome (SIDS) claims between twelve hundred and fifteen hundred children a year. Surviving siblings must deal with these losses and with grieving parents at the same time.

In *Empty Cradle, Broken Heart*,* Deborah Davis lists four factors that influence how children respond to the death of their baby sibling:

---

*Deborah Davis, *Empty Cradle, Broken Heart*, Golden, CO: Fulcrum Publishing, 1991.

- Their level of understanding about death
- Their relationship with the baby
- Their reaction to the parent's grief
- The support and reassurance they receive

Above all, be honest; explain death in age-appropriate ways. If you are too upset and can't manage to be supportive, find someone who can. It will take time for you to recover enough to give the support you want to give; losing a child is a tragedy unlike any other. You may work hard to maintain your stability, but this is unrealistic during a time of great sadness.

PROCEDURES FOR PARENTS

- Take time to talk. Explain death even to nonverbal infants and toddlers.
- Talk about yourself and what you are experiencing.
- Assure the children that you are still there to take care of them and love them. Explain that you are not upset because of something they have done.
- If the death was from a car wreck or similar accident in which the surviving sibling was also injured, try to be as attentive as possible—hospital visits, shared TV time, reading out loud, and so forth. As the child recovers, expect regressions and choose toys, books, accordingly. The child may be afraid he or she might die, too.
- Don't anticipate how surviving siblings may react. So much depends on age and understanding.

Be on the lookout for symptoms of fear, inasmuch as young children may not understand death. It is not unusual for them to fear that something will happen to them, especially if they become ill. Fear of sleep or of illness, fear about dead bodies, and fear of separation and abandonment are common.

Allow expression of anger—one predictable child's reaction to loss. Prepare yourself to respond to the question, "Can we get a new baby?" (See *The Replacement Child*, page 77.)

After the baby died, my three-year-old Zach would climb into the baby's crib and cry and cry and cry. We decided that this was his way of expressing his grief. This went on for about two weeks. Then, one day, he walked out of the baby's room, slammed the door, and announced, "Me feel better." That moment helped our recovery more than I can say.

REASSURANCES

The key reassurances must be for you, the parent. As your energy returns and your despair, anger, and grief subside, you will gradually resume your positive, stable interactions with the surviving family members. Give yourself time. Join support groups. The surviving children will manage these difficult, dysfunctional times even though it is a struggle.

Welcome the support of friends and family. Sharing mutual grief can strengthen ties and perhaps trigger improvements in relationships. Unfortunately, the shared experience of grief may demand an intimacy between survivors that causes discomfort or conflict for some.

Grief will continue to come in waves. Reestablishing stability is your goal. It may take months. During recovery, professional support persons are appropriate targets for your feelings. Try not to break the communication with your spouse or children. That only makes matters worse—and no one deserves that.

16

The Family on the Move
Here Today, Where Tomorrow?

ONE IN EVERY FIVE FAMILIES in the United States moves every year, whether it's across town or across a continent. For some families it is a matter of putting their few possessions in a truck or a trailer and heading to unfamiliar places, with no guarantees of a job for the parents or a place to live. These disruptions threaten the stability of everyone. The family unit itself may be the only remaining security. However, a move frequently follows parental separation, a serious quarrel, or a loss of employment. Relationships suffer, feelings are raw. Uncertainties are overwhelming and the needs of the children may be overlooked. Reassurances are important. Fears of abandonment are common. Separation from familiar surroundings is scary.

Not all moves create problems, however. A move may represent upward mobility, an improved living situation, adventure, and the opportunity for growth. It may be welcomed by everyone. Uncertainties can represent adventure rather than instability.

Moving is a time of loss. *Parents' attitudes strongly influence the children's adjustment.* When the adults feel overwhelmed, children reflect their insecurities. When adults feel devastated and defeated, the children find it difficult to feel optimistic— much less excited. When adults feel comfortable and have a positive attitude, children are more likely to feel the same way. The major problem facing most children is fear of the unknown.

Sometimes it is necessary for a child to adapt to a new environment that he or she perceives as cheaper or more rustic than the previous surroundings. The majority of moves that result in a lower standard of living are preceded by serious family problems or by a breakdown of the family structure. This means that the child has multiple adjustments to make. Complaining about the move and the new setting may be symptomatic of more deeply seated conflicts and instability.

Studies of fourth- to sixth-grade children who have moved several times have shown that they are often better adjusted than children who have not moved at all.

If the move involves moving in with grandparents, point out the pluses and the minuses. One result of the economic crunch of the late 1980s was the necessity for thousands of families to move in with grandparents. That trend continues.

INDICATORS OF INSTABILITY

Before departure, a child may be irritable; cry, tell stories, or daydream; exaggerate dependency on family members by clinging or being disobedient; show signs of anxiety, anger, and discouragement; run away; hang on to pets; hide out; or avoid new and close relationships. These same symptoms may be seen for weeks after the move.

66.
Safeguarding Stability During a Move: Children's Needs

There are many ways grownups in a family can help the children accept a move. Even if moves are frequent, each move entails saying good-bye to the familiar and facing the unfamiliar. Some children can handle this more readily than others. Most children will ask a lot of questions that denote both curiosity and concern. That concern can affect stability.

A child needs:
- To be informed of the move ahead of time. A spur-of-the-moment move that is a total surprise can be very, very upsetting. Some children have come home from school in the afternoon to discover most of the family possessions in a truck ready to pull away. Even though the family may be sticking together, such disruption can hurt badly.
- As much reassurance as possible. Children need help in leaving friends, school, or family members. If the move represents the breakup of a family, the child must be told what the breakup is all about. A child may need to be told repeatedly, "You can still love daddy very much, even if he lives many miles away." If you know that the move will be a break from someone close, be certain to arrange for ways to keep in touch, such as scheduled long-distance phone calls or giving friends addressed postcards to fill out so that they can write. Older siblings may help in such matters if the parents are too busy or unable to do so.
- To be involved in as many of the decisions as possible. Depending on the age of the children, many can help pack, or choose what to keep and what to discard, for example.
- Time to say good-bye.
- Adult understanding that a move represents loss—loss of friends and favorite play places. When parents share their own feelings, it helps. There may be times, however, when the parents are anxious to get out of *this house* or get out of town and the children do not want to. The decision to move is an adult decision. Again, children need to know what the adults are feeling and vice versa.
- To be encouraged to express anger and grief and to cry. The expression, "Not again!" denotes disbelief and may trigger the instability.
- To hang onto security blankets and other items of importance without being chided.
- To be involved in the placement of a pet that will not be taken along, unless this means a heartbreaking trip to a an animal shelter.
- As many reassurances as possible that this move is not a temporary one—that the child will stay long enough to finish the school year (at least), to make friends, to feel at home, and to feel safe from disruptions.

- To keep family routine as steady as possible during preparation time—bedtimes, chores, church, and sports, for example.

> *The attitude of the parents strongly influences a child's adjustment to a move.*

PROCEDURES FOR PARENTS

Take time to consider what you will need for your own comfort. This will benefit everyone. Make checklists, including medications, books, and other emergency supplies.

For Infants

Babies will be the least affected by a move. It is important to keep them comfortable and maintain their routine as much as possible. If the family is to fly, allow for delays and minimal service. Some infants are very aware of unfamiliar surroundings and need to be held, comforted, and reassured. If the child is greeted by grandparents who are total strangers, do not assume that the child will adjust readily.

Infants may cry a lot, refuse to eat, or require holding as symptoms of the insecurities they are experiencing.

For Toddlers

Tell the child as many of the plans as he or she can understand. Emphasize that the family will be together (if this is the case).

Keep the child with you as much as possible while preparations for the move are being made. If a child is aware that certain things, even pets, will be left behind, he or she may be fearful of the same fate.

Let the child pack a few of his or her most treasured possessions. Keep some out for the trip, whether it is by car or by plane.

Take time to listen to the child's questions and answer as factually as possible. Don't make any false promises such as, "We'll get a new doggy," if this is not what you plan to do.

Arrange for small children to find time to say good-bye to grandparents, friends, babysitters, and other relatives. You may anticipate expressions of anger, sadness, and bewilderment. The child may not use words, but behavior and facial expressions may reveal feelings. Anticipate some problems such as bedwetting, thumbsucking, and unexpected or prolonged crying, disturbed sleep, or refusal to go to preschool.

Elementary School-aged Children

Some persons state that this age group is particularly vulnerable to the unsettling effects of moving, especially for the first time. The child has made adjustments, established his or her place with teachers, other families, activities, sports, and church groups outside the home. Many people and places feel familiar. It is difficult to give them up. Children are not mature enough to anticipate that in a new place there can be happy times ahead. In anticipation of the break, the children may be angry, uncooperative, and stubborn. Some may pretend to be sick so they don't have to leave the house.

Before moving, shy children may become even more shy, aggressive youngsters may signal even more aggressiveness, and you may expect pleas to be close to you. Younger children may start to shadow older siblings, wanting uncharacteristic physical closeness.

Children may ask many questions, seeking answers that no one may be able to give. If possible, share all the facts that you have, such as a picture of the new house or new school. Where once it was considered advisable to move during the summer after school is out, many today recommend the move while schools are still in session, so that there are other children for them to meet immediately. The child isn't marooned in a new neighborhood, and you may predict a lively interest in a mid-term "new kid" in the class.

The Middle-School-aged Child

The promotion from elementary school to middle or junior high school represents a giant step for many boys and girls even when a move isn't involved. They have graduated from the relatively protected environment of a self-contained classroom to impersonal halls and computerized schedules. They feel more independent, more challenged, and more responsible. This attitude may contribute to a cooperative involvement in a family move.

If your child enters middle school at the beginning of the year, he or she may notice immediately that there are lots of others who get lost or feel strange. This helps to give the feeling of being "just like the other kids." School entrance at any other time may be somewhat more difficult for children in this age range. Preteen children are open to meeting new classmates and are usually not as critical and standoffish as many high school students tend to be. For the entering student, this means that if he or she is open and friendly, the chances are that adjustments to school will be relatively easy.

As a parent, show your interest in what is happening at school. Take time to ask questions. If your child adjusts well at school, his or her positive attitude may be contagious at home. If the child has difficulties, take time to go to school and get acquainted with teachers or counselors. The fact that you went to the school, and that you took time to meet the teachers, carries an important message to your boy or girl—*in spite of the mess at home, my parent(s) really cares!*

The Adolescent in the Family of Mobility

High school days are for exploration and discovery. But students want to be in their own bailiwick, protected by the nest called "home."

A move for many high school students represents relinquishment of special friendships, love affairs, special student-teacher relationships, and, for some, the end of special endeavors. They may miss the band concert or won't be able to go to the senior prom. School events may be the most important parts of their lives, and being wrenched away from them may be profoundly unsettling.

Teenagers whose families have been mobile as a way of life may, for the first time, express anger and disappointment at having to move again. Or they may be resigned to the pattern of short-term friendships and outwardly accede to the move, vowing inwardly not to get close to anyone because leaving them is too painful. And why bother to study because chances are school will be interrupted in the middle anyway? The next school will probably be some dumb place where they don't know anything anyway—and so go the sour grapes.

The other side of the coin may be that the adolescent hates

the school he or she is attending now. It is too large, kids are unfriendly, and the teachers disinterested. A move to another school may be a dream come true!

For a teenager, the move may:

- Expedite self-discovery, present ideas to such questions as, "What is most important in my life today?" "How much do I help my parents or my brothers and sisters?"
- Be regarded as a lesson on how to separate from loved ones, as a dress rehearsal for what is ahead at graduation. "Can I manage by myself? I'd better figure out how to keep up communication."
- Be an opportunity to develop new relationships—again, a dress rehearsal for possible dormitory life or meeting people on the job.
- Be an opportunity to put extra effort into academic achievement, to discover that he or she can be successful in any school, that skills and talents don't go away just because you have to move. It can also be a time to face up to deficiencies and what to do about them.

That's a tall order; parent and teacher support is vital. No matter what patterns your adolescent may display, it is important to remember that teenage years are years of rebellion. Mobility may bind the student into family dependency at a time when he or she has been struggling to be free. Displays of outrage are not unusual, along with accusations that parents are cruel, heartless, selfish, or whatever. Parents are still the decision-makers and though their reasons may be unacceptable to the teenager, the plans proceed. Try to get your child's understanding and help. "This too shall pass," is a handy cliché to remember. Talk about the future. Make plans for friends to come and visit. If possible, offer options. In some instances, the teenager might be better off remaining in the old location with a relative or friend for a prescribed time. This can eliminate the pitfalls resulting from leaving a school, loss of friends, or the negative impact the angry teenager may have on brothers and sisters. By listening to what your adolescent wants, and negotiating accordingly, you show respect. When you work together, you make the best of a difficult situation. *Express your thanks and appreciation to teenagers who are cooperative and helpful.*

67.
School Placement

It would be wonderful if every school were to possess all the desirable attributes imaginable. Such is not the case. Nevertheless, all schools have caring teachers (some have more than others). Information about a school district and the local school is obtainable. Parents should be made aware of this and proceed to look at:

- Appearance of the building. Make-up of the pupil population.
- Range of programs (classes for the handicapped, vocational or career guidance, provisions for the gifted and talented, extracurricular activities, outdoor education).
- Class size (twenty-five or under is preferable).
- Services—bus (if needed), breakfast and lunch programs, media center/library, provisions for textbooks and materials, field trips.
- The school's philosophy—open classes, self-contained classes, back-to-basics, individualized learning, methods of discipline, rules, basic attitude. Do the teachers and kids appear happy or dreary?
- Possible dress code.
- Busing considerations. Will the child be bused across town at the same time he or she is trying to adjust to the new house and neighborhood?

Parents should talk to administrators, other parents, and district personnel regarding school. More than one option may be available, and school is so important that it merits more than cursory attention. Because a smooth school placement diminishes stress, take the following steps.

Before the move, try to obtain the following:
- Transfer card or latest report card or transcript
- Birth certificate
- Medical records
- List of textbooks and educational materials used
- Written descriptions of special programs the child may have been in (such as Title I, remedial math, visual-motor training, gifted and talented program)

- Grading method; statement from teachers describing achievement level and interests
- Standard test scores and results of any special testing

When admitting the child to school, the staff should be made aware of past placements and needs. For example, if the child has been in a program for the gifted, a similar type of placement should be requested. Most states have open-record laws guaranteeing parents access to all school records. Don't hesitate to ask. The information can be used to your child's advantage at the time of placement.

Teachers can help transfer students make a smooth transition.

The First Day of School

The first day in a new neighborhood, the child should not be forced to go to school. He or she may need time in the house, time with family, or time to rest. One day, more or less, will not affect learning and may help diminish stress.

On the first day of school, the parent should:
- Accompany the child to school.
- Meet the child's teacher(s).
- Supply the child with basic pencils, papers, and similar items appropriate to his or her grade level.
- Make certain the child knows the way home—what bus to take or what sidewalks lead home. A rehearsal beforehand is a good idea. Point out landmarks such as "the house with the white fence" or "the store on the corner."
- Remind the kids that few schools are ideal, but there is lots to learn and new friendships to be made.

If you should discover that your child is depressed and you believe that this reflects school problems, get in touch with the principal, teacher, or social worker. A teacher may not recognize that the new child is depressed or may have been too busy to notice. He or she may have perceived the child as naturally quiet or withdrawn and will be grateful to you for pointing out the depression. Teachers work on the premise that it takes about six weeks for some children to adjust or perk up, and they may not assess the seriousness of the situation accurately. Parents are urged to be assertive, introducing themselves and the children to the neighbors. One should not wait for the neighbors to reach out. People are not unfriendly and rejecting, just very, very busy keeping up with the demands of everyday life.

Pam, a fifteen-year-old girl, moved to Denver from Columbus, Ohio, with her mother after a divorce, leaving behind an older brother and her father. Her protests never ended. She showed all the indicators of instability.

Several months later, I ran into Pam in a store. She told me that she had gone back to visit in Columbus. All of a sudden, her friends didn't seem close to her anymore. The reunion was fun but disappointing. Then, with a smile, she admitted, "When I got on the plane, I realized I wanted to come home, and home, now, is here." Kids are wonderful, aren't they?

REASSURANCES: GOOD THINGS THAT CAN COME FROM A MOVE

- Family ties are strengthened. "We may be in a new house, but we are still a family."
- The child feels competent. "It was hard to leave, but I've made new friends already."
- The child may have to be more independent. "I used to have to depend on mom for everything. Here, she has to work, so I do more things for myself."
- The child and the whole family may take time to talk about what's most important in their lives, or their values. "Living in Denver was neat, but I like this place better because it is so much smaller. People are friendlier," or "We were the only black family in that neighborhood, and occasionally that was hard for us. In this racially diverse area, the kids seem much happier."

- A chance to see new sights, meet new people, and learn what's unique. "I never heard of grits before. Since we've been living here, we eat them every day," or "I'd only seen mountains on TV, and here they are right in our own backyard."
- A move gives parents a clearer picture of the child's personality, coping style, and needs. "In the old house, I was too busy to notice that Alice is afraid of dogs and stays by herself a lot. Now that we have a smaller house and less housework to do, I can spend more time with Alice. This is enjoyable for both of us," or "I never imagined that Jenny would be so unhappy about moving. At least now we can talk about our feelings."

Part V

THE DOWNSIDE OF INSTABILITY
INSTABILITY SIGNALS A CRY FOR HELP

SOME CHILDREN CANNOT withstand the onslaught of chronic instability or recover from terrorizing, destructive tragic events. They may be especially vulnerable to upsets for an assortment of reasons—health, temperament, past history, impaired bonding, or others. No one is to blame. There is no objective, scientific way to determine precisely what went wrong. What we do know is the children must have help.

This part is concerned with the child whose history of instability has resulted in serious dysfunction, delinquency, or emotional illness. It includes suicide issues, the habitual liar, the child who steals, the child addict, and the child in crisis. Important information about professional therapy is described. The many guidelines and suggestions for parents are offered in order to help support an optimistic approach, balanced with a realistic appreciation of the price some children pay when instability saturates their lives.

17

Help for Children Who Hurt

LIFE ISN'T ALWAYS FAIR. Some babies never feel wanted and secure. They are deprived of the bonds that denote trust and safety. Their symptoms of instability make them sad and frightened. They don't have a chance to become stable unless, when school age or older, they are provided intensive, long-term therapy. I call them *Children Who Hate.*

Other youngsters may feel bonded, but experiences or personal problems undermine their stability. Certain strengths survive and traces of self-esteem provide enough stability that the children learn in school, may have friends, and may cope quite well with difficulties at home. However, their signs of instability signal a cry for support. Their trust in adults needs repair, their self-esteem needs a boost, or they are feeling overwhelmed by what's going on in their lives. I call them *Children Who Hurt.* These children can benefit from a series of brief, purposeful, one-to-one talks with a caring adult. Both their trust in adults and their self-esteem may improve measurably. *They do not require long-term therapy.* Such a program is described in detail in Appendix A.

It is important to distinguish between *Children Who Hurt* and *Children Who Hate.* Their symptoms may overlap, but frequent observations help to evaluate the depth of instability.

INDICATORS OF INSTABILITY

Children Who Hurt: low self-esteem children who need support	**Children Who Hate: critically unstable children who need therapy**
Immature	Cruel, callous, not *able* to empathize
Able to empathize	
Impaired ability to memorize and concentrate	Seek rejection as a way of life
	Lose touch with reality (may be multiple personalities)
Poor self-concept	
Occasionally tell lies, steal	Profoundly depressed, require medicine, hospitalization, or institutional support
Destroy property	
Some impulsive, manipulative behavior	Habitual liars, kleptomaniacs
Under control most of the time	Danger to self or others
	May be suicidal, explosive or isolated, withdrawn

A Trust-Building Program for Children Who Hurt

The Trust-Building Program is designed for Children Who Hurt. Parents may want to be informed about the program just as they want information about child therapies. This program is designed for teachers, counselors, youth workers, foster parents—someone outside the family. In addition to understanding how the Trust-Building Program works, it is important that parents be supportive—even if it means making special transportation arrangements or reserving the home telephone for your child's scheduled telephone appointments.

The success of the program depends on a warm adult-child relationship that develops though the contacts are limited to twice a week for eight to ten weeks. This is a *short-term program.* Do not consider your child's relationship with another adult as a threat to your parent-child relationship. It is not a rejection of you. On the contrary, the parent-child relationship may benefit because the purpose of the trust-building meetings is to strengthen self-esteem. With improved self-esteem, a child will be more stable and can relate to you in a more steadfast way.

> *If your child needs a boost, it does not mean you have failed. Many things contribute to instability.*

Intensive therapy for Children Who Hate is in the domain of trained professionals, psychiatrists, psychologists, social workers, and some counselors—often offered in a residential setting or in connection with a hospital, clinic, or detention facility. Outpatient long-term therapy can be successful as well.

THREE SERIOUS SYMPTOMS OF CHILDREN WHO HATE

In my years as a child therapist, there were three indicators, among others, that were relatively easy to observe and portrayed a potential for serious troubles ahead. These boys and girls may be regarded as *victims* of unstable parenting. They represent the downside of instability. These were the child who lies habitually, the child who steals, and the child addict.

68.
The Habitual Liar

Little Cissy comes home from school and tells her mother that her teacher shoved her. Her mother is sympathetic. She is also irate. Cissy explains that Billy was behind her in line and pulled her hair. She jumped out of the line to escape him and her teacher shoved her. A plausible story, but it was totally untrue.

Cissy is a habitual liar. She makes up stories on a daily basis. She tells tales about her mom and dad, too. She is in fourth grade. Her parents and her teachers have the attitude, "There she goes again," yet they react in protective ways. "That teacher is mean," dad comments to mom. "Those mean parents," the teacher remarks to herself. No one confronts Cissy. Cissy is in trouble. Her habitual lying is a sign of marked unhappiness, a hallmark of instability.

Most children up to six years of age have wonderful imaginations. They learn the game of, "I can do that, too!" or "My dad is president of an airline!"—something fantastic or glamorous that has nothing to do with reality. They learn to play "let's pretend." They tell stories that are real to them, based on dreams, fantasy, or TV. When a parent or an older brother says, "That's baloney," they are bewildered. Yet unhappy, unstable children as young as five can become habitual liars, fully aware that they *are* lying. They may give any answer that pops into their heads; to them credibility is not an issue. *Or they may have learned to protect themselves or someone else by covering up the truth or denying what has happened.* The habitual liar is displaying marked insecurity, fear, and severely damaged self-esteem.

> *The main reason children of all ages tell lies is fear. They are afraid if they tell the truth, they will be punished. Sometimes they are afraid parents or other important adults will stop loving them. The habitual liar endures nonstop anxiety.*

Telling lies is a bad habit. When the child is prone to blurt out an answer, a defense, with the hope that others will not question the truth, every tale is clouded with uncertainty. This creates anxiety. The child needs to remember what story he or she told about what situation to cover his or her tracks, and that's hard to do. Children really don't care. They believe that a reckless answer isn't going to make things better or worse. There is no reason to be honest.

Parents must confront lies. Many will simply say, "Hey, I don't believe you." Others may try to get the child to confess or even make a joke of it. "Better luck next time, Buddy!" They may or may not discipline the child. They may talk about trust and occasionally make threats such as, "The next time you lie to me, I'll wash your mouth out with soap." Threats and punishments are to no avail. The child who has become a habitual liar feels boxed in. "If I lie, I'll be in trouble; if I tell the truth (I did throw the snowball) I'll be in trouble too." When they learn to value themselves, they will value the truth. Children need help before they can stop lying.

PROCEDURES FOR PARENTS

In conjunction with the therapy that is required, these procedures for parents may be helpful.

- *Don't ask for confessions or explanations about events when you already know the truth.* You know that Jim knocked the plant off the table or Helen got into trouble on the school bus. Forget the confession and confront the behavior. The pathological liar may appear to be immune to consequences, but parents must not ignore blatant lies.
- Do not be manipulated by lies. Make certain there is no payoff for being a liar. Commend children for admitting to lies. Children must understand that you will question what they say. Work together to establish interactions that can be handled truthfully. "Thanks for telling me that you put the mail on the table. I like it when you tell me the truth."
- Take time to consider what you may be doing that contributes to the child's sense of insecurity. Is the discipline in your house too severe? Does this child feel unloved? Does this child use lies to compete with others? Could this child be lying to cover up for someone else? Does this child tell lies to cover up deep feelings of inferiority?

Your answers indicate changes that need to be made. Confer with a professional. Counseling may extend to all members of the family.

Pathological liars have an intense need for people to like them.

69.
The Child Who Steals

Your preschooler is not doomed to be a lifelong thief if he or she slips a nickel out of your purse. Most children do not distinguish between the nickel on the kitchen table and the cookie on the counter; they are equally available. An older child who steals habitually displays significant indicators of instability.

You may have tried punishing this child for stealing but to no avail, or perhaps you have made up excuses such as, "He is such a loving child, but he does help himself to things that don't belong to him. I do wish he would just ask." This may sound soft and loving, but this child is a thief and cannot stop by himself. This child is called a kleptomaniac.

It is important to notice *what* the child steals and *from whom.* A little girl I worked with always took things that were soft—stuffed animals from stores, baby blankets, or wool scarves. She was telling the world, "I need affection. I need to be held and cuddled." Not all children give such clear messages.

Young children steal for a variety of complex reasons:
- Poor self-esteem runs their lives.
- They have no regard for the property of others.
- They crave love. Possessions make them feel better—at least temporarily.
- They need food, clothes, money—the things that they steal.
- They want to get caught to get attention or to have someone set limits.
- It is the only thing they do that makes them feel successful.

Older children have additional reasons for stealing:
- They are subject to peer pressure.
- They discount social pressures and values.
- They are thrill-seekers.
- They need to support a habit such as drugs.
- They want to emulate a hero.

By the time a child becomes a confirmed thief, the problem is beyond parental influence and control. Home punishment has had no long-lasting effect. The child's basic needs are still not being met. Ongoing instability in this child's life forces him or her to adopt an unsuccessful, antisocial coping style, one that is potentially self-destructive.

When you become aware of this serious problem, *do something immediately. To do nothing is to condone.* Seek help. Authors in the past have suggested that stealing is a symptom of a character disorder and have been pessimistic about how effective therapy might be. I am convinced that significant therapy plus well-managed behavior modification programs can help some young persons learn, accept, and use socially acceptable ways to ask for love, approval, and acceptance. I realize that few offenders have the opportunity to get intensive help. Many do not come from middle-class or affluent families where costly therapy or admission to residential treatment is possible.

Many young thieves get in trouble with the law. If your child should be apprehended, remember that parental support is essential. It does not mean that you condone the behavior when you back your kids but it does convey the important message that you care about them. Everyone will be embarrassed and upset. The work ahead will focus on building self-esteem and breaking a disastrous habit.

70.
The Child Addict

Many kids today are hooked on drugs and alcohol. There are more than five hundred thousand teenage alcoholics. Unlike so many other reactions to stress, physical, emotional, and mental processes are harmed by the use of drugs. More important, few persons can go cold turkey and recover from these habits by themselves. They need to have someone help them accept that they have a problem, guide them into recovery, and stand by them as they go through a difficult treatment regime. They must understand that they are ruining their lives.

> *One hundred twenty-five thousand elementary-school-aged children get drunk at least once a week.*

Drugs are available in any city. They are a bit more difficult to acquire in some rural settings. Nevertheless, alcohol can be found anywhere. Why have these children (and there are now many alcoholics in the fifth and sixth grades) become addicts? In most cases, they learn from the other kids. Peer persuasion is immeasurable. Addicted parents are setting bad examples for their children. Many have had to make a series of adjustments and for one reason or another became vulnerable. They were introduced to drugs as the emotional painkiller. (Refer to *Living with an Alcoholic Parent*, page 148.)

Whether rich or poor, child addicts are exhibiting self-defeating behavior. Next to suicide, there is no more dramatic way to exhibit that they are not maturing appropriately and that they are acquiring habits that will only produce more instability. For example, the person with an addiction cannot relate to others with honest feelings. When feelings are distorted, relationships will be erratic and unsatisfactory. This agenda is inescapable unless the person is off drugs.

> *Parents hurt when their children hurt. Parents are a child's main defense against the pressures of a drug culture. It is hard to remember that kids start on drugs because they think it is cool. It may or may not be rebellion against parents.*

PROCEDURES FOR PARENTS

What parents can do? *If uncertain that the problem exists:*
- Observe your child. Look for changes. Note the hours he or she keeps, attitude about school, appetite, and appearance.
- Talk to your child and note if he or she acts muddled, inconsistent, unduly irritable, or complains about unhappy relationships.
- Express your concern. Tell what you have observed. Don't pretend that you don't notice things or that you will stay with the, "That's just kids (adolescents)" approach. Confront inappropriate behaviors. State your expectations. See if the behaviors improve.

When certain that your child is an addict:
- Do not assume that the child will stop of his or her own accord. You must be convinced this is so and that it is now too late to lecture and cajole.
- Take action. Consult your physician, the school counselor, or whoever will help you find a place where your child can get help.
- Make certain your child understands you are not helpless. You are the family manager. You are free to talk about your

concerns or your intentions and plans to get help. If necessary, this may include law enforcement people. Do not be persuaded by arguments such as, "Oh, mom, I know you'd never do that!" or "You really don't love me, do you?"

- Be aware that any limits or punishment you now propose are after the fact. Action must be geared to stopping the habit and promoting emotional and personal recovery.
- *Be a model of responsible behavior.* If you continue to drink or smoke marijuana, this may discourage children from treatment. If you use pills, such as antidepressants or sleeping pills, be certain you know why. Do your habits with so-called legal drugs (and alcohol is a legal drug) give you credibility?
- Don't look for appreciation from your child. There may be months of fury and rejection of you.

The child in recovery needs your support. *You have identified the problem. You have taken action. You must stay involved.*

Recovery from substance abuse is very difficult. Prevention is a much better course to take. Prevention *must focus on your ability to take an* in-charge *position with your children and stick to it. Be relentless—insist your children be drug free.*

71.
The Child in Crisis

Crisis behavior is a breakdown or severe reaction to ongoing family instability or a traumatic event. In a crisis, the person who is upset cannot picture a happy outcome. This is terrifying.

A crisis, whether an accident or a sudden, dangerous display of uncontrolled emotions, fractures stability. Although many parents may have witnessed serious indicators of instability, they are surprised when a crisis occurs. "I never imagined that Dick was so upset," or "I guess I never noticed that Marie was depressed, and now she's attempted suicide!" Use the crisis as a springboard to repair or start to *change what needs to be changed,* after the child has been given immediate and significant support.

You may ask, "Did this kid run away or deliberately kill the cat just to get to me?" Perhaps the answer is yes, in part. Whatever the reason behind a crisis episode or event, I implore you to see the child's desperation and show love. This may be difficult. Your stability is suffering. Don't blame yourself. Parents do the best they can and are sometimes understandably overwhelmed.

You may rationalize that teenage girls are naturally emotional and impulsive. You consider an episode (such as bursting out of the school building, cursing a teacher, or destroying her notebooks) as something that will pass. Most teenage girls, however, do not resort to crisis behaviors. Any crisis—for girls or boys—denotes intense, overwhelming frustration, defeat, or fear.

What brings on a crisis?
- Family problems, such as an announced divorce
- Termination of a friendship or love affair
- Death of someone important
- School stress—exams ahead
- A humiliating incident, such as a poor athletic performance or a temper tantrum witnessed by others
- Anxiety overload—money, illness, family problems, all combined
- Reaction to drug or alcohol use
- Peer pressure, gang power, or a breaking away from them
- Fear of pregnancy, venereal disease, herpes, AIDS

Take Charge!!!*

These suggestions may be helpful:
- Take care of any emergency. Make necessary decisions.
- Focus on the problem, not the person. Avoid name-calling.
- Listen to what your teen has to say. *This is not a time for lectures or preaching. Kids can be very hard on themselves when they make a mistake.*
- Don't humiliate anyone. Embarrassment adds stress to an already stressful situation.
- Vent your anger appropriately. *Don't invoke punishment that you may regret later.*

---

*Ruth P. Arent, *Take Time To Talk*, Littleton, CO: Arent & Associates, 1992.

- Avoid statements like, "I'll never trust you again." A crisis which results from immaturity or poor judgment *does not indicate that teen-parent trust is in trouble.* A teen may not have respected your judgment or values—that is part of learning to be independent.
- Don't use a crisis as a reason to pry into the teen's other affairs if they are not related (for example, if a teen is caught shoplifting, this does not give a parent license to ask personal questions about sexual interests.)
- *Avoid self-pity.* "Why did you do this to me?" is an inappropriate question. *Kids do what they do to please themselves—not to make you angry.* Disastrous decisions are determined by many influences.
- Don't look for appreciation. That may have to come later.
- Accept surliness or short tempers. They are only symptoms that the teen is upset.

Keep in mind the benefits of hospitalization. Short-term hospitalization (a few days) gives the patient time to calm down, be away from home, receive medicine if necessary, feel safe and be evaluated, and dry out, if drugs are involved. Short-term hospitalization helps the entire family understand the seriousness of the breakdown and the need to discover the sources of the instability.

When a crisis occurs, your job as a parent is to provide immediate, unconditional support.

—Joel and Lois Davitz

Listen to what the child has to say. Maybe all the child asks is for someone to take the time to be involved in his or her turmoil. After a crisis is over, make certain that your communication encourages frank sharing in order to prevent further episodes. (See *Therapy Is a Must,* page 304.)

72.
Suicide: The Choice with No Return

There is no more dramatic way for a child to show instability than to attempt or commit suicide. Everyone who has known the child feels guilty. The universal question is, "What could I have done?"

Childhood suicide (children under twelve) is a rare occurrence, but it is becoming more prevalent. In the seventeen to twenty-five age group, it is second only to automobile accidents as a cause of death. Over fifty-five hundred suicides were reported in 1992. At least four times as many youths reported considering or attempting suicide. The reason: stress can be overwhelming; hopelessness can take over. What more startling way is there to cope with stress than to attempt to end life? *It is the ultimate display of hostility, grief, despair, and instability.*

Young Children

Many young children who commit suicide never acquired stability—were never bonded. Such children:
- Had a history of feeling unwanted
- Felt worthless and unloved
- Recently (within three months) lost someone close, usually by accident or suicide
- Were failures in school
- Lived in a stress-saturated environment with emotionally unstable parents; often encountered violence at home and had strained relationships
- Had a history of foster homes, or adultless homes, or dependence on immature older siblings for care
- Were frequently exposed to pills and drugs
- Intended to die; did not harbor the hope that they would be rescued
- Planned to commit suicide; gave away toys, pets, made elaborate preparations

Most children who take their own lives hang themselves or take a drug overdose. Some use guns. The suicides are almost always a total surprise to the family, though afterward, the loss of a loved one may be the ascribed reason. Frequently, these children have had a series of losses in their lives—through abandonment, by parental separation and divorce, and perhaps subsequent loss of one or two stepparents.

We also read a very different picture of seemingly well-adjusted, motivated, middle-class youngsters who kill themselves. They may have known family turmoil, but outward appearances indicated that they had made reasonable adjustments. Something triggered momentary despair, irrational behavior, or rage. The unknown explanations add to the stress of the survivors.

Suicidal Teenagers

Not all who attempt suicide want to die. Many teenage girls, in particular, take pills to manipulate others. The message is, "If someone sees how desperate I am, I will get what I want." This message may apply to boyfriends, parents, or rules in school. Unfortunately, some of these attempts are successful and fatal. Unlike most of the younger children, teenage suicidal behavior is often impulsive, showing up in one-car auto accidents or drug overdoses. Many are high or drunk. Suicide among Native American youths is a major source of concern to tribal and community leaders. It is frequently blamed on the conflict between tribal and nontribal lifestyles and the struggle to adjust to two cultures. Unemployed black youths constitute the largest group of adolescents who take their own lives. They were unable to visualize a happy, productive future.

The most common reasons for teenage suicidal behaviors are:
- Intolerable, bleak uncertainty about the future: a job, family, car, or spouse; hopelessness
- Feelings of inadequacy
- Feelings of alienation from parents or others; an attitude that "no one cares"
- A divorce in the family
- Cumulative frustration resulting from neighborhood problems, such as slum conditions
- A history of learning disabilities (dyslexia, for example)
- A specific emotional blow, such as poor grades in school, loss of a girlfriend or boyfriend, a minor car accident
- Depression following a drug episode
- The recent loss or death of an important relative, friend, or public hero
- Lack of an adult model for an appropriate coping style; inappropriate adult models

- Utter frustration, among the more gifted, at being unable to change depressing world conditions such as starvation or poverty
- Sexual conflicts and anxiety

There are four kinds of death: natural, accidental, homicide, and suicide. Suicide is the most lethal in terms of effect on survivors.

PROCEDURES FOR PARENTS

Remain alert! Note:
- Remarks such as, "I wish I were dead."
- Marked personality changes (for example, from outgoing to withdrawn).
- Prolonged depression.
- Inability to sleep or sleeping too much.
- Marked change in school performance.
- Indications of putting things in order; giving away prized possessions, comments such as, "Take care of my dog."
- Conversation about suicide or death that indicates prolonged interest or overconcern.
- Unresolved grief; frequent visits to a cemetery; repeated expressions of guilt, emptiness.
- Severe reactions to family disruption or a move to a new place; a sense of aloneness or of having no friends.
- Unabated fury about something. "I'll get back at you; just you wait and see!"

Should you observe such symptoms, please:
1. Listen.
2. Do not chide, scoff, belittle, or joke about the child's feelings.
3. Ask direct questions such as, "Are you thinking of hurting yourself?" A child contemplating suicide may get significant relief by having a chance to talk over fears or despair. Rest assured, you are not planting the idea in the mind of a person under severe stress.
4. If a person is threatening suicide, try to determine whether

he or she has a plan. What, if any, method is mentioned (pills, gun, car, rope, carbon monoxide)? The more detailed a plan, the higher the risk. Be direct. "Flush those pills down the toilet now!" "Give me that gun now."

5. Involve a "significant other"—a friend, teacher, coach, or counselor—*but do solicit help.* Talk to the person in crisis. Be positive. *Find nice things to say;* the upset, depressed child may reject these words, but they must be said repeatedly.

6. Use community services, hotlines, and similar programs.

All suicidal persons are ambivalent. Part of them wants to die, but even the most severely depressed persons cling to some hope that things will get better. *This hope must be uncovered and nurtured.* Emphasizing the hope, plus your directives and persistent involvement, may help the person through the crisis. The cry for help has been heeded.

18

Therapy Is a Must for Critically Unstable Children

ARE THERE MORE CHILDREN who display mental illness today? And is that because people are more aware of signs or as a result of commercial promotions for hospitalization? Regardless of the reason, *it is a fact that some disturbed, unstable children need a protective hospital environment, especially adolescent addicts.* They may require medicine, supervision, structure, individual, and/or group therapy and a reprieve from a dysfunctional, damaging home situation. Further, they may need to be in a place where they can dry out from drugs or alcohol, recover physically, and be launched into a treatment program for the repair of self-esteem and improvement of coping skills.

Living in unstable times can be overwhelming for everyone. Don't wait for a crisis to consider asking for help. If a crisis or breakdown should occur when your child displays indicators of exaggerated instability, an evaluation is essential. Hospitalization may be recommended (or, in some cases, ordered by the courts).

The thought of your child requiring a stay in a mental hospital may be heartbreaking or devastating—a final declaration that one has failed as a parent. Do not equate a child in treatment with parental failure. There are *multiple reasons* a child falls apart and/or becomes an addict. Nevertheless, parental distress is real. The decision to hospitalize a child is painful.

There are three important sentences for every parent to read and memorize:

Be proud of your decision to use help.
It is a difficult decision.
It reflects your good judgment and maturity.

This positive support position needs to be repeated many times. It may abet the child's recovery because it provides validation to the parents.

In the course of long-term therapy, a child may develop a close, meaningful relationship with a therapist or other staff member, and parents may feel displaced or envious. Parents are urged to reflect on the part they play in the decision to use hospitalization and *be proud* that the child is benefiting from the experience. Almost without exception, this would not have occurred without the parental decision. Parental attitude is pivotal to the child's attitude. As stated, don't wait for a crisis to consider therapy. Try to remain aware of your child's indicators of instability and ask others to evaluate them, too. You can also be certain that when you are upset, the children will react—an echo of the phrase that *instability can be a contagious disease!*

Family therapy is no longer taboo. It emphasizes family strengths, family confidence, and family wellness. It doesn't deal with blame but how to solve problems.

It takes hard work.

It can provide useful, specific suggestions on how to handle situations. The self-esteem of children and parents may benefit.

Let go of any "embarrassment" or "fear" you may have. Open your minds and hearts to finding new ways to develop or enrich mutual respect.

Goals of Therapy

Whether in an office, detention center, juvenile hall, drug center, or school for offenders, the therapy must be structured to:
- Establish or repair at least one important adult-child relationship. The child must be convinced that one person really cares. Without this belief, there will be little motivation to cooperate, change, or grow up.
- Help a child get through a severe crisis or a breakdown. Treatments may include medication, hospitalization with twenty-four hour supervision, or temporary placement in a mental health facility or foster home. It may call for advice in solving such problems as an unwanted pregnancy, threats to run away, peer fights, or irrational anger. Parental involvement will vary.
- Restore a sense of self-discipline and responsibility, a sense of impulse control.
- Improve the family system.
- Help the child emancipate or change his or her life circumstances if the family system will not work.

Often a parent wants to know what a therapist really does with a child. Therapists work on the theory that what goes on in the office cannot and will not be disclosed. Without violating confidentiality, a therapist may share basic concepts. By being informed of concepts and goals, a parent can relate to how difficult and complex therapy really is. It may also be painful for a child and the parents. The therapist will have to help the child to:
- Trust the therapist. This entails confidentiality, availability, and the freedom to express feelings. This takes time and patience. It will be tested.
- Take responsibility to control himself or herself in the office. "You may not hurt me, you may not hurt yourself."
- Tell the truth. "I do not accept lies in this office."
- Put aside self-pity. Develop a philosophy that almost every child experiences rough times in growing up.
- Come in drug free. "If you are stoned, you are wasting my time and your money." This is essential in order to stay reality-oriented and be able to think clearly.
- Transfer a lot of anger from the parent to the therapist so that the child can let go of it.

- Accept that he or she can be a fine person, even when at odds with parents. Acknowledge friendships.
- Recognize where fears and feelings originate; view parental attitudes and treatment with objectivity.
- Acknowledge some positive things the parents have done on his or her behalf.
- Accept the parents' faults without having to emulate them.
- Set goals for self and be open to suggestions on how to achieve them. "Get a job," or "Go get your high school equivalency certificate," or "Move in with a friend."
- Lean less on parents for support and strive to become independent.
- Accept that perhaps he or she is more mature than one or both parents. This needs careful explanation because it may result in further parent-child alienation.

If your youngster has been unhappy at home and your relationship has been difficult for some time, a decision for the child to be *away from home for a protracted period of time* may be the decision most beneficial for all. Adolescents do pull away. Your child may need placement away to help his or her thrust toward independence.

The parent-child relationship never ends. Being apart may be an important phase intended to stabilize the situation. It is an expeditious plan indicated for this family, this child, at this time.

FINAL REASSURANCES

Kids are resilient. Tens of thousands of kids benefit each year from sensitive, skillful, professional help. Keep aware of what's happening if you can, and stay involved in ways that may prepare these kids for improved mutual respect and stability in the years to come.

Bibliography

Abrams, Richard S., M.D. *Will It Hurt the Baby?* Reading, MA: Addison-Wesley, 1990.

Ackerman, Robert S. *Children of Alcoholics, A Guide for Parents, Educators and Therapists*, 2nd edition. New York: Simon & Schuster, 1987.

Arent, Ruth P. *Take Time To Talk, A Plan for Parent-Teen Communication.* Littleton, CO: Arent & Associates, 1992.

Brazelton, T. Berry, M.D. *Families: Crisis and Caring.* Reading, MA: Addison-Wesley, 1989.

Clarke, Jean Illsley. *Self-Esteem: A Family Affair.* San Francisco: Harper, Collins, 1978.

Cline, Foster and Jim Fay. *Parenting with Love and Logic.* Colorado Springs, CO: Navpress, 1990.

Coles, Robert. *The Spiritual Life of Children.* Boston: Houghton Mifflin Co., 1990.

Colfax, David and Nicki. *Homeschooling for Excellence.* New York: Warner Books, 1988.

Collins, Emily. *The Whole Single Person's Catalog.* New York: Peebles Press International, Inc., 1979.

Coons, John E. and Stephen D. Sugarman. *Education by Choice.* Berkeley: University of California Press, 1978.

Davis, Deborah. *Empty Cradle, Broken Heart.* Golden, CO: Fulcrum Publishing, 1991.

Elkind, David. *Miseducation, Preschoolers at Risk.* New York: Alfred A. Knopf, 1987.

Faber, Adele and Elaine Mazlish. *Siblings Without Rivalry.* New York: Avon Books, 1987.

Fontana, Vincent, M.D., and Valerie Moolman. *Save the Family, Save the Child.* New York: E. P. Dutton, 1991.

Friedrich, Elizabeth. *The Parent's Guide to Raising Twins.* New York: St. Martins Press, 1984.

Frith, Terry. *Secrets Parents Should Know About Public Schools.* New York: Simon & Schuster, 1985.

Gesell, Arnold and Frances L. Ilg. *The Child From Five to Ten.* New York: Harper and Bros., 1946.

Goldberg. Ronald. *Sit Down and Pay Attention: Coping with Attention-Deficit Disorder Throughout the Life Cycle.* Washington, DC: The PIA Press, 1991.

Gordon, Sol, Ph.D., and Judith Gordon, M.S.W. *Raising a Child Conservatively in a Sexually Permissive World.* New York: Simon and Schuster, 1986.

Gritter, J. *Adoption Without Fear.* San Antonio, TX: Corona Publishing, 1989.

Harrison, Helen. *The Premature Baby Book.* New York: St. Martins Press, 1983.

Hewlett, Sylvia Ann. *When the Bough Breaks, The Cost of Neglecting Our Children.* New York: Harper Perennial, 1992.

Isaacs, Marla B., B. Montalvo, and D. Abelsohn. *The Difficult Divorce: Therapy for Children and Families.* New York: Basic Books, 1992.

Jones, Clare B. *Sourcebook for Children with Attention Deficit Disorder.* Tucson, AZ: Communication Skill Builders, 1991.

Kappelman, Murray, M., M.D., and Paul R. Ackerman. *Parents After Thirty.* New York: PEI Books, 1980.

Kelley, Marquerite and Elia Parsons. *The Mothers' Almanac,* revised edition. New York: Doubleday, 1992.

Kozol, Jonathan. *Rachel and Her Children: Homeless Families in America.* New York: Crown Publishers, 1988.

Krementz, Jill. *How It Feels When a Parent Dies.* New York: Alfred A. Knopf, 1981.

Kubler-Ross, E. *On Death and Dying.* New York: Macmillan, 1969.

Kuzma, Kay. *Working Mothers.* New York: Harper and Row, 1980.

Matthews, Andrew. *Being Happy! A Handbook to Greater Confidence and Security.* Los Angeles: Price Stern Sloan, 1988.

Morse, Melvin, M. D., with Paul Perry. *Closer to the Light.* New York: Ivy Books, 1990.

Neifert, Marianne. *Dr. Mom's Parenting Guide.* New York: Signet, 1987.

Noble, Elizabeth. *Having Twins*, Second edition. New York: Houghton Mifflin, 1991.

Plutzik, Roberta and Maria Laghi. *The Private Life of Parents.* New York: Everest House Publishers, 1983.

Poe, Leonara M. *Black Grandparents as Parents.* Berkeley, CA: 2034 Blake St.,1992.

Rando, T. *Parental Loss of a Child.* Champaign, IL: Research Press, 1986.

Reed, Ronald F. *Talking with Children.* Denver, CO: Arden Press, 1983.

Rhodes, Sonya, D.S.W., with Josleen Wilson. *Surviving Family Life.* New York: G. P. Putnam's Sons, 1981.

Rubin, Theodore Isaac. *Not to Worry, The American Family Book of Mental Health.* New York: The Viking Press, 1984.

Schaffer, H. Rudolph. *Making Decisions About Children, Psychological Questions and Answers.* Cambridge, MA: Basil Blackwell LTD, 1990.

Shreve, Anita. *Remaking Motherhood, How Working Mothers are Shaping Our Children's Future.* New York: Fawcett Columbine, 1988.

Silber, K. and P. Speedlin. *Dear Birthmother.* San Antonio, TX: Corona Publishing, 1989.

Silber, Kathleen and Patricia Martinez Darner. *Children of Open Adoption.* San Antonio, TX: Corona Publishing,1990.

Silver, Larry B., M.D. *The Misunderstood Child, A Guide for Parents of Learning Disabled Children.* New York: McGraw-Hill, 1984.

Silverman, P. *Help Women Cope With Grief.* Beverly Hills, CA: Sage Publications, 1981.

Smith, Manuel J., Ph.D. *Yes, I Can Say No, A Parents Guide to Assertiveness Training for Children.* New York: Arbor House, 1986.

Sullivan, S. Adams. *The Fathers' Almanac,* revised edition. New York: Doubleday, 1992.

Varenhorst, Barbara S. *Real Friends.* San Francisco: Harper and Row, 1983.

Vine, Phyllis. *Families in Pain.* New York: Pantheon Books, 1982.

Ware, Ciji. *Sharing Parenthood After Divorce.* New York: Bantam Books, 1984.

Weiner-Davis, Michele. *Divorce Busting: A Revolutionary and Rapid Program for Staying Together.* New York: Summit Books, 1992.

Appendix A

A Trust Building Program

ABSTRACTED FROM the detailed guidebook, *Trust Building With Children Who Hurt,** the facts and protocol of the program are as follows.

Purpose: To build a child's self-esteem through a series of sixteen to twenty brief one-to-one meetings or talks. Meetings range from ten to twenty minutes—no longer—and are protected by confidentiality.

Protocol: Each session has five parts.

1. Initial greeting: warm, cordial—not to rehash the past or refer to specific problems (personal, family, or academic).

2. Adult will talk about self, using good judgment and common sense; self-disclosure denotes respect and humanism. This will model openness since some parents do not tell their children about personal history, feelings, hopes, talents, dreams, and the like. It helps build trust.

---

*Trust Building with Children Who Hurt, Ruth P. Arent, M.A., M.S.W. © 1992. Reprinted by permission of the publisher, The Center for Applied Research in Education/A division of Simon & Schuster, West Nyack, New York.

3. Subject matter selected by the adult or the child. In the course of sixteen meetings, the adult will introduce the importance of honesty and facts, limits, dependency, managing what you do and say (Stop!, Think!, and Choose!), social skills and separations. Children may introduce whatever they choose. Some children are more verbal or expressive when free to handle clay, crayons, sand, pipe cleaners, or paints while talking.

4. Affirmations. The child will learn to recognize and accept *good* things about self *and* verbalize them. "I deserve friends." When self-initiated and frequently repeated, positive concepts become believable—are internal—not phony.

5. Reminder of next meeting or appointment. A commitment is not a commitment without a plan. A child's self-esteem benefits from knowing the adult has put aside time especially for him or her. This builds respect and trust.

Other Features of the Program

There are written activities, sheets the kids can enjoy filling out—no pressure; handwriting and spelling don't count.

There is a chart to record the improvements that take place. This chart is called a "Struggles Chart." Affirmations can be scribbled on each sheet as well.

Bud is an eight-year-old who hurts. His father deserted the family when he was three months old. He has welcomed two stepfathers and wept when each one said good-bye. His relationship with his mother has weathered her problems with the men in her life. Her concern for Bud, an awareness of his sweetness and his alert mind, and a fervent drive to have him succeed in school have not wavered. But Bud feels that Mom is unpredictable, her temper is scary, and lately she's been drinking a lot. Because of her schedules as a nurse and part-time cosmetics salesperson, she isn't available very much, and Bud thinks she is selfish. She has provided a home and encouragement but no closeness, affection, or good humor. He doesn't trust her to care. He doesn't trust any adult. He does well in school and this masks his loneliness and fears. He needs one adult to make him feel important. *He is not a candidate for long-term therapy.*

In a series of meetings, the child is helped to *stop* saying or doing things that are unfriendly or inappropriate, *think* of his options or choices, and *choose* the best one. This is behavior management. "I didn't swear at Henry today. I'm learning control. Pretty good for an eight-year-old man," Bud announced. This elevates self-esteem. His teacher, whom he sees after school on Wednesdays and talks with on the phone on Fridays from 4:15 to 4:30, repeatedly coaches him, and he's beginning to trust that she really cares.

At the beginning, the adult tells the child, "We'll only talk together about sixteen times," so that the child will not anticipate long-term dependency. When the time approaches to end the meetings (three or four more to go), the adult and child will discuss how they are feeling (both will be a bit sad) and review all the good things that have happened. Children take improved self-esteem with them wherever they go—even home where things may be uncaring or disturbed. The ability to choose not to misbehave or be inappropriate supports the new sense of competency. Devotion to the helping adult spells *trust.*

Stability is the goal; *learning to trust is step one.*

Appendix B

Too Many Experts Undermine Parental Self-Confidence

PARENTS ARE BOMBARDED by books—each intended to be helpful. I feel sad when I read a book entitled *What Did I Do Wrong? Mothers, Children, Guilt* (Lynn Caine) or *Why Good Parents Have Bad Kids* (E. Kent Hayes) or *Perfect Women—Daughters Who Love Their Mother but Don't Love Themselves* (Colette Dowling) or *Mothers Who Love Too Much* (Anne F. Grizzle).

The negative titles bother me, although each book is practical and constructive. The negative titles can create self-doubt and guilt. I prefer descriptions that convey a positive message and project optimism.

Parents can recite their weaknesses. Each of us was short-tempered after a no-sleep night when Bobby was teething or Mary had the chicken pox. You are urged to practice the fine art of giving yourself pats on the back *and to pick and choose sections of the guidebooks* that are useful—but good old common sense may be your best friend of all.

A Collection of Reassurances for You

- A child's self-esteem is determined by an accumulation of life experiences and relationships.

- Children will react differently to their parents according to their individual personalities, ages, perceptions of what they think is loving or unloving, feelings about their brothers and sisters, and so forth. Some children are far more flexible and understanding than others.
- Children adapt to a predictable way of life. Little ones do not sit in judgment of their parents. If, for example, going to the sitter is their daily routine, they can be most accepting and feel secure. Older children may complain but still feel secure because their continuous relationship with a parent is not in jeopardy.

Certain reassurances are frequently included in the advice of the experts; I've selected some that encourage you to confer with outsiders when you feel baffled or overwhelmed.

- Most complexities in society that undermine stability are not of your making—such as economic problems, social tensions, violence, and discrimination. When you are caught up in family struggles, you may lose sight of the broader picture. Let others remind you that one can be a victim of racial prejudice, sexual harassment, unfair hiring policies and so forth.
- Competition in schools, on playgrounds, in Little League, at piano recitals, dance contests, and beauty contests affects everyone. Even when you and your child carefully plan these activities and you are perceptive about overload, anxiety can result. It's hard for a child to be on a team that always loses or to play a minor role to another's *stardom.* You have to give appropriate approval and support in order to offset feelings of incompetency or inadequacy—even arrogance. If your efforts prove ineffective, the support of a counselor, coach, or teacher should be considered.
- If a member of the family is so unhappy that everyone else suffers, professional help can turn things around. One cruel family member or cruel act can undermine the stability of everyone in the family. It is important to ascertain why the person is obnoxious and find out what to do about it.
- Almost every family faces one or more crises—a grandparent gets hurt in an accident or Bob is suspended from school because he was caught smoking in the locker room. Large or small, chances are the crisis will disrupt stability.

> *Be proud of your decision to use help. It is a difficult decision. It reflects good judgment and maturity.*

Experts plead for you to enhance your sense of well-being. I encourage you to answer these questions.

- How long has it been since you watched a sunset or a dramatic lightning display, or read a book, wrote a poem, played the piano, or listened to music that you selected?
- Do you give yourself permission to spend money on yourself, even though your family has many needs? Even an inexpensive pair of pantyhose can boost your morale.
- Are you learning to be a selective perfectionist—to let some things go and just get by with others and feel okay about that?
- Do you take time to meditate, write a journal, or read the bible or other books or materials that nurture your spirituality?
- How recently have you reached out to a friend or visited your mother or *mother-in-law* just for pleasure? You are not being self-indulgent when you take time to write a letter. The return mail may indeed be cheerful.
- Do you take care of yourself by helping others? Given your busy schedule, what volunteer things do you manage to squeeze into a week or a month?
- Are you nourishing your relationship with your spouse or significant other?
- Have you managed to let go of "your own old stuff?" Are you free of most of the anger and disappointments that bothered you badly when you were a child?

Please note that none of these questions has to do with parenting. The stability of the family is a reflection of your well-being. You need a reprieve from nonstop analysis of what you do and do not do as a mother or father.*

You are taking care of you when you set realistic goals and *dream the impossible dreams*. Try to avoid getting buried in overwhelming responsibilities and defeatism. Don't let life break your smile.

---

*See Section 1, *Take Care of Yourself,* page 9.

Appendix C

Preparing for Death
Kubler-Ross' Theory

A PARENT WANTS to do everything possible to prevent children from suffering. When someone is killed or dies suddenly, one has to focus on the crisis and adjust to the loss. That is after the fact. However, when a child must confront his or her own death or the approaching death of a relative or friend, a parent wants desperately to minimize trauma effectively.

The most constructive way is to understand and experience together the processes described as the five mental stages of the dying person. These were identified by Dr. Elisabeth Kubler-Ross and first published in *On Death and Dying* in 1969. The five stages represent the emotional responses of an individual who faces certain death. They offer insights for use with patients and caring family and friends.

Not every terminally ill person goes through the five stages in the described order, and not every person goes through every stage. Furthermore, some persons return to stages they passed through earlier, such as denial. The family of the dying patient goes through essentially the same stages, though perhaps with more or less intensity. The stages are:

1. Denial. When a person first realizes that he or she has a terminal illness, the reaction is, "No, it can't be! Not me!" This denial can last from a few seconds to a few months and recur again and again.

Denial serves an important purpose. It provides time to sort things out emotionally, to process the possibility that one is going to die. It may be important for the person to deny the seriousness of the situation because those around him or her are not ready to face the truth. They express denial to each other. Or sometimes a dying person is more open to talking about the situation than are relatives, spouses, children, or even nurses and doctors.

2. Anger. After a person has passed through the "No, not me!" stage, feelings of anger are expressed. "Why me? Why not Mack? He's never done anything for anybody. Why not him?" There is no comforting answer to this question.

The patient may be irritable and cantankerous when people come to visit, especially in a hospital. Criticism of doctors, nurses, the food, and the noise are commonplace. The patient seems intent on making well people feel guilty that they are well and he or she is ill. But people do not enjoy visiting with someone who is unpleasant or openly hostile, so the visits may be fewer and the length of each visit noticeably shorter. As a result, the person now experiencing rejection begins to feel sorry for himself or herself.

Sometimes a need to scream and rant and rave becomes imperative. Caretakers should expect this and understand that this is a normal stage the dying person goes through.

Family and friends go through anger too. "Why my husband (or child or best friend)?" They may curse God or become physically violent.

3. Bargaining. As the person becomes increasingly ill, he or she begins to realize that the rage and the anger do not change things. At this point, bargaining begins. Most patients make a bargain with God, usually in private, a direct plea for more time from God; in return, the patient will dedicate himself or herself to the service of God. Or the person bargains with the doctors, promising to give his body to science or work for funds for the medical school.

The message behind bargaining reads, "Yes, I've been told I'm going to die, but ..." When this frame of mind moves on to, "Yes, me ... period," without a need to bargain, to plea, to deny, the next stage begins.

Meanwhile, during the bargaining stage, the spouse, children, and friends may notice brief times of marked improvement. This may result in false encouragement and bring up feelings of denial again. At some point, however, everyone will head into stage four, depression, though this may not be synchronized between patient and loved ones.

4. Depression. When people die, they lose everyone and everything they have known. Survivors lose one person whom they have loved very much. The dying person is very much alone. Survivors have each other for support. Depression is to be expected. Not only does the person face death, but he or she also must deal with the damaged self-esteem that results from a debilitating condition. Loss of virility, less attractive appearance, unrehearsed dependency, pain, relinquished ability to care for others, and many other factors contribute to depression. For a parent, guilt about child care and the high cost of hospitalization are two other important factors.

Many dying patients change in appearance (skin color or weight loss, for example) or lose mobility or take on an unusual odor. Relatives finding this all too painful may turn their backs on the patient. Patients need compassion, and yet it is almost impossible for some relatives or friends to come through. They should make every effort not to reject or desert the dying.

One way to help is to listen, or if that is too painful, to make certain that the dying person has someone to talk to.

A second way to help is to comply with requests a person may have, such as, "Please bring the photograph album so I can finish it," or "Bring my will for me to change." Kubler-Ross says, "We are always impressed by how quickly a patient's depression is lifted when these vital issues are taken care of."

A third way to help is to *show* your feelings. Cry together. Participate in expressions of regret, sorrow, and guilt. Don't be artificially cheerful. Kubler-Ross labels these manifestations of depression as "reactive depression."

She has identified a second phase of depression *preparatory depression* or *preparatory grief.* Now the focus is on grieving over the losses that lie ahead. This is not a time for a lot of words. The patient is letting go of the ties that have been his or her way of life.

5. Acceptance. Kubler-Ross says that when a person contemplates the very end, some expression of grief is expected.

Physically, the patient may seem exhausted, dozing a lot and restless or disturbed by too much noise in the room. He or she has given up hope of recovery or even of living a few more weeks or months. Terminal patients who are in great pain, steadily or intermittently, are tired of enduring the pain.

The survivors-to-be need reassurance that the peaceful attitude of the dying person must not be equated with rejection of them. They need to understand that the long fight for life is almost over and peace is at hand.

Children want to be understanding, and too often they are not allowed to be. They are often shut off from this kind of information with the excuse that it would be too painful or that they are too young to understand. There is no age at which a child acquires instant awareness or suddenly becomes capable of understanding death. But the child should be given the benefit of the doubt. Attempting to discuss death with a concerned child is preferable to avoiding the issue. Be sure to use a vocabulary that the child can understand.*

---

*Adapted with the permission of Macmillan Publishing Company from *On Death and Dying* by Elisabeth Kubler-Ross. Copyright © 1969 by Elisabeth Kubler-Ross.

Epilogue

CHILD REARING TECHNIQUES are not infallible. Increasing evidence reveals that parents simply do not have that much control over a child's personality and development; too many other influential factors—especially genetics—are at work. There was a time when moms, in particular, were blamed for every family blemish. Renowned authors, fiction writers, screenplays and the kids themselves, especially teenagers, formed an anti-mother chorus. Mothers were blamed for a child's schizophrenia, sexual preference, drug problem, failed relationships, and even suicide attempts. An anti-mom attitude still persists among many and, sadly, among mothers themselves.

It is time to stop this nonsense. Mothers, fathers, grandparents and all other caregivers have inadequacies and admit feeling confused about how kids should be raised. Blame, guilt, and confusion can negate commendation and applause. Don't let that happen to you. Do the best you can. Enjoy the kids. Take care of yourself. Strive for stability, work for harmony, and keep your fingers crossed. That's how it was meant to be.

Index

Collins, Emily
  Whole Single Person's Catalog,
    138-39
Commercials, 39-40
Communication
  in affluent family, 197
  and divorce, 241
  parent-teacher, 184
  with teenager, 51
  and television, 200
Community grief specialist, 272
Competition
  in affluent family, 197
  school, 168, 172, 177
Conformity, 50
Consistency, 24, 133
  in alcoholic family, 148-49
Continuing education, 218
Corporal punishment, 24
Counselor, high school, 183
Crack (drug), 52
Crisis behavior, 297-99
Cult, 209-10
Curfew, 46
Custodial parent, 141
  remarriage of, 245
Custody issues, 232-35
Cystic fibrosis, 89
  separation and divorce and, 90

— D —

Dating by divorced parent, 243
Davis, Deborah
  Empty Cradle, Broken Heart, 274
Daycare, 36-38, 134. *See also* Care-
    takers
Dear Birthmother (Silber and
    Speedlin), 78
Death, 130, 264-75
  of child with illness, 104, 105
  crisis behavior, 298
  gifted child's reaction to, 121
  grief symptoms, 266-68

of parent, 264-65
and religion, 212
replacement child, 77
violent, 272-73, 274
Decisions by children, 7
Depression
  and attention deficit disorder or
    learning disability, child
    with, 113
  and gifted child, 118, 121
  and teenager, 48, 49, 50-51
Devil worship, 209
Diabetes
  adult, 156
  childhood, 89, 96
Disabled child, 89-100, 208
  at school, 174
Disabled parent, 153-56. *See also*
    Chronic illness: parent with
Discipline. *See also* Limits
  mutual respect, 23-24
  school, 172
  teenager, 48-49
Discrimination, 203-8
Disease, invisible, 96. *See also*
    Chronic illness
Divorce, 226-32
  and chronically ill or disabled child,
    90
  crisis behavior, 298
  and move, 278
  and suicide, 301
*Divorce Busting: A Revolutionary and
    Rapid Program for Staying
    Together* (Weiner-Davis), 223
Down's syndrome, 161, 163
Dreams, 213
Drinking. *See* Alcohol abuse; Alco-
    holic parent
Dropout, school, 45, 180, 181, 217
  gifted child, 117
Drug abuse, 45, 180, 295-97
  crisis behavior, 298